Tibetan Magic

Also Available from Bloomsbury

Buddhism and Waste, Edited by Trine Brox and Elizabeth Williams-Oerberg
Rethinking "Classical Yoga" and Buddhism, Karen O'Brien Kop
Tibetan Sky-Gazing Meditation and the Pre-History of Great Perfection Buddhism, Flavio A. Geisshuesler

Tibetan Magic

Past and Present

Edited by
Cameron Bailey and Aleksandra Wenta

BLOOMSBURY ACADEMIC
LONDON • NEW YORK • OXFORD • NEW DELHI • SYDNEY

BLOOMSBURY ACADEMIC
Bloomsbury Publishing Plc, 50 Bedford Square, London, WC1B 3DP, UK
Bloomsbury Publishing Inc, 1359 Broadway, New York, NY 10018, USA
Bloomsbury Publishing Ireland, 29 Earlsfort Terrace, Dublin 2, D02 AY28, Ireland

BLOOMSBURY, BLOOMSBURY ACADEMIC and the Diana logo are trademarks of Bloomsbury Publishing Plc

First published in Great Britain 2024
Paperback edition published 2025

A catalogue record for this book is available from the British Library.

Library of Congress Cataloging-in-Publication Data
Names: Wenta, Aleksandra, editor. | Bailey, Cameron, 1985– editor.
Title: Tibetan magic : past and present / edited by Cameron Bailey and Aleksandra Wenta.
Description: 1st. | New York : Bloomsbury Academic, 2024. |
Includes bibliographical references and index.
Identifiers: LCCN 2023036378 (print) | LCCN 2023036379 (ebook) |
ISBN 9781350354944 (hardback) | ISBN 9781350354982 (paperback) |
ISBN 9781350354968 (ebook) | ISBN 9781350354951 (pdf)
Subjects: LCSH: Magic–Religious aspects–Buddhism. | Buddhist magic. |
Magic–China–Tibet Autonomous Region.
Classification: LCC BQ4570.M3 T53 2024 (print) | LCC BQ4570.M3 (ebook) |
DDC 294.3/43–dc23/eng/20230808
LC record available at https://lccn.loc.gov/2023036378
LC ebook record available at https://lccn.loc.gov/2023036379

ISBN: HB: 978-1-3503-5494-4
PB: 978-1-3503-5498-2
ePDF: 978-1-3503-549-51
eBook: 978-1-3503-5496-8

Typeset by Newgen KnowledgeWorks Pvt. Ltd., Chennai, India

For product safety related questions contact productsafety@bloomsbury.com.

To find out more about our authors and books visit www.bloomsbury.com and sign up for our newsletters.

Contents

List of Illustrations vii
Acknowledgments viii
Note on Transliteration ix

Introduction 1
Cameron M. Bailey and Aleksandra Wenta

1 The *Zla gsang be'u bum*: A Compendium of Ritual Magic and Sorcery 13
Amanda N. Brown

2 Magical Results of the Rituals in the *Tārā-mūla-kalpa*'s *Continuation Tantra* 35
Susan Landesman

3 The *Vajrabhairavatantra*: *Materia Magica* and Circulation of Tantric Magical Recipes 61
Aleksandra Wenta

4 The Magic That Lies within Prayer: On Patterns of Magicity and Resolute Aspirations (*smon lam*) 85
Rolf Scheuermann

5 The *Yogin*'s Familiars: Protector Deities as Magical Guides 103
Cameron M. Bailey

6 Emic Perspectives on the Transubstantiation of Words in Tibetan-Script Textual Amulets 125
Valentina Punzi

7 The Magical Causality of Poison Casting and Cancer among Tibetan Communities of Gyalthang 149
Eric D. Mortensen

8 Is There Magic in *Gcod*? An Expedition into (Some of) the Complexities of *Sādhana*-Text Enactments 169
Nike-Ann Schröder

9 "Trainings for Sorcery, Magic, Mystic, Philosophy—for That Which Is Called 'the Great Accomplishment' ": Alexandra David-Neel's Written and Unwritten Tibetan Grimoires 193
Samuel Thévoz

Afterword: Conceptualizing the "Magical" in Tibet and Beyond 221
Nicolas Sihlé

List of Contributors 245
Index 249

Illustrations

1.1	Appended illustrations of the *garuḍa*, frog, and human effigy for rite number 1 from the *Zla gsang be'u bum*. Image provided by the Buddhist Digital Resource Center (BDRC)	18
6.1	The color-scanned copy used by Cidanji to make the two amulets	135
6.2	Cidanji drawing the wheels of the amulet	135
6.3	The two amulets placed in the basket	136
6.4	The materials prepared for the ritual	137
6.5	The glue made of flour and water	137
6.6	The amulet is spread with glue	138
6.7	The amulet stuck on the wall	138
6.8	The eggs prepared for burning	139
6.9	The eggs are burnt with the juniper branches in the backyard	139

Acknowledgments

This volume stems from the panel on Tibetan Magic that took place during the sixteenth seminar of the International Association for Tibetan Studies (IATS) held in Prague in 2022. The editors are grateful to all the people involved in this event who contributed to the fruitful discussion and intellectual exchanges. The editors are especially thankful to the organizers of the IATS conference in Prague and to the IATS Advisory Board for accepting their panel proposal and giving them a public forum to engage in the controversial topic of magic in Tibetan contexts. The editors' special thanks go to Robert Mayer for his unwavering support in this project and for being a rock to lean on through the intellectual ups and downs of our research work more generally.

Both editors would like to express their gratitude to Bloomsbury editorial staff, especially Stuart Hay, Lily McMahon, and Emily Wootton, for their support, efficiency, and professionalism in making the publication of this volume possible.

Note on Transliteration

Transliteration of Asian languages is based on the systems commonly accepted in the academic community, namely, Wylie for Tibetan, Pinyin for Chinese, and IAST for Sanskrit. For Naxi, for which there is no accepted standardization, we adopted the system developed by Pan Anshi in 1998 in collaboration with Anthony Jackson. See Michael Oppitz and Elizabeth Hsu. 1998. *Naxi and Moso Ethnography: Kin, Rites, Pictographs*. Zürich: Völkerkundemuseum Zürich. Pan Anshi's system was derived from the work of Joseph Rock. See Joseph F. Rock. 1972. *A Na-khi—English Encyclopedic Dictionary*, Part II. *Gods, Priests, Ceremonies, Stars, Geographical Names*. Rome: Serie Orientale Roma, 28. For Lisu we use the system developed by Bradley. See David Bradley. 1994. *A Dictionary of the Northern Dialect of Lisu (China and Southeast Asia)*. Canberra: Pacific Linguistics Australian National University. For Mosuo (also known as Moso), for which there is also no broadly accepted system of transcription, we use the system developed by Mathieu and Lamu Gatusa in 1998. See Michael Oppitz and Elizabeth Hsu. 1998. *Naxi and Moso Ethnography: Kin, Rites, Pictographs*. Zürich: Völkerkundemuseum Zürich. While for ease of consistency we chose to use Wylie as the standard system of transliteration for Tibetan in most of the chapters, the author of the afterword opted to use both Wylie and phonetic systems of transliteration to provide greater cross-disciplinary accessibility.

Introduction

Cameron M. Bailey and Aleksandra Wenta

The present volume is a collective study of magic in Tibetan culture, examining a range of magical practices both in historical and modern Tibetan and Himalayan contexts and employing a variety of definitional models and theoretical angles. "Magic" is a term easily utilized but very difficult to precisely define. Scholars and laypeople alike commonly use the word with an intuitive, if vague, understanding of what magic is. In an academic context, however, when it comes down to explaining the definite features of magic, the use of the term can quickly become controversial, even problematic, especially in fields studying non-Western cultures. Some scholars, particularly in the field of Buddhist and Tibetan studies, have questioned not only the applicability of the term "magic" to their subjects but even the value of it as a universal category entirely.

Reviewing how most people tend to define magic, or use the term intuitively without a strict definition, an approximate, simple, and diplomatic definition one could easily make is something along the lines of "the (purported) techniques for producing, or the display of, a supernatural or supernormal power or effect." However, this definition is so general that, depending on the context, it could include everything from ordinary, normative religious prayer to the practice of pharmaceutical medicine (and many other things besides), the practitioners or performers of which may be unlikely to agree that their actions constitute "magic." Hence, where "religion" or even "science" ends and magic begins (or vice versa) has long been a subject of controversy and debate. Therefore, if the term "magic" is going to be used as a universal heuristic and/or a cross-cultural category, it seems necessary to identify its more specific features.

To solve this problem, some scholars, notably (especially for the subject of the present volume) Sam van Schaik in his recent monograph *Buddhist Magic*,[1] have proposed using a Wittgensteinian "family resemblances" approach to the definition of magic, pointing out certain elemental features of magic that tend to recur in similar practices historically in cultures across the planet. Otto and Stausberg (2013) propose a somewhat similar organizational principle they term "patterns of magicity," which allows for an examination of certain common features across times and cultures.[2] Some of these more specific features tend to be things such as the ritual use of special words believed to possess inherent power, the appeal or reference to esoteric or occult knowledge, and a belief in (or awareness of) nonobvious sympathetic bonds between objects at a distance that can be manipulated through special methods.

The difficulty in precisely defining what "magic" is, however, is insufficient by itself to explain the disregard, dismissal, or sometimes outright contempt for the subject that exists in academia. Speaking from within the Tibetan or Buddhist studies context, critics of the term "magic" often point to the fact that there is no Tibetan word (or a word in any other Asian language) that can be precisely mapped onto the concept of "magic." However, the same could be said for other Western cultural terms and categorical concepts that are routinely used comfortably in our discipline. "Dharma" (Tib. *chos*) is often translated as "religion," but a host of objections to such a translation could be raised depending upon what definition of religion one is using, such as the fact that historically *chos* almost always specifically refers to the Buddha's teachings and is not the same kind of universal cross-cultural category that "religion" is usually considered to be. Like "magic," "religion" is a similarly imprecise term with a similarly significant amount of cultural baggage, and yet with the exception of certain pedantic post-structuralists, humanities scholars usually use the term "religion" quite comfortably, without feeling the need to constantly justify it. In our more specific Buddhist and Tibetan studies context here, the same could be said for the category of "Tantra," which, while it has the advantage of being an emic term, can still be an extremely imprecise and problematic conceptual category. Yet "magic," more than these other categories, always seems to require special caveats before it can be taken seriously. It is a kind of orphaned stepchild of social science heuristics.

There are good historical reasons for this, but the negative connotation of "magic" relies on a very particular cultural bias that is in fact somewhat out of tune with how the word "magic" is used in the vernacular. In any basic discussion of magic and its definitions within a scholarly context, the names of the same handful of twentieth-century theorists always, inevitably, come up. Among them, James Frazer and Émile Durkheim are almost always mentioned, rightfully so, since for better or for worse (mostly for worse) they were instrumental in the way "magic" has been shaped and come to be understood as a scholarly category. Today, their theories are also almost always broached in order to show how inapplicable they are in the face of real-world data, especially in the way both of them defined magic in hard contradistinction to "religion." Frazer is also known, and regularly criticized, for his association of magic with primitivism to the point that his use of the term "magic" was effectively a cultural pejorative.

The Frazerian and Durkheimian conceptual frameworks of magic lie firmly within a tradition going all the way back to the origin of the word itself, in which magic (Greek *mageia*) meant by definition something primitive, culturally alien, and unfavorably distinct from the beliefs and practices of normative/proper religious authority. From Platonists in the early common era dismissing popular magical practices as a technically effective but ultimately pointless manipulation of sympathetic bonds to later Christian authorities condemning magic (however it was precisely identified) as something inherently sinister and immoral, the work of demons, magic has accumulated significant negative cultural baggage. This definitional tradition continued during the colonial and Orientalist periods when European observers would implicitly condemn or at the very least chauvinistically exoticize the practices of non-Western cultures as "mere magic," in distinction with proper religion (usually based on Protestant Christian models). Thus, there is a good argument to be made, as Otto and Stausberg point out (2013: 6–7), that since the term's inception in ancient Greece, "magic" is an inherently ethnocentric concept.

It is not surprising then that (post)modern, post-colonialist scholars, especially in formerly so-called Oriental fields, might be uncomfortable reading and interpreting their subjects through a concept like magic. For all their difficulties, other cross-cultural categories do not invoke the specter of primitivizing and "othering" on quite the same level that magic can, and does. However, magic's poor reputation as a scholarly category in large part stems from, or is influenced by, a normative, conservative Christian-influenced worldview. Within Tibetan studies, since our application of the term "magic" is almost always used in the context of texts, rituals, and other practices that were produced or at least influenced by a self-consciously esoteric tradition, it may be more useful to draw on the Western esoteric tradition and its understanding of magic, which was (and still is) quite different from "magic" as conceptualized by what became mainstream Christianity, and by some extension early anthropologists. Occult philosophers and practitioners in the West did not view magic as bad science and primitive religion in Frazerian terms, or pit religion and magic against each other in hostile, mutually exclusive Durkheimian terms. Quite the contrary, they often viewed magic as the pinnacle of religion and natural philosophy (i.e., science). According to Heinrich Cornelius Agrippa, following Giovanni Pico, in his encyclopedic *Three Books of Occult Philosophy*:

> Wonderful effects are produced from magic, uniting virtues by applying things with each other and by accepting their congruity, and everywhere binds and marries inferior and superior gifts and virtues. This is the most perfect and highest science, the highest and most sacred philosophy. Finally, it is the absolute consummation of the noblest philosophy, for all regulative philosophy is divided into natural science, mathematics, and theology.[3]

The latter disciplines, Agrippa goes on to insist, are ones in which a magic practitioner is necessarily skilled. Similarly, Maslama al-Qurṭubī, the likely author of the highly influential Arabic grimoire of astral magic best known by its translated Latin title *Picatrix*, believed that "magic is the inevitable consequence of a zealous philosophical life."[4]

Similarly, Buddhist scripture and Buddhist commentators held similar views with regard to supernormal powers as the fruits of soteriological and philosophical accomplishment. To summarize one brief example, the eighteenth-century Tibetan tantric master Sle lung Bzhad pa'i rdo rje in a commentary appended to a book of magic spells (i.e., short rituals featuring mantras meant to produce a special, supernormal effect) states that:

> All animate and inanimate phenomena lack true existence. Furthermore, they amount to nothing more than interdependent origination. If you realize that essentially magic ["*'phrul*"] is the union of appearance and emptiness, you will accomplish the ordinary and supreme *siddhis* [super powers] without too much effort.[5]

Obviously, this kind of interpretation of magic is an elitist one that ethnographic scholars especially may find unhelpful, even counterproductive, when interpreting their data. But the point here is that the term "magic" should not necessarily be seen in the negative, primitivizing, antireligious light that so often unfairly hounds its usage. Examining the work of figures like Agrippa or Sle lung, we can see that there are plenty of historical examples and theoretical models, etic and emic, which can be invoked to counter this stereotype. This esotericist or "occultist" framework also has other advantages. There is still a strong tendency, in Buddhist studies especially, to think of magic as an extraneous cultural epiphenomenon adhering to some supposedly pure doctrinal and philosophical "core" of a religion. An esotericist model of magic, which is much more in line with the actual emic viewpoints of the writers and practitioners of the texts and methods we are studying, recognizes magic not as opposed to religion but as a specialized form of it.

Returning to the fact that there is no single term in Tibetan to which we can necessarily cleanly map the concept of magic, we have already mentioned the similar problem with the cross-cultural concept of "religion" that comes with a massive amount of cultural and historical baggage of its own, but we could also note that there is no single word for "ritual" in Tibetan either. Rather, there is a constellation of more or less interrelated terms and concepts for what we tend to think of and interpret as different *types* of ritual, with *sgrubs thabs*, *mchod pa*, and *gsol mchod* being but a few examples. Similarly, there is no one word for "magic" in Tibetan, yet there are numerous, often related concepts that at least roughly parallel how magic (and related terminology) has been understood and conceptually isolated in the West. *Las 'byor* invokes the concept of the manipulation of sympathetic bonds central to the Frazerian (and also, significantly, Platonian) understanding of magic.[6] *Las tshogs* and *Be'u 'bum* are examples of terms for collections of spells that are often structurally extremely similar to rituals found in collections like the *Greek Magical Papyri*, and grimoires like the *Picatrix*. *'Phrul*, used in the excerpted quote above, is difficult to translate without some reference to the concept of magic.

As scholars using European languages to discuss Asian texts and oral accounts, one of our primary jobs and skills must necessarily be translation. Translation is unavoidably an imperfect process of interpretation using imperfect linguistic and conceptual models to approximate meaning as best as we can. "Magic" is one such conceptual model, perhaps rougher than some, but undeniably culturally potent and familiar to the point that its explanatory power is undeniable. By carving out a space for the category of magic, we allow special attention to be paid to, and have an opportunity to set the record straight about, certain texts, traditions, historical figures, and other cultural facets that especially in Buddhist and Tibetan studies have historically been ignored, unfairly downplayed, or misunderstood (sometimes purposefully) through the corrupted lens of lurid exoticism.

In Chapter 1 of this volume, "The *Zla gsang be'u bum*: A Compendium of Ritual Magic and Sorcery," Amanda Nichole Brown explores a Rnying ma collection of Yamāntaka rites, known also as "Yama's handbook" attributed to Gnubs chen Sangs rgyas ye shes and Mañjuśrīmitra. This handbook is an example of aggressive magic or rites directed against specific targets to cause harm. In the beginning of the chapter, Brown delineates a working definition of magic, consisting of four aspects, that is, manipulation of a target, activation of power, employment of sympathetic means, and mitigation, and advocates for the usefulness of applying this definition for a cross-cultural study of magic. She then analyzes three rites dealing with the destruction of an enemy, inflicting a target with leprosy, and hail-casting—a rite meant to suppress speech of a hail-chaser who protects the community against hailstorms. She demonstrates that these three rites adhere to a certain "arc of narrative," distinguished by their specific repeatable syntax, including a homage, accumulation of materials, mantra recitation, and so on. In the end, she discusses the efficacy of magic rituals, which rely on the activation of power through the employment of contaminated substances and inversions.

Chapter 2 is Susan Landesman's textual study of the early Buddhist tantra, the *Tārāmūlakalpa*'s *Continuation Tantra*. In it she discusses the concept of magical attainments (*siddhi*s) that, although not classified as "magic" per se, may be regarded as such, for they display all types of magic-like characteristics, including flying in the air, becoming invisible, living for an eon, and so on. The *Tārāmūlakalpa*'s *Continuation Tantra* refers to the three signs of obtainments of *siddhi*s: first, when the object begins to heat up (*uṣme*); second, when the smoke arises (*dhūme*); third, when it bursts into flames (*jvalite*). These three types of *siddhi*s belong to the "ritual syntax" of the early tantric milieu, commonly found in the early Buddhist tantras, such as the *Mañjuśriyamūlakalpa* and the Śaiva *Niśvāsa*-corpus (Goodall and Isaacson 2016). The *Tārāmūlakalpa*'s *Continuation Tantra* follows the pan-Indic template of classifying magical rituals into four divisions, namely, pacification (*śāntika*), generating wealth or long life (*pauṣṭika*), subjugation under one's own will (*vaśīkriyā*), and retaliative magic (*abhicāra*), which interestingly receives only one mention in the text. In Landesman's contribution, the material aspect of early tantric Buddhist magic, which relies on the usage of various materials "consecrated" with the mantra, comes to the forefront. One can notice that certain materials, such as, for example, salt for making an effigy of a person targeted in the rite of subjugation, or the use of honey, butter, and milk (or yoghurt) in the rites of *śāntika* and *pauṣṭika*, conform to a consistent ritual syntax also found in other Buddhist and Śaiva tantras discussed in the next chapter of this volume.

In Chapter 3, "The *Vajrabhairavatantra*: Materia Magica and Circulation of Tantric Magical Recipes," Aleksandra Wenta approaches the same topic of early tantric Buddhist magic from a comparative lens of magical recipes that are found both in Buddhist and Śaiva tantras. She demonstrates that the early Buddhist tantra, the *Vajrabhairavatantra*, shares parallel recipes with the early

Śaiva tantras, such as the *Guhyasūtra* of the *Niśvāsatattvasaṃhitā* and the *Vīṇāśikhatantra*. These parallel recipes not only provide the evidence of the shared magical technology that crossed sectarian boundaries but also shed insight onto the practice of adopting the recipes as a type of "magical" genre, distinguished by their formulaic language, recycled phrasing, and adaptive "repackaging" to different tantric cults. Wenta focuses on the material aspect of tantric magic and demonstrates that the manipulation of materials seems to be embedded in the taxonomies of correspondences related to a specific semantic construction derived from Brahmanical and literary cultures.

In Chapter 4, "The Magic That Lies Within Prayer: On Patterns of Magicity and Resolute Aspirations (*smon lam*)," Rolf Scheuermann examines a popular Mahāyāna practice of resolute aspirations, known in Tibetan Buddhist communities as *smon lam*. *Smon lam* is a form of prayer that focuses on an altruistic wish to attain enlightenment for oneself and for others, and as such it is commonly associated with the realm of "religion." In his contribution, Scheuermann undertakes an intellectual exercise and applies the concept of "magicity" developed by Michael Stausberg and Bernd-Christian Otto in their informative reader, *Defining Magic* to *smon lam*. He demonstrates that many of the patterns discernible by Stausberg and Otto as aspects of "magicity," such as efficacies of words, objects, and miraculous capabilities, can be found in *smon lam* as well, but this does not necessarily mean that one can reduce *smon lam* to magic. Rather, the existence of "magicity" is purported to show that *smon lam* is merely one among many practices of Tibetan Buddhism where religious and magical aspects interlock. In conclusion, Scheuermann advocates for the usefulness of applying "magicity" to different cross-cultural contexts, arguing that this concept not only allows us to transcend the contested categories of magic and religion but also permits to extend its application to those aspects of practice that are not usually associated with magic.

In Chapter 5, "The *Yogin's* Familiars: Protector Deities as Magical Guides," Cameron M. Bailey examines narrative and ritual context of the eighteenth-century Tibetan Buddhist master Sle lung Bzhad pa'i rdo rje (1697–1740) and his relationship with his personal protector goddess, Lha gcig Nyi ma gzhon nu. In discussing the nature of this bond, Bailey applies the concept of daemonic magic, derived from the Platonic tradition, where daemons were regarded as important nonhuman intermediaries between humans and the gods, to the Buddhist context. He argues that the daemonic magic, that is, magic that relies on the intercession of unenlightened *laukika*, or worldly, *daemons* as opposed to the invocation of enlightened *lokottara*, or transcendent, buddhas and bodhisattvas, is a useful heuristic tool to describe protector deities. Bailey argues that the protector deities are often depicted not as servitors but more as spiritual friends, whose appearance is not generated through ritual means but rather occurs in spontaneous encounters. As such, they seem to resemble the familiar spirits of witches and so-called cunning folk in the vernacular religion of medieval and early modern Europe, particularly in the British Isles, who, at least initially, appear outside of witches' control. He then discusses three rites that were taught to Sle lung by Nyi ma gzhon nu and deliberates on the applicability of the label "magic" to them.

In Chapter 6, "Emic Perspectives on the Transubstantiation of Words in Tibetan-Script Textual Amulets," Valentina Punzi comparatively discusses two ethnographic cases related to the crafting of Tibetan textual amulets based on the author's fieldwork undertaken in eastern Qinghai Province (PRC) and in a Baima community in western Sichuan Province (PRC). She argues that the making of amulets and their transformation into magical devices meant to protect the household and livestock against diseases are linked to the personal authority of a ritual specialist who operates in a private, domestic sphere without any official authorization from religious establishments. Punzi locates the crafting of amulets between the informative and performative aspects of ritual practice and demonstrates that although authoritative texts retain their semantic value and legitimize the authority of a ritual specialist, the efficacy of amulets derives from the authoritative use of texts, rather than from the texts themselves. The ritual specialist may, therefore, depart from textual injunctions through adherence to metonymy and substitution. Punzi theorizes her research findings in a larger context of magic as a semiotic domain where the authority of a ritual specialist is linked to the affinity group sharing the same cultural framework and values. It is this affinity group that recognizes certain actions as ritual magical actions, therefore legitimizing the authority of a ritual specialist who has mastered the grammar of complex meanings.

In Chapter 7, "The Magical Causality of Poison Casting and Cancer among Tibetan Communities in Gyalthang," Eric D. Mortensen discusses the concept of *dug* as cancer and poison casting based on his ethnographic fieldwork in the Gyalthang region in the southern Khams of Tibet (PRC). Mortensen examines *dug*, a pre- or non-Buddhist phenomenon officially considered to be a superstition, through the interconnected concepts of prognostication and *dug*-transmission, which can take on multifold forms, including a matrilineal transmission from a mother to a daughter, transmission through gaze, and, most commonly, transmission through food served to the visitors to the household, which has been inflicted with *dug*. Mortensen discusses the gender practices of feeding *dug*, with sweat or menstrual blood, and a magically sublimated practice of growing *dug* in a jar through the recourse to crematory practices of exhuming the corpse, as well as the use of code words to speak about *dug* in a manner incomprehensible to others. He focuses on different aspects of social stigma associated with *dug* and theorizes the construction of accusations connected with a *dug*-caster as an example of "invisible ontology," the concept applied to the witchcraft accusations attested also in the Azande communities of Africa. He also examines *dug* in the context of the semantically loaded terms such as *rten 'grel* and *grib*, the former denoting "coincidence" or "fate," the latter, "contamination," and demonstrates that a distinction between being stricken with *dug* and raising *dug* is established through moral framework.

Chapter 8 of this work, "Is There Magic in Gcod? An Expedition into (Some of) the Complexities of Sādhana-Text Enactments," Nike-Ann Schröder combines ethnographic fieldwork and textual study to examine intricacies associated with the etic–emic understanding of "magic" in the enactments of the *gcod sādhana* practiced in contemporary Tibetan Buddhist communities in Ladakh (India) and Nepal. In it she explores the history of representing *gcod* in Western academic literature initiated by the ethnographic accounts of Alexandra David-Neel in her book *Magic and Mystery of Tibet*. She demonstrates that the image of *gcod* as "magic," that is, something backward, primitive, and therefore, opposed to religion, stemmed from the theories developed within cultural anthropology as well as evolutionist models of human development and was perpetuated in the West in colonial times. She also delineates several causes that contributed to the emic and etic classifications of *gcod* as a non-Buddhist "other." Motivated by a clearly stated purpose to decolonize *gcod*, Schröder then proceeds to examine the opening verses of the *gcod sādhana*, *The Outspreading Laughter of the Ḍākinīs*, in which she deconstructs the division between magic and religion. Combining the emic and etic approaches to the conceptualization of "magic" and linking them together into what she calls the "fields of magic," she demonstrates that the divide between religion and magic is not only fluid but also depends on the context and situation in which a person enacting or examining *gcod* finds herself. She then constructs *gcod* as "magic" because of its being a transformative practice that changes the mode of the practitioner's operation in the world, and also as a "miracle," something unexpected that changes people's perception.

In Chapter 9, "Trainings for Sorcery, Magic, Mystic, Philosophy—for That Which Is Called 'the Great Accomplishment': Alexandra David-Neel's Written and Unwritten Tibetan Grimoires," Samuel Thévoz deals with the invention of

Tibetan magic by a French-Belgian explorer to Tibet, Alexandra David-Neel. Relying on the archival material, including David-Neel's letters, notebooks, and published and unpublished book projects, Thévoz carefully analyzes various historical and personal factors that contributed to David-Neel's construction of Tibetan magic. He argues that it was the intellectual climate of the time in France, with its mixture of scientific, occultist, and artistic trends, that contributed, to a large extent, to David-Neel's magic project. In David-Neel all the contradictions of her age seem to have become incarnate—the age of transition from magic as supernatural to the "scientific magical culture," expressed through a peculiar marriage of scientists and spiritists joined together in their shared endeavor to launch the new study of parapsychology. Beyond the historical determinants, David-Neel's interest in magic was also motivated by her personal ambitions to self-position herself in the growing, male-dominated literature on Tibet and challenge the gender stereotypes. In so doing, she projected an image of a valiant Parisian woman, who traveled to Tibet and engaged in Tibetan Buddhist practices for the purpose of spiritual illumination. Thévoz's contribution paints a complex picture of David-Neel's public, personal, and literary personas mingled together in her attempts to establish herself as the authority on all things Tibetan, at the same time identifying aspects of occultism and tantric and Tibetan Buddhism that, in equal measure, contributed to her formulation of Tibetan magic.

Notes

1 See van Schaik (2020: 17–18).
2 A concept explained and utilized by Scheuermann in this volume.
3 Agrippa (2021: 67).
4 Attrell and Porreca (2019: 8).
5 See Bailey (2020: 545–6) for a broader discussion of this quote and Tibetan concepts of magic.
6 See Cuevas (2010: 169–70).

References

Agrippa, H. C. (2021), *Three Books of Occult Philosophy* (Eric Purdue, trans.), Rochester, VT: Inner Traditions.

Attrell, D., and D. Porreca (trans.) (2019), *Picatrix: A Medieval Treatise on Astral Magic*, University Park: Pennsylvania State University Press.

Bailey, C. (2020), "The Magic of Secret Gnosis: A Theoretical Analysis of a Tibetan Buddhist 'Grimoire,'" *Journal of the Korean Association of Buddhist Studies* 93: 535–70.

Cuevas, B. (2010), "The 'Calf's Nipple' (Be'u bum) of Ju Mipam ('Ju Mi pham): A Handbook of Tibetan Ritual Magic," in Jose Ignacio Cabezon (ed.), *Tibetan Ritual*, 165–86, New York: Oxford University Press.

Goodall, D., and H. Isaacson (2016), "On the Shared 'Ritual Syntax' of the Early Tantric Traditions," in D. Goodall and H. Isaacson (eds.), *Tantric Studies: Fruits of a Franco-German Project on Early Tantra*, 1–76, Pondicherry: EFEO/IFP/Asien-Afrika Institut Universität Hamburg.

Otto, B. C., and M. Stausberg (2013), "General Introduction," in B.-C. Otto and M. Stausberg (eds.), *Defining Magic. A Reader*, 1–13, Sheffield: Equinox (Critical Categories in the Study of Religion).

van Schaik, S. (2020), *Buddhist Magic: Divination, Healing, and Enchantment through the Ages*, Boulder, CO: Shambhala.

1

The *Zla gsang be'u bum*: A Compendium of Ritual Magic and Sorcery

Amanda N. Brown

The *Zla gsang be'u bum* (*The Moon's Mystery Handbook*), also known as the *Gshin rje be'u bum* (*Yama's Handbook*),[1] is a collection of approximately sixty different magical rites invoking the power of the Buddhist deity Yamāntaka, a wrathful version of Mañjuśrī, the bodhisattva of wisdom. This compendium is a handbook of *magic* outlining specific ritual acts that are meant to accomplish the manipulation of the external world through sympathetic means. Rather than having a direct soteriological aim, these rites are practical in nature and are meant to deal with a variety of worldly concerns. Furthermore, the *Moon's Mystery* is unique in its emphasis, particularly on fierce destructive rites. And as such, the compendium includes rites with a variety of hostile aims, including suppressing speech, causing confusion, destroying crops with hailstorms, and even killing. This compendium is a prime example of a Tibetan magic *grimoire*, a collection of instrumental magic rituals. In this chapter, I will introduce the collection and then highlight the specific content of three rituals that typify the category of magic, a category I contend ought to remain in the academic's repertoire of scholarly analysis. Specifically, I will suggest a narrow category of magic that is useful for cross-cultural analysis, using these three rituals as examples of that categorical distinction. I will conclude with a discussion of common themes of the collection that are elucidated by these examples, including the use of contaminated substances, inversions, and the power of the serpentine spirits, the *klu* (Skt. *nāga*).

The *Moon's Mystery*: A glimpse of the Rnying ma Yamāntaka tradition

In addition to the fierce, magical nature of the content, this collection is also noteworthy as an example of a specifically Rnying ma collection of Yamāntaka rites.[2] The compendium is attributed to Gnubs chen Sangs rgyas ye shes and Mañjuśrīmitra, two prominent figures in the Rnying ma Yamāntaka lineage. The individual rites of the collection are drawn from a variety of sources, most notably, the Mahāyoga tantras found in the *Rnying ma rgyud 'bum*, for example, the compilation's namesake, the *Zla gsang nag po'i rgyud* (*The Black Moon's Mystery Tantra*). The compendium is from the library of the late Smin gling khri chen, 'Gyur med kun bzang dbang rgyal (1931–2008). I propose that he likely compiled the edition himself, and as of yet I have not found any evidence to the contrary.

Each individual rite in the compilation is separated by a title page, marked with a specific alphabetic code.[3] Many of the rites cite specific Rnying ma tantras. The citations in the first half of the collection (rites labeled in a linear sequence from *ka* through *ki*) generally follow the order of the *Rnying ma rgyud 'bum*. Subsequent rites are also labeled with an alphabetic code but without a discernible pattern. This latter half represents a hodgepodge of Rnying ma Yamāntaka materials, most notably a section from Rgya Zhang khrom's treasure cycle called the *Hundred Neck Pouches of Gnubs*.[4] Thus, I contend that the first half of the compendium was compiled in a single instance, while the remaining rites were added at a later date, possibly over time.

The *Moon's Mystery*: A collection of magic and sorcery

Despite the lack of patterns in the arrangement of the collection, the nature of each rite displays a similar structure outlining the basic elements of performance that accomplishes a specific goal. Thus, here I will utilize the *Moon's Mystery* as a case study on magic as an apt category to describe ritual action in the context of Tibetan Buddhism and Buddhism more broadly. The study of Buddhist ritual magic remains a relatively nascent field of academic inquiry.[5] In fact, some scholars dismiss the term "magic" altogether, claiming magic to be an inherently denigrating term and/or a remnant of nineteenth-century colonialist anthropology. Some dissenters additionally claim that the term is too diffuse and thus not an academically useful category.[6] Here, I will argue for the utilization of the term "magic" as a useful analytical category, specifically as an apt category to describe the rituals that constitute the *Moon's Mystery*. Following this, I will discuss the prominent magical mechanisms employed in the collection, highlighting their internal logic and discussing the specific content of three rites, noting features that typify my proposed definition of magic.

From the very beginning magic was an emic term to describe the "other"—a group differing from the main, authoritative group's tradition. Subsequently, the term transformed into a fully pejorative category specifically to describe activities distinct from "religion" proper (M. Bailey 2006: 7–8; Copenhaver 2015: 25–6). However, I argue that if we accept that magic is a category that falls within the broader category of religion, it then becomes a useful tool for scholarly analysis.

In a colloquial sense, most of us have a working concept of what actions or ideas constitute magic. However, in a scholarly sense, it is difficult to construct a precise definition. Early discourse on magic, specifically work in anthropology, described magic by its relationship to other conceptual entities such as religion and science. Particularly, dichotomies between religion and magic and between magic and science are problematic since they show an inherent value judgment against acts deemed magical. Certainly, it would be difficult to separate the acts outlined in the *Moon's Mystery* from the religious elements of Buddhism. These acts are woven into the very frame of Buddhism and Buddhist ritual. For example, the rites contained in the *Moon's Mystery* require meditative visualizations of primary Buddhist deities such as Mañjuśrī-Yamāntaka; furthermore, these acts are ideally only to be performed by high-level Buddhist practitioners,[7] defined as such through the religious system as a whole.

Following the work of various scholars outside of the field of Tibetan studies who have addressed the subject,[8] I want to highlight two important factors when considering "magic" as a useful term and also present a tentative definition of the term. For my purposes, the two most important components of the concepts of magic are (1) that magic and ritual action are related, and (2) that magic is best framed as a category within and/or overlapping the category of religion itself, rather than being in contrast to it. Thus, describing the rites of the *Moon's Mystery* as rites of magic means that they are firmly embedded in the overall religious milieu of Buddhism, and furthermore, that these rites are defined by an element of instrumentality. In other words, they are functional through performance of specific, ordered actions. I suggest that magic can be loosely defined as a repeatable ritual action, operating within (and not against) the larger category of religion. Such action has the following four key features:

1. Manipulation and/or coercion of a specified target
2. Activation and communication of power (*mantra*, burning, spinning, mechanical, and so on)
3. Utilization of sympathetic means and employment of symbols of interrelatedness[9]
4. Mitigation (or intensification, in the case of sorcery) of risk and/or misfortune (i.e., apotropaic)

Notably, this definition excludes miraculous powers that are gained through meditative realizations, as these powers are part of the very identity of Buddhahood and are not accomplished via a specific, external ritual program.[10] This narrower description of magic matches the content of the *Moon's Mystery* and employing a polythetic, flexible etic definition of magic allows scholars to maintain a point of reference for cross-cultural analysis, while providing enough ambiguity to account for the multitude of nuances that accompany any large umbrella categories.

Importantly, the *Moon's Mystery* not only represents a collection of Buddhist magic but particularly also a collection of aggressive magic or "sorcery." In other words, the rites in the *Moon's Mystery* are directed at specific targets (humans, demons, etc.) to cause harm.[11] These rites are extremely important to the practitioners that utilize grimoires like the *Moon's Mystery* to combat a variety of threats to the community and to themselves. From a scholarly point of view, the study of these rites can thus illuminate concerns of the community. The rites I will discuss below will uncover two main concerns—climate and disease. Tibet's harsh climate is fraught with tough growing seasons and frequent hailstorms. Also, the threat of skin diseases like leprosy (Tib. *mdze*)[12] is apparent in these rites. Notably in this context of sorcery, these concerns are inverted and thus weaponized toward enemies. Furthermore, these rites unveil methods of harnessing and unleashing power within the Buddhist cosmological framework. It will become clear that these rites summon the power of entities like the *klu* to sabotage enemies.

Tibetan Buddhism delineates four types of mundane actions that fit neatly in the category of magic as outlined above. These four acts (Tib. *las bzhi*) are: pacification, augmentation, subjugation, and ferocity. The latter two of these four acts, subjugation and ferocity, are aggressive in nature, hence the classification "sorcery." Subjugation rites include acts such as suppressing demons that are thought to cause weather disturbances or other calamities. The rites of ferocity, on the other hand, include the euphemistically termed "liberating" (Tib.

sgrol ba) rituals. These rites are meant to kill the target, whether it be a human or demon. From the perspective of the tradition, this is not an unethical act. In fact, this is ideally an act of great compassion, an act that is only employed by high-level tantric practitioners. The targets are usually demons or extremely deluded individuals who have no hope of their own to properly engage in Buddhist practice. In the first two examples below, vow breakers (Tib. *dam nyams*) are the targets.

A practitioner who utilizes the *Moon's Mystery* performs the overall ritual through a series of both speech acts and the manipulation of tangible, material objects. The handbook serves as an instructional guide to the basic layout of the performance, having key components available to review as the practitioner performs the acts. The most prominent magical objects employed in the rites of the *Moon's Mystery* are effigies (*liṅga*), curse charts (Tib. *gtad khram*), and various magical circles or wheels called *yantra*s (Tib. *'khrul 'khor*) and "action wheels" (Tib. *las kyi 'khor lo*; Skt. *karmacakra*). Many of the rites include drawings of the magical device in order to further guide the practitioner in the correct construction and preparation of the materials. Drawings of effigies are appended to several of the rituals. The effigies are usually humanoid, nude, with hands and arms bound in chains.[13] They are depicted as helpless victims. Crosshatches are usually above the head with the binding syllable "*dza*" in between each of the four spaces created by the cross (Cuevas 2011: 77). The illustrations also direct where specific syllables should be placed on the various body parts. For example, "*phaṭ*" is usually drawn at the genital area. Curses and the name of the victims are also written on the bodies of the effigies. The rites below utilize effigies to symbolize the actual victim, creating a connection to that victim in the world beyond the ritual space.

Three rites in the *Moon's Mystery* that typify the category of magic

Here I will introduce three specific examples from the *Moon's Mystery* to demonstrate the magical techniques employed in the handbook. Also, these rites will serve as an example of the major themes present in this collection, namely, the use of contaminated substances and the prominence of the *klu* (serpentine spirits) and leprosy-related materials.

Rite number 1: *Garuḍas* and *nāgas*

The first rite I will discuss is entitled "Wild mantra of a female *preta* (hungry ghost), for causing confusion: a curse chart which joins the *garuḍa* (mythical bird; Tib. *khyung*) and the *nāga* (serpentine spirit)."[14] This ritual is four folios in length and contains an illustration of the images one must draw—a human effigy, a *garuḍa*, and a frog (see Figure 1.1).[15] The colophon of the text states that it is from the pith instructions (*man ngag gnad*) of Zhang, hidden in the mind by Chos kyi grags pa.[16] In addition to the effigy, this rite employs a curse chart (*gtad khram*). In this rite it seems this "chart" refers to the illustrations of the *garuḍa* and frog that lock in malign forces.

This rite gives specific instructions for drawing the three different images (the *garuḍa*, the effigy, and the frog) on birch bark (Tib. *gro ga*) or paper (Tib. *shog bu*). On the *garuḍa* and the frog, the practitioner must draw three circles on each entity's stomach. Important in the context of their later union, the *garuḍa* here is identified as a female, while the frog is identified as a male. On the *garuḍa*, the practitioner must write *khroṃ*, a seed syllable specifically associated with the *garuḍa*. He will also write the specific mantras given in the ritual manual and the name of the enemy who is the vow breaker (Tib. *dam nyams*)—the target of this ritual. The mantra along with the name is written on all three objects. This mechanism of writing the name is clearly a case of utilizing sympathetic means to affect the physical, tangible world. This act is a performance of intent, aiming to bind the victim to the representational effigy (and the rest of the ritual space) through laws of sympathy. Thus, in doing so, whatever act the practitioner does to the effigy, it affects the victim. In this case, the effigy is locked in between the *garuḍa* and the frog.

The coupling of the *garuḍa* and the frog is very significant here. Firstly, the frog (Tib. *sbal*) can be considered serpentine (*klu*) in the Tibetan worldview (Bell

Figure 1.1 Appended illustrations of the *garuḍa*, frog, and human effigy for rite number 1 from the *Zla gsang be'u bum*. Image provided by the Buddhist Digital Resource Center (BDRC).

2020: 13). In fact, the terms *klu* and *sbal* are used interchangeably in this ritual (but the image is clearly an amphibian). Furthermore, the protective circle (Tib. *srung 'khor*) for the *klu* is a frog (Nebesky-Wojkowitz 1996: 5), and therefore it is not surprising that the *klu* is physically represented by the illustrated frog in this rite. Both the *garuḍa* and the frog each have eight-spoked drawings in the middle circle of their wheels. The *garuḍa*'s eight spokes are as follows: the seven planets of Tibetan astrology—Sun, Moon, Mars, Mercury, Jupiter, Venus, and Saturn, with an addition of Ketu (the setting node of the moon, often called a shadow planet) (Cornu 2002: 143–6). On the frog, the eight-spoked image is a lotus leaf. Each of these petals represents one of the eight *nāga* kings.[17] Again, this reinforces the fluid nature between the Tibetan categories of the frog (pictured in the rite's images) and the description of the *nāga* within the text of the rite.

This ritual also utilizes various contaminating and harmful substances. The ritual directs the practitioner to put various poisons on the *garuḍa* circle. Interestingly in contrast, on the frog, one puts the "three whites" (Tib. *dkar gsum*; curds, milk, and butter) and the "three sweets" (Tib. *mngar gsum*; molasses, honey, and sugar).[18] These are used as a food offering to spirits. Thus, in this configuration there is a positive offering, coupled with the poisons. Perhaps this arrangement entices the spirits in, divides them from their protection, consequently locking the entity inside the constructed trap. Also, various types of blood are smeared on the effigy. After reciting the complete female *preta* mantras, the practitioner then completes the act by folding the frog and *garuḍa*, again locking the *liṅga* in between this union.

The choice in this rite to implement the *garuḍa* and frog/*klu* (Skt. *nāga*) is a powerful inversion of their normal roles in Indic folklore.[19] Generally, the *garuḍa* and the *nāga* are sworn enemies consistently locked in a battle.[20] As is the case in the rite, the *garuḍa* is often depicted with a *nāga* in its mouth. In an Indic myth found in the *Suparṇādhyāya* and the *Mahābhārata*, the *garuḍa* and *nāga*'s enmity begins with a case of half-sibling rivalry, as Kaśyapa impregnates two different women, resulting in two lines of progeny—the *garuḍa*s and the *nāga*s (Zimmer 1955: 52–3). Furthermore, in terms of cosmology, the *garuḍa* and the *nāga* represent the opposing ends of a vertical schema of the Tibetan world: the upperworlds (here symbolized by a bird-like creature, the *garuḍa*), the earth-bound realm (where the effigy is locked), and the underworld (the realm of the *klu*).[21] In regard to the folding of the material paper during this rite, the title of the rite uses the terminology "*kha sbyor*"; this phrase literally means "join at the mouth." This is also a phrase utilized to describe the *yab yum*, the sexual union of the male with his female consort. As mentioned above, it is integral that there is a sex assigned to each entity, the *garuḍa* as the female and the *nāga* as the male. This allows their union to be a symbol of sexual yoga, a *yab yum* formation. In an inversion of their mythic rivalry, they become partners in destroying the humanoid effigy in the middle.

After this union is created, next the practitioner binds the paper and inserts it into a skull, a yak horn, or an ox horn. There is an integral geospatial component here as well, as it is important to place the materials in a specified location. The best place is identified as bodies of water occupied by spirit entities such as the *klu*; the middling option identifies religious structures including a temple and a *stūpa*, and the last resort is to place the object in a *vajra*-crossed path (Tib. *lam rgya gram*), a tree root, or a bridge.

Interestingly, the ritual instruction acknowledges the dangerous nature of this performance and thus insists to spread *bdud tsi* (Skt. *amṛta*) in front of oneself for protection. Once these actions are completed, three platforms are constructed and they are to be circumambulated counterclockwise weekly. It is important to correlate the performance of this ritual with the malignant stars and planets (Tib. *gza' skar ngan*); in other words, the rite ought to be performed on inauspicious days. The text explicitly states that this rite will devour the enemy, as this is a rite of *rbod gtong* (inciting and dispatching, also translated as liberation[22] sorcery).

A rite such as this is a prime example of the proposed narrowed category of magic that I have outlined above in four features truncated here as: target, activation of power, sympathetic means, and intensifying effects. There is a clear target—a vow breaker. The name of this target is written on all three illustrations. It is clear that the illustrations are set as a guide to conduct this ritual multiple times (namely, it is expected to be a repeated action). One clue of its transmutability is the replacement phrase for the target name "*che ge mo*" (such and such person), thus alerting the practitioner that he can insert anyone's name into this standard formula. As mentioned above, the connection to the victim is created by writing this name on the ritual objects as they are manipulated in the ritual space. The mantras and the physical acts of folding the charts and inserting them into other objects transform the items into power objects that provide the conduit to affect the physical world. The ultimate aim is to increase the risk toward the victim, here specifically to kill him.

Throughout this ritual, the practitioner is presented with various choices of materials. This supports the case that these rites are actually meant to be physically performed. The outline of the steps for the ritual defines an ordered structure, yet it remains malleable to fit various scenarios. For example, at the beginning, the rite calls for a special kind of bark or simply regular paper. If this was not meant to be truly performed, what reason would there be to introduce alternatives to the main option? I contend that this is evidence of actual performance and reflective of the realities of the magician on the ground; the magician is an individual that is limited by his surroundings and hence available materials. Perhaps birch bark is the most desirable and effective writing medium due to its ancient use.[23] The natural birch bark represents a material connected to a purer and distant past that transmutes to a higher-powered medium. However, the writer of this text is aware that the optimal material may not always be available to the practitioner, thus an alternative is suggested—regular paper (Tib. *shog bu*) made from a pulp-pouring process. A presentation of a choice appears again toward the end of the ritual, as the practitioner chooses whether to put the folded illustrations into a skull, a yak horn, or an ox horn. The text explicitly states that the skull is the best vessel, followed by the yak horn, then the ox horn. This three-tiered hierarchy is introduced again in the context of placement. As outlined above, the practitioner can choose between placing the conglomeration into a body of water, a religious site, or a natural area like the roots of trees. Important to note here too, besides the pragmatic concerns of acquiring various substances and objects, this "choice" could be related to narratives of efficacy. If the ritual does not seem to cause the desired result, perhaps the reason for this lack of efficacy is using an object that is the least desirable and thus not as effective. This shifts the responsibility from the practitioner's power and abilities to the power of the objects themselves (or the lack thereof).

Rite number 2: Lepers and frogs

The second rite I will present immediately follows rite number 1 in the order of the compilation. This second rite is called "The ritual of the live leper and live frog from the *Nāga's Moon's Mystery*."[24] It exists in three folios. The colophon attributes this rite to Padmasambhava, and it contains three different sets of actions. The first two implement a male leper. The third includes a living frog as the main instrumental mechanism of the rite.

The first living-leper action requires the practitioner to thinly peel the flesh from the ribs of a black-haired bull. On this slice of flesh, the practitioner draws an effigy with the resin of an evergreen tree (Tib. *rgya skegs*). At the heart of the effigy, he must write the given and family name of the victim. Again, like the ritual above, this provides the sympathetic connection between the image and the essence of the victim. Next, he writes the mantras and curses on the effigy. Then, the practitioner must anoint the material with the "three whites" and the "three sweets." After this, he performs the division from the protections and completes the summoning. He recites ten thousand mantras and scatters mustard seed (Tib. *yungs dkar*). Interestingly, the practitioner is warned that this recitation will cause boils to rise on his own body, mouth, and tongue; however, he should not be concerned about that outcome. After finishing the recitation, he must roll up the effigy, bind it with sinews, and dip it in blood. Then he must give this effigy to a live male leper to ingest; specifically, he offers twenty-five of these effigies to the leper, one day at a time. Like the first rite, it is essential that this process occurs on inauspicious days. The rite notes that after scattering and making the final offerings, the effigies must be anointed with whatever is suitable. In this case the effigy is anointed with the six wastes of the body (Tib. *dri ma drug*)—excrement, urine, eye mucus, ear wax, saliva, and/or nasal mucus.

The next living-leper act within this rite particularly outlines the aim of killing; thus, I interpret the previous action of this rite as simply giving the enemy leprosy, matching the aim given in the first line of the ritual. This second act is similar in preparations to the last. The practitioner must construct an effigy. In this prescription, the writing medium is the blood from the sliced ribs of the black ox. Again, the effigy is offered to a leper.

The third act of this rite, the living-frog action, requires a variegated blue frog from the mouth of a spring. The practitioner constructs an effigy and draws the name and mantras on the effigy with uterine blood. The effigy is also rolled up and anointed with the "three whites" and the "three sweets." Then, the six wastes of the enemy are added. The effigy is inserted into the mouth of the frog. The frog is then released in a spring, a lake, or a cascading waterfall. If the frog returns to the release point, the practitioner is instructed to merely do the general offerings (namely, there is no need for deity meditation, *gtor ma* offerings, or reciting the mantras). This is an interesting passage, as it outlines other actions that are usually part of these types of ritual programs but are assumed rather than outlined in the recipe. The final comment in the rite is that this act should result in the victim contracting leprosy.

This series of instructions for the three acts of the second rite is similar to the first rite. Mantras and effigies are used to activate the magical connection to the victim; however, in this instance a living being is used as the main conduit of that power. The digestive system of the living entities provides the mechanism of transformation, projecting the intent out into the world. These rites have a specified target, again the vow breaker (Tib. *dam nyams*). The intent of misfortune here is specifically to bestow leprosy upon (or kill) others. In the first section a living leper is utilized to provide a point of infection. In the second, the frog is utilized. Since the frog and *klu* are interchangeable in this worldview, it is not surprising this animal is used since the *klu* are connected to skin diseases like leprosy. This will be discussed more thoroughly in a later section below.

Rite number 3: Hail casting

The final rite I will discuss is "From the *Secret Tantra of the Poison Mountain, Ocean of the Glorious Black Moon's Mystery*: The ritual application of the planetary demon Black Lord of Death for causing hail to fall, destroying the yearly grain."[25] This rite appears in the latter half of the collection in four folios. The main tantra this text cites, the *Secret Tantra of the Poison Mountain, Ocean of the Glorious Black Moon's Mystery*, can be found in the Mtshams brag edition of the *Rnying ma rgyud 'bum* in volume 45 (text 5).[26] Specifically, the rite claims this ritual is based on chapter sixteen of this tantra. The mantra included in this chapter matches the mantra in this rite; however, the content is not exact, thus it is more appropriate to utilize the terminology "inspired" by these Rnying ma tantras to indicate this discrepancy. This tantra is a Mahāyoga tantra translated by Gnubs chen sangs rgyas ye shes.[27]

This ritual instructs the practitioner to procure a head of a wild animal or a skull of a leper or beggar; one must shave it, then smear blood inside of the bald skull. This blood must be from a human, a horse, and a dog. Then to affect the harvest land, since this is to destroy grains, poisons and blood from a person who has been killed by a weapon (Tib. *gri khrag*) are poured onto the ground. Next, in a hollowed-out frog carcass, the practitioner must smash these substances with poison. After that, the frog is inserted into the skull, and then this conglomeration is placed inside of a triangular hearth, the hearth shape that is common in hostile rites. Next, the practitioner is instructed to offer *gtor ma* to Yamāri, the *nāga*s, Rāhula, and the eight classes of spirits. Then the practitioner must abide in the pride of Yamāri,[28] an essential indicator that these types of magical actions are woven into the very framework of religious practice and not in contrast to the Buddhist religion as a categorical distinction. Similar to the examples above, the rite highlights the best time to complete these actions. Here, the optimal timing is on a day of the full moon, the fifth day, the ninth day, or the third day in this lunar cycle.

The aim of this rite is to suppress the speech of a specific target—the hail chaser (Tib. *ser bsrung*), a practitioner who is responsible for protecting the community against hailstorms. Again, the rite is activated via recitation of mantras and manipulation of special objects. In this case, there is activation through burning in a triangular hearth. Furthermore, this rite serves as another example of sympathy; the practitioner pours substances out on the area he hopes will receive the hailstorms and utilizes the same substances in his ritual space to activate that connection.

Ritual narrative arc

Prior to discussing the major themes of the collection, I want to emphasize the nature of these rites as repeatable, identifiable formulas of action. To be sure, each of the above rituals outlines an order of performance following a specific syntax, or "arc of narrative."[29] Generally, these rites form the following syntax: homage, preparation of power materials, mantra recitation and activation of materials, placement outside the preparatory space, a time specifier, and a brief colophon.

The first aspect of each ritual is to pay homage to Yamāntaka. In the three example rites, this is in the form of the phrase "Ya mā ri *na mo*." After the homage, the title is usually restated, frequently including the related tantric text. Then, each rite gives instructions on preparing the ritual materials, whether it be to procure a skull or make an effigy, and so on. This preparation creates sympathetic connections, aligning intent toward the victim. It also sets the stage for action and provides a ripe ritual space for supermundane entities to enter the area. The mantra recitation is integral to activating and communicating power. In the second ritual above (the live-entity rites) it is apparent that the mantra is specific to the individual action. The mantras used to activate the ritual in the first two sections of this rite dealing with the live leper differ from one another. The first mantra notably begins with the syllables "*nā ga*."[30] Firstly, although in some cases syllables in mantras do not form any syntactical meaning, there are important syllables incorporated into the utterance that are specifically signifying through a recognizable word. As witnessed in this case, it is directly related to the entities being invoked in the process, the *nāga*s (the leprosy-related serpent deity). Secondly, even though these mantras are present in the same ritual, they are prescribed for two very different results. The first mantra aims to infect the victim while the second mantra aims to kill. Even within the same rite one can see that the mantra is imperative for a unique identity of this particular aim. After the recitation of the mantra, a final step usually sets the object in the world, that is, outside of the initial ritual space. This establishes where the ritual mechanism will reside and transmit its power. At the closure of the rite, the instructions usually suggest a time period that is best for performance and then the final inclusion is a brief colophon. This colophon typically notes the author of the rite and restates the name of the rite, including any information about the tantras in which it takes its inspiration. Any illustrations that will help the practitioner construct the preparatory materials are appended here. Importantly, one can assume there are parts to this performance that are not explicitly prescribed here in this bare-bones structure. In other words, it is not necessary to have a written account of their instruction because the practitioners are so familiar with these other components that these actions are just assumed. This is apparent in the living-frog rite. Recall the rite states that if the frog returns there is no need to perform the deity meditation, the *gtor ma* offerings, or recite the mantras. The deity meditations and *gtor ma* offerings were not previously mentioned in the first part of this rite; thus, they are components that are assumed to take place (but of course here highlighting that the practitioner does not have to perform them again). Therefore, what is explicitly included must be necessary, a basic reminder of the important specific identity of each ritual. For example, the nature of the mantra is included because it is an element that changes from rite to rite and it is important to that individual identity. Other parts are more formulaic and appear in many of the rites, for example, the division and summoning.

Power through transgressing the boundaries of purity: The contaminated and the inverted

The efficacy of these rituals relies on power activation and communication through a variety of means. In addition to the mechanisms such as effigies and mantras described above, there are two other modes of power conveyance operating in these rites—the use of contaminating substances and inversions. As demonstrated in the example rites, certain contaminated[31] or polluting substances and/or objects are prominent in these rituals. In fact, many if not all of the rites in the *Moon's Mystery* employ these contaminated substances, for example, the blood of lepers, feces, poison, skulls, and so forth. These impure substances in many cases serve as an activator, as in the first example of the effigy, aiding in bringing a polluted or dangerous enemy's essence to the ritual space.

I contend that the contaminated substances are operating on two levels here, firstly in a more pragmatic operation within the logic of the tradition—the contaminated attracts the corrupted. This logic is another sympathetic connection that supports the use of the term "magic" as outlined in my tentative definition. In other words, it simply makes sense to attract and attack "bad" individuals (like the vow breakers or a competing sorcerer) with anything deemed counter to mainstream ideas of the pure (e.g., any diseased substances, substances related to excrement, or substances related to death). Secondly, in tantra, the macabre and the grotesque transmute to ritual power. Indeed, in the general tantric Buddhist context, the wrathful is a symbol of overcoming afflictions and death. In this ritual context, the macabre is exemplified by invoking a Yamāntaka deity, literally "the slayer of death." The macabre is visceral; these items signal the crudeness of our mundane reality, our material reality of the process of life and death. Take, for example, the above prescriptions for procuring a skull, a yak horn, or an ox horn. In a general sense the skull may be the more macabre as a direct signifier of death, but in fact, all of these items are related to death and particularly causing death. Since these animals do not shed their horns, these items are difficult to procure without transgressing the boundaries of normative Buddhist ethics.[32] Since these contaminated items are socially toxic materials, ideally it is only the high-level adepts that can handle them. The contamination is active in the world, while the adept remains unphased. These acts thus signal the adepts' realization of nonduality and the ability to manipulate the world.[33]

Relatedly, many inversions are utilized in the *Moon's Mystery*, which represent a recurring theme in this collection and another mechanism of power. As discussed above, the aversion between the *nāga* and the *garuḍa* is turned upside down, presenting the pair in a *yab yum* formation. Another prime feature is the prominence of "black" (Tib. *nag po*) as a qualifier. The animals used in the rituals are specified as black-haired. Furthermore, many of the tantras that inspire these rites contain "black" in the titles, most notably the namesake tantra *The Black Moon's Mystery*. This notion of "black" is generally related to sorcery as "black" magic, that is, magic that harms. Although this notion is not limited to the Tibetan world, a prime example from Tibetan sources is the color designation of the various "beryl" (*bai dūrya*) collections attributed to Sangs rgyas rgya mtsho (1653–1705), the famous regent of the Fifth Dalai Lama (1617–1682). For example, the *Black Beryl* is a collection of curses, in other words, black magic. Also, in the *White Beryl* (his treatise on Tibetan astrology) Sangs rgyas rgya mtsho uses a tripartite distinction of incest—the black, the white, and the motley. These are presented in a hierarchical nature, black being the most detrimental form, designating relations between individuals of the paternal group (Samuels 2021: 28–32). Thus, in the most general sense, it seems that the color black connotates the harmful or impure.

There are a few other notable inversions throughout the manual. For example, once the practitioner constructs the platform/altar he must circumambulate it counterclockwise. Generally, circumambulations in the Tibetan Buddhist world occur clockwise, as in the direction one would go around a *stūpa* (reliquary). Furthermore, the rite specifies that one must perform the ritual during the time of the "malignant stars, and the deceptions of the earthly lords" on the twenty-ninth of the month. This is a reference to specific days that are determined through divinatory practices to be suitable for certain activities. For example, Tibetans will only hang prayer flags on certain days of the month. Otherwise, hanging them on days not deemed auspicious could bring about extremely bad luck. Here, it is clear that performance of these rites must occur on an inauspicious day, contrary to other types of ritual action or devotion. A significant part of this type of ritual program is creating a world to invite and manipulate the dangers of the spirit world; these elements of inauspiciousness facilitate that.

Prominence of the *Klu* in the *Moon's Mystery*

Leprosy and the *klu* are a recurrent theme in this collection, which is not surprising since the traditional Tibetan view is that the *klu* cause these sorts of skin diseases. Many of the rites require the blood and skull of lepers; these items serve as a powerful symbol. In the past, and even in some instances today, leprous individuals were socially shunned. Not only was there a fear of acute transmission, becoming infected oneself, but from the tradition's perspective, contracting leprosy is a sign of moral weakness. To be sure, the individuals who contract the disease are susceptible to attacks by spirit entities such as the *klu* because of their moral failings.[34] Following this logic, when the ritual calls for a skull of a leper, a beggar's skull will also suffice, namely, anyone who is outside of the mainstream social structure is a good connector to attack others like vow breakers.

Furthermore, in relation to this collection, the *klu* (specifically the king of the *klu*) are directly connected to protecting the treasure cycles of Gnubs chen. In the *Gnubs kyi rgya bo che*, believed by the tradition to be an autobiography, Gnubs chen describes entrusting the king of the *klu* with his earth treasures and binding them with a bundle of snakes (Dalton 2014: 154). The ambivalent characteristics of the *klu* are thus exemplified here and in the context of the compilation; the *klu* are clearly both a protector of the teachings and a disease vector (in the case of the *Moon's Mystery*) used as a weapon against others.

Accordingly, many of the effigies employed in the handbook include serpentine aspects. Some of the human effigies have serpents encircling the body, devouring the hands and arms. One particular grouping of rites that cite the *Black Moon's Mystery* has separate images of *klu* demons. The *klu* demons are depicted with a human torso and head but with a serpentine tail replacing the lower body. They have nine snakes on the crown of their heads (Brown 2021; 80–4). These images have similar attributes to another wrathful form of Mañjuśrī, 'Jam dpal Nā ga rakṣa and to Rāhula.[35] Nā ga rakṣa is mentioned in the handbook, particularly in mantras, but this entity is included along with spirit entities or dharma protectors such as Yama and Rāhula, not as an enlightened being. Further research would have to be conducted to verify whether this form of Mañjuśrī is connected directly to any of these materials or their related textual cycles.[36]

Conclusion

The *Moon's Mystery* is a fascinating collection of rites that challenges the basic stereotypes of Buddhism as the quintessential nonviolent religion. In fact, this ritual program uses the power of those normative views by inverting them. The *Moon's Mystery* is unique both as a collection of Rnying ma Yamāntaka rites and as an example of a collection of aggressive Buddhist magic or sorcery. Although there are merits to conducting highly specialized studies for specific sets of practices in their own cultural context, it is integral to expand those conversations outside of those boundaries both for cross-cultural analysis and pedagogical purposes. I hope this study provides future avenues of research in which similar compendiums of magic can be compared in the contexts of other traditions, even outside of the Buddhist world. Maintaining the category of "magic" as a tool for scholarly analysis aids in this endeavor. I contend that using a narrowed and responsible definition of magic as outlined in this chapter can facilitate these important conversations.

Notes

1 This compilation, attributed to Gnubs chen sangs rgyas ye shes and 'Jam dpal bshes gnyen (published in 1975), can be found at the Buddhist Digital Resource Center W2CZ7967.

2 See Siklós (1996); Wenta (2020); and Cuevas (2021) for a history of Vajrabhairava/ Yamāntaka text cycles.
3 A catalogue for the *Zla gsang be'u bum* can be found in my master's thesis (Brown 2021: 78–135).
4 Cited in the text as *Pha chen snubs kyi gong khug* (Brown 2021: 130–4). See Esler (2022) for an introduction to the ritual program of Rgya Zhang khrom.
5 Notable studies include Beyer (1978) and van Schaik (2020).
6 For example, see J. Z. Smith's critique of the term (2004).
7 The general "ideal" here is a practitioner who is considered a tantric bodhisattva. This is an individual who has the ability to transgress normative Buddhist ethical systems, following a higher sense of compassionate morality and thus transcending duality. However, in the lived traditions, various local village priests engage in this sort of practice, and, as Nicolas Sihlé has described, these individuals would not always fall into the category of a "high-level" adept (2010).
8 See Tambiah (1968); Goudriaan (1989); Versnel (1991); Glucklich (1997); Thomassen (1997); Hoffman (2002); M. Bailey (2006); Sørensen (2014); White (2017).
9 See Ariel Glucklich's theory of interrelatedness (1997: 22, 96).
10 See Gomez (1977); Granoff (1996); Clough (2012); and Fiordalis (2012) for discussion of these various "miraculous" and "wonder-working" powers.
11 I am following the classic anthropological definition of "sorcery" as outlined by Evans-Pritchard, that is, actions that are employed against others via a specific ritual program. This is distinct from the innate ability connotated by the word "witchcraft" (1976: 1). Furthermore, I am purposely avoiding the term "witchcraft" here due to its use in academic sources on medieval Europe from the fifteenth century onward that discuss specific accusations toward practitioners who perform harmful magic (Lat. *maleficium*) (M. Bailey 2019: 487). This use of the term strongly suggests activity of "demons" and the "devil" in contrast to the power of God (M. Bailey 2001: 961–5). This agency of a definitive good or evil entity does not translate well to a Buddhist context. Sorcery too can have this valence, but the origin (a divinatory valence from Lat. *sortilegium*) and history of this term in a Western context carry a milder connotation and a broader meaning.
12 Note *mdze* can have a more general meaning of "skin disease."
13 See Cuevas (2011) for an excellent study on human effigies in Tibetan ritual.
14 *Ma gshin 'chol ba'i sngags rgod khyung klu kha sbyor gyi gtad khram* (Brown 2021: 86–8, rite no. 08).
15 The illustration appended to this rite is also shown in Cuevas (2010) as an example of destructive, fierce rites (which are interestingly not included in the ritual manual compiled by 'Ju Mi pham).

16 Perhaps this is the first *chung tshang*, 'Bri gung Chos kyi grags pa (1595–1659). This is likely given his connection to Yamāntaka text cycles, most notably the rites of the "Black Tortoise," the "Red Wind," and the "Red and Black Faced Rāhula" (Fitzherbert 2018: 66). Chos kyi grags pa is credited in other rites of the collection, but in these rites his dates are specified; thus, the identification in these instances is more conclusive than it is here. The qualifying phrase of the pith instructions in the text is mostly illegible, but it may read "*ba thu mkhan zhang gi*." There is a Yamāntaka tradition in Tibet known as the Zhang lineage, the lineage from the translator Zhang cog gru Shes rab bla ma (Cuevas 2021: 35–40). He is responsible for the prominent 49-Deity Vajrabhairava practice. But if this is referring to Zhang Lo tsā ba, it leaves the question of a direct relation to teachings received by Chos kyi grags pa. Thus, the absolute identity of both individuals in this context remains unknown without further research.

17 The eight *nāga* kings are as follows: Mtha' yas, Rigs ldan, Dung skyong, Padma chen po, Padma, Stobs rgyu, 'Jog po, and Nor rgyas. A similar lotus is described in Nebesky-Wojkowitz's discussion of rain-making rituals (1996: 476–8).

18 For a discussion of the "three sweets," see Wenta's contribution in this volume (pp. xx–xx).

19 For a discussion of the *khyung*'s usual role as a subduer of the *klu* in Tibetan texts of the *Rnying ma rgyud 'bum*, see Hillis (2002).

20 See Wenta's related discussion of "The Logic of Archenemies" in Chapter 3 (pp. 61–84).

21 Robert Wessing discusses this Indic tale and similar themes of place in Southeast Asia (2006). Also see Vargas (2013: 111–15).

22 An euphemism for killing, signaling the greater compassionate motives and techniques of an adept who can utilize *'pho ba* techniques to guide someone's consciousness to a superior realm.

23 van Schaik (2020: 50, 79) describes the use of birch bark in old *dhāraṇī* manuscripts and other Buddhist manuscripts found along the Silk Road, some dating perhaps as early as the first century CE.

24 *Klu'i zla gsang mdze po dang sbal pa'i gson gtad* (Brown 2021: 88–9, rite no. 09). The title of this related tantra appears as *'Chi bdag klu'i zla gsang* in the first line of the rite.

25 *Dpal zla gsang nag po rgya mtsho dug ri kha'i gsang rgyud las / lo 'bras brlag byed gza' 'chi bdag nag pos skyin thang dbab pa'i las sbyor* (Brown 2021: 117, rite no. 34).

26 In the Dpal Brtsegs edition: Volume 52 (text 12).

27 This "oceanic cycle" is associated with a particular form of Yamāntaka, the Black Longevity Lord (Tib. Tshe bdag nag po/'Chi bdag nag po; Skt. Āyuṣpatikāla). This form is associated with the treasure cycles of Gnubs's reincarnation Rgya Zhang khrom.

28 This indicates that the practitioner must rise up in the form of the deity.

29 This discussion is inspired by Daniel Stevenson's description of Chinese Buddhist rites for securing rebirth in the Pure Land (2008: 173–5).
30 Interestingly, the second mantra appears in the *devanāgarī* script with the Tibetan-script equivalent noted in the margin. I posit that this is a technique to signal Indic provenance and thus legitimacy.
31 I use contaminated meaning substances that one would avoid in any mundane setting (i.e., any substances thought to cause illness or invite unsavory spirits to the area).
32 In the worldview of the Tibetan pastoralist, all three of these items (the skull and various horns) are known to be what Toni Huber (2019: 5–8) calls "the killer's share." This is the share that the hunter takes when a large animal like a yak is killed. Huber argues that the head and horns have the highest ritual value and that their ownership signals the highest moral burden that is taken on by the actual slayer (compared to the rest of the hunting party). Also note, some ethnographic material suggests that certain magicians recognize the problematic nature of procuring these substances (Klein and Khetsün Sangpo 1997: 543).
33 See Wedemeyer (2013: 117–32) for a discussion of interpreting tantra via semiotics.
34 For a robust discussion of leprosy, disease, and the *klu* see Vargas (2003: 66–9; 2010; and 2013). Vargas notes that disruption of the natural environment and violation of sexual norms particularly agitate the *klu*.
35 See C. Bailey (2015: 61–5) for a discussion of Rāhula's relation to Yamāntaka.
36 I would like to thank Stéphane Arguillère for bringing this form of Mañjuśrī to my attention at the sixteenth annual International Association for Tibetan Studies Conference 2022.

References

Primary source

Gnubs chen sangs rgyas ye shes and 'Jam dpal bshes gnyen (1975), *Zla gsang be'u bum*, Dehra Dun: D. G. Khochchen Trulku, BDRC W2CZ7967.

Secondary sources

Bailey, C. (2015), "The Demon Seer: Rāhula and the Inverted Mythology of Indo-Tibetan Buddhism," *Journal of the International Association of Buddhist Studies* 38: 33–72.

Bailey, M. (2001), “From Sorcery to Witchcraft: Clerical Conceptions of Magic in the Later Middle Ages,” *Speculum* 76 (4): 960–90.

Bailey, M. (2006), “The Meanings of Magic,” *Magic, Ritual, and Witchcraft* 1: 1–23.

Bailey, M. (2019), “Superstition and Sorcery,” in S. Page and C. Rider (eds.), *The Routledge History of Medieval Magic*, 487–501, London: Routledge.

Bell, C. (2020), *Tibetan Demonology*, New York: Cambridge University Press.

Beyer, S. (1978), *The Cult of Tārā: Magic and Ritual in Tibet*, Berkeley: University of California Press.

Brown, A. N. (2021), “Hail-Casting and Other ‘Magical’ Rites from a Compendium of Nyingma Rituals Invoking Yamāntaka: A Study and Catalogue of the *Moon's Mystery Handbook* (*Zla gsang be'u bum*),” MA thesis, Florida State University.

Clough, B. S. (2012), “The Cultivation of Yogic Powers in the Pāli Path Manuals of Theravāda Buddhism,” in K. A. Jacobsen (ed.), *Yoga Powers: Extraordinary Capacities Attained through Meditation and Concentration*, 77–95, Leiden: Brill.

Copenhaver, B. P. (2015), *Magic in Western Culture: From Antiquity to the Enlightenment*, New York: Cambridge University Press.

Cornu, P. (2002), *Tibetan Astrology*, trans. H. Gregor, Boston, MA: Shambhala.

Cuevas, B. J. (2010), “The Calf's Nipple (*Be'u bum*) of Ju Mipam ('Ju Mi pham): A Handbook of Tibetan Ritual Magic,” in J. I. Cabezón (ed.), *Tibetan Ritual*, 165–86, New York: Oxford University Press.

Cuevas, B. J. (2011), “Illustrations of Human Effigies in Tibetan Ritual Texts: With Remarks on Specific Anatomical Figures and Their Possible Iconographic Source,” *Journal of the Royal Asiatic Society, Series 3*, Vol. 21, Part 1: 72–97.

Cuevas, B. J. (2021), *The Rwa pod and Other 'Lost' Works of Rwa lo tsā ba's Vajrabhairava Tradition: A Catalogue of Recently Acquired Tibetan Manuscripts from Mongolia and Khams and Their Significance*, Wien: Arbeitskreis für Tibetische und Buddhistische Studien Universität Wien.

Dalton, J. (2014), “Preliminary Remarks on a Newly Discovered Biography of Nupchen Sangyé Yeshé,” in B. Bogin and A. Quintman (eds.), *Himalayan Passages: Tibetan and Newar Studies in Honor of Hubert Decleer*, 145–61, Boston, MA: Wisdom.

Esler, D. (2022), “Yamāntaka's Wrathful Magic: An Instance of the Ritual Legacy of gNubs chen Sangs rgyas ye shes on the Byang gter Tradition via the Figure of rGya Zhang khrom,” *Revue d'Etudes Tibétaines* 62: 190–215.

Evans-Pritchard, E. E. (1976), *Witchcraft, Oracles, and Magic among the Azande*, Oxford: Clarendon Press.

Fiordalis, D. V. (2012), “The Wondrous Display of Superhuman Power in the *Vimalakīrtinirdeśa*: Miracle or Marvel?,” in K. A. Jacobsen (ed.), *Yoga Powers: Extraordinary Capacities Attained through Meditation and Concentration*, 97–125, Leiden: Brill.

Fitzherbert, S. G. (2018), “Rituals as War Propaganda in the Establishment of the Tibetan Ganden Phodrang State in the Mid-17th Century,” in A. Travers and

F. Venturi (eds.), *Cahiers d'Extrême Asie* 27: 49–120, Kyoto: École française d'Extrême-Orient.

Glucklich, A. (1997), *The End of Magic*, New York: Oxford University Press.

Gómez, L. O. (1977), "The Bodhisattva as Wonder-worker," in L. Lancaster (ed.) and L. O. Gomez (assoc. ed.), *Prajñāpāramitā and Related Systems: Studies in honor of Edward Conze*, 221–61, Berkeley: Buddhist Studies Series.

Goudriaan, T. (1989), "Magic in South Asia," in L. E. Sullivan (ed.), *Hidden Truths: Magic, Alchemy, and the Occult*, 131–5, New York: Macmillan.

Granoff, P. (1996), "The Ambiguity of Miracles: Buddhist Understandings of Supernatural Power," *East and West* 46 (½): 79–96.

Hillis, G. (2002), "*Khyung* Texts in the *Rnying ma'i rgyud 'bum*," in H. Eimer and D. Germano (eds.), *The Many Canons of Tibetan Buddhism*, 313–34, Boston, MA: Brill Academic.

Hoffman, C. A. (2002). "Fiat Magia," in P. Mirecki and M. Meyer (eds.), *Magic and Ritual in the Ancient World*, 179–96. Leiden: Koninklijke Brill.

Huber, T. (2019), "Dismemberment and sharing of game meat by pastoralist hunters on the Tibetan Platueau," *Études mongoles et sibériennes, centrasiatiques et tibétaines*, March 4, 2019. Available online: http://journals.openedition.org/emscat/3969 (accessed November 14, 2022).

Klein, A., and Khetsun Sangpo (1997), "Hail Protection," in D. S. Lopez Jr. (ed.), *Religions of Tibet in Practice*, 538–47, Princeton, NJ: Princeton University Press.

Nebesky-Wojkowitz, R. (1996), *Oracles and Demons of Tibet: The Cult and Iconography of the Tibetan Protective Deities*, Reprint, Kathmandu: Pilgrims Book House.

Samuels, J. (2021), "Incest, Classified: A Seventeenth-Century Tibetan Ruler's Perspective on Sexual Proscriptions and the Boundaries of Kinship," *Inner Asia* 23: 21–50.

Sihlé, N. (2010), "Written Texts at the Juncture of the Local and the Global: Some Anthropological Considerations on a Local Corpus of Tantric Ritual Manuals," in J. I. Cabezón (ed.), *Tibetan Ritual*, 35–52, New York: Oxford University Press.

Siklós, B. (1996), *The Vajrabhairava Tantras: Tibetan and Mongolian Versions, English Translation and Annotations*, Tring: The Institute of Buddhist Studies.

Smith, J. Z. (2004), "Trading Places," in J. Z. Smith (ed.), *Relating Religion: Essays in the Study of Religion*, 215–29, Chicago: University of Chicago Press.

Sørensen, J. (2014), "Magic Reconsidered: Towards a Scientifically Valid Concept of Magic," in B. C. Otto and M. Stausberg (eds.), *Defining Magic: A Reader*, 229–42. New York: Routledge.

Stevenson, D. B. (2008), "The Ties That Bind: Chinese Buddhist Rites for Securing Rebirth in the Pure Land," *Hōrin: Vergleichende Studien zur japanischen Kultur* 15: 139–202.

Tambiah, S. (1968), "The Magical Power of Words," *Man*, New Series 3, no. 2: 175–208.

Thomassen, E. (1997), "Is magic a subclass of ritual?," in D. R. Jordan, H. Montgomery, and E. Thomassen (eds.), *The World of Ancient Magic: Papers from the First*

International Samson Eitrem Seminar at the Norwegian Institute, 55–66. Bergen: The Norwegian Institute at Athens.
van Schaik, S. (2020), *Buddhist Magic: Divination, Healing, and Enchantment through the Ages*, Boulder, CO: Shambhala Publications.
Vargas, I. (2003), "*Falling to Pieces, Emerging Whole*: Suffering Illness and Healing Renunciation in the Dge slong ma Dpal mo Tradition," Ph.D. diss., Harvard University, Cambridge, MA.
Vargas, I. (2010), "Legitimising Demon Diseases in Tibetan Medicine: The Conjoining of Religion, Medicine, and Ecology," in S. Craig et al. (eds.), *Studies of Medical Pluralism in Tibetan History and Society*, 379–404, Leiden: E.J. Brill.
Vargas-O'Bryan, I. (2013), "Falling Rain, Reigning Power in Reptilian Affairs: The Balance of Religion and the Environment," *Religions of South Asia* 7: 110–25.
Versnel, H. S. (1991), "Some Reflections on the Relationship Magic-Religion," *Numen* 38 (2): 177–97.
Wedemeyer, C. K. (2013), *Making Sense of Tantric Buddhism: History, Semiology, & Transgression in the Indian Traditions*, New York: Columbia University Press.
Wenta, A. (2020), "The *Vajramahābhairavatantra*: Its Origins, Intertextuality, and Transmission," Ph.D. diss., University of Oxford.
Wessing, R. (2006), "Symbolic Animals in the Land between Waters: Markers of Place and Transition," *Asian Folklore Studies* 65 (2): 205–39.
White, E. (2017), "Contemporary Buddhism and Magic," in M. Jerryson (ed.), *The Oxford Handbook of Contemporary Buddhism*, 591–605, Oxford: Oxford University Press.
Zimmer, H. (1955), *The Art of Indian Asia: Its Mythology and Transformations*, ed. Joseph Campbell, New York: Bollingen Foundation.

2

Magical Results of the Rituals in the *Tārā-mūla-kalpa*'s *Continuation Tantra*

Susan Landesman

Magical results of the rituals in the *Tārā-mūla-kalpa*'s *Continuation Tantra*

Whether rituals are performed to acquire gold or land, exert control over kings, live for an eon, or travel through the sky, such results won't manifest until suitable conditions are met. According to passages from the *Tārā-mūla-kalpa*, practitioners who wish to realize such attainments (*siddhi*s) must ensure that their rituals are perfectly performed, religious commitments are maintained, and respect for teachers, teachings, and tradition is upheld.[1]

The early Buddhist tantra with the abbreviated title *Tārā-mūla-kalpa* (TMK) documents the emergence of the female Buddha Tārā. Composed in Sanskrit during the seventh–eighth centuries in India, the text was brought to Tibet by Atīśa in 1042 and translated into Tibetan by Bu ston in 1361.[2] A chapter from the TMK entitled "The Eleventh Extensive Ritual of Prayer Beads"[3] provides the material for discussion. Its contents are attributed to "The Ritual Text of Ūrdhvajaṭā,"[4] a work that predates the *Tārā-mūla-kalpa* and serves as one of its sources.[5] Its rituals supplicate a form of Tārā with her locks (*jaṭā*) bound up (*ūrdhva*) or flowing skyward, and the word "kalpa," which means "ritual text," is an older word for "tantra."[6]

The chapter opens with the Buddha Bhagavān seated on the Potala King of Mountains.[7] There, he summons the Bodhisattva of Compassion Avalokiteśvara and asks him to explain the practices of " 'The Ritual Text of Ūrdhvajaṭā' and the *vidyā* shared by all Tārās."[8] In the long narration that follows, Avalokiteśvara explains how these rituals are performed, where, when, by whom, and for what reasons. He also explains the materials used, the varied results, and even why rituals fail. Ultimately, the reader learns how properly enacted rituals bring about the desired attainments (*siddhi*s). Although the text does not explicitly refer to its rituals as forms of magic, the resulting "attainments" could be interpreted as such (namely, acquiring gold and land, subjugating kings, becoming invisible, traveling through the sky, living for an eon, and so forth).

What definitions of magic emerge from studying Tibetan Buddhist text-cultures?

Building upon a general definition of magic will help to elucidate elements of Indo-Tibetan Buddhist magic that are unique. A general definition of magic entails "a belief in the role of invisible forces and the techniques that invoke these forces to influence events and change conditions."[9] From the viewpoint of Indo-Tibetan Buddhist rituals, the role of "invisible forces" would indicate the deity of the tantric ritual, that is, a Buddha or Bodhisattva. The "techniques" that invoke these forces would be the sacred syllables (*mantra*s and *vidyā*s) used to invoke the deity, and the practice of visualizing the deity in meditation (*sādhana*). Although the "deity" may be invisible to others (in a literal sense), it is clearly seen in the minds of practitioners. Thus, the *sādhana* enables the practitioner to access the mind's eye in order to harness a "visionary insight that permits the manipulation of unseen forces lying beneath the surface of things."[10] When asked to explain the practices and applications of the distinguished "Ritual Text of Ūrdhvajaṭā," Avalokiteśvara enacts a *sādhana*, whereby he cultivates a one-pointed concentration (*samādhi*) called "Viewing all sentient beings [with compassion]" and visualizes Bhagavatī Tārā, locks bound up, a third eye, four arms, and Bhagavān Amitābha seated on her head.[11] Avalokiteśvara further describes "[Tārā's] immense, divine body as the source of all the Tathāgatas, liberating all living beings and eliminating even the slightest [danger] whatsoever."[12] This visualization meditation (*sādhana*), accompanied by such things as vows, offerings, and *vidyā-mantra* recitations, comprise the tools with which the practitioner achieves attainments (*siddhi*s), many of which may be deemed magical in nature.

Comparing the major characteristics of magic with aspects of tantric rituals will also help to identify elements of magic in the TMK. The four major characteristics of magic are: (1) spells, namely, a word or phrase supposed to have magic power, (2) ritual performers, (3) rituals, and (4) materials, whether naturally "potent" or empowered via incantation or ritual.[13]

Regarding the first major characteristic of magic (spells), Malinowski underscores that words serve as the fundamental building blocks of magic: "From the very use of speech men develop the conviction that knowledge of a name, the correct use of a verb, the right application of a particle, have a mystical power which transcends … mere utilitarian convenience."[14] Within Buddhist context, sacred syllables constituting *mantras* and *vidyās* function as the "sound body" of the deity and its "animating essence."[15] These syllables, when intoned, do not simply embody magic power—as does a spell,—but invite an enlightened being to reside at the ritual (within a sacred image) and favorably influence its outcome. *Mantras* and *vidyās*[16] are traditionally obtained from one's guru during initiation: having embraced the three refuges, generated *bodhicitta*, and viewed the *maṇḍala*,[17] the practitioner is initiated with commitments (*samaya*), practices as the means to achievement (*sādhana*), and empowerment. "Having offered a gift to one's guru, and having accepted the *vidyā* of whichever [aspect of] Tārā is suitable—inside the *maṇḍala*, and in the presence of the painted cloth, or in front of an image—beginning from the first day of the waxing moon, the practitioner should recite [the *vidyā*] 100,000 [times]."[18] The repetition and ritual application of mantras facilitate the attainment of mundane magical powers and the ultimate goal of enlightenment.[19]

The second major characteristic of magic, the ritual performers, also appears in the "Ritual of Prayer-Beads." Herein, the practitioner (Tib. *sgrub pa po*) or the *vajra*-master (*ācārya*) who may be a lay devotee (*upāsaka* and *upāsikā*), a novice (*śrāmaṇera* and *śrāmaṇerī*), a monk (*bhikṣu*), or a nun (*bhikṣuṇī*)[20] either performs a variety of rituals for specific purposes. Practitioners who achieve superior attainments (*siddhi*) with superior powers are referred to as *vidyādharas*.[21]

Rituals comprise the third major characteristic of magic, which Brown defines as "procedures intended to produce palpable effects in the physical world."[22] In the TMK, three of the four major types of worldly rituals are featured: rituals to pacify or appease the deity (*śāntika*), prosperity rituals to yield everything desired (*pauṣṭika*), and rituals that subjugate or exert control over others (*vaśīkriyā*). A fourth type of worldly ritual, that is, fierce rites or destructive magic (*abhicāra*), is only found once in this chapter,[23] and two verses warn the reader to refrain from enacting fierce rites, which are repudiated by the sages (*muṇi*).[24]

The TMK's rituals are associated with three categories of "sacredness": sacred time, sacred place, and sacred object. Sacred places that are specified in the text include mountain peaks, the banks of a river or lake, the ocean shoreline, or charnel grounds. Often, a particular direction is indicated, whether a cardinal or intermediate direction. Sacred times of rituals are generally coordinated with celestial events, that is, during the full moon or new moon, the eighth, fourteenth, or fifteenth day of the waxing or waning moon, a span of time from the first day of the waxing moon to the full moon, and vice versa, as well as during lunar and solar eclipses. Rituals also take place in the presence of sacred objects which "house" the presence of the deity, whether a Buddha or Bodhisattva. During a ritual, the practitioner invites an enlightened being to inhabit an image; this can be a painted cloth (Skt. *paṭa*, Tib. *ras bris*, *thangka*), a *maṇḍala* (i.e., deity's "residence," Tib. *dkyil 'khor*), a *stūpa* with relics (Tib. *mchod rten*), or a sculptural image (Skt. *pratimā*; Tib. *sku gzugs*). Herein, the deity's presence favorably influences the ritual's outcome.

The fourth major characteristic of magic consists of the materials—whether naturally "potent" or empowered via incantation or ritual—that are used in the rituals. Here, the questions one may ask include: What magical technologies were employed to cause supernormal effects? Why were certain materials deemed "magical" while others were not? Although the list of materials for the rituals in the *Tārā-mūla-kalpa* is quite extensive, the effectiveness of these materials depends, in part, upon their consecration by means of recitations (a characteristic of magic), their role as an offering, and their use in combination with other materials. Initially, materials must be "consecrated" by reciting a *vidyā* or *mantra* over them multiple times, making them "potent" within the context of the ritual. Because a *vidyā* or *mantra* evokes the presence of an enlightened being, reciting it over a material offering infuses the offering with a divine presence. The number of recitations varies, depending upon the ritual. Usually, a practitioner recites a *vidyā* or *mantra* from one to 10 million times. The most commonly occurring numbers of recitations are 21, 800, and 100,000. Once consecrated, the material offerings are placed in the fire. The procedure of placing offerings in a fire may be repeated up to 2,100,000 times, with the most commonly occurring number of procedures being 8,000 and 100,000. Consequently, a complete set of ritual instructions mentions the type of sacred image, time, place, direction in which the ritual is to be performed, the number of times the practitioner is to recite a *vidyā* or *mantra*, the number of ritual performances that must be completed, as well as the specific material(s) that are to be offered for specific results. Because there are hundreds of rituals in this chapter, many rites are abbreviated, and certain categories of information are sometimes lacking. Generally, after a complete ritual appears in the text, variations of that ritual follow, which may only mention the items or parts that vary. In conclusion, the fire sacrifices, whose offerings are imbued with power via mantra recitations, performed at sacred times and places, and near sacred images (painted cloths, *maṇḍalas*, sculptures, or *stūpas*) housing the presence of a Buddha, Bodhisattva, or tantric deity, constitute the magical technologies of the ritual.

Types of rituals, offerings, and materials

The primary types of offerings recorded in this chapter include burnt offerings (Skt. *homa*, Tib. *sbyin sreg*); offerings associated with the five senses (Skt. *pūjā*, Tib. *mchod pa*), such as flowers, incense, fruit, butter lamps, and so forth; offering cakes (Skt. *bali*, Tib. *gtor ma*); and magic pills (Skt. *gulikā*; Tib. *ril bu*). Categories of offering materials include special types of wood, flowers, metals, minerals, pills, incense, ashes, leaves, seeds, cow products, and honey. Materials used for specific rituals are discussed below.

Pacifying rituals: Introduction (Skt. *śāntika*, Tib. *zhi ba*)

Rituals to pacify or appease the deity include offerings of milk, butter, lotuses, sweet-smelling flowers crushed with yogurt, honey, and butter, and jasmine flowers crushed with curd, honey, and butter.[25] Wood used in burnt offerings to pacify the deity is required to be freshly cut, including *pālaśa* wood or *aśoka*-tree wood.[26]

> Perform 8,000 burnt offerings of lotuses in the presence of a painted cloth, [and] it will pacify [the deity]. Perform 8,000 burnt offerings of jasmine flowers (*mālatī*) crushed with curds, honey, and butter in the presence of the painted cloth, [and] it will pacify [the deity].[27]

Pacifying disease

Rituals that dispel, pacify, or liberate from disease and pain emphasize mantra recitation, burnt offerings (8,000 to 100,000), consecrated water,[28] and white earth.[29] Materials for burnt offerings to dispel disease vary.[30] Two examples follow:

> In the presence of the painted cloth, eat cooked barley with milk and remain silent. [Then], on a cushion of *kuśa* grass that is spread out, starting from the first day of the month until the full moon, one should recite 1,600,000 [times

> and] perform 8,000 burnt offerings with *udumbara* firewood. It will dispel all diseases.[31]
>
> Perform 100,000 burnt offerings of white mustard seeds to liberate one from diseases. Perform 100,000 burnt offerings of mango leaves with a vessel of milk to liberate one from all diseases.[32]

Pacifying for long life

One ritual for "long life" (*tshe ring po*) requires 100,000 burnt offerings of coral and *dūrva* grass.[33] Rituals to attain a life span from thousands of years to an eon are discussed in section on attainments (*siddhis*).[34]

Prosperity rituals: Introduction (Skt. *pauṣṭika*, Tib. *rgyas pa*)

Most prosperity rituals in the TMK are performed for coins, gold, land (i.e., villages or kingdoms), wealth, and treasure. The wood used for the burnt offerings must be freshly cut,[35] and offerings consist of food[36] and fragrant substances, including incense[37] and flowers. Most prosperity rituals generally require that offerings, performances, and recitations be 8,000 or 100,000 in number. Examples of prosperity rituals performed to obtain coins, gold and silver, or land are discussed below.

Prosperity: Offerings to obtain coins, (pieces of) gold or silver

In the most successful rituals, practitioners may obtain from 1,000 pieces of gold[38] or silver[39] to 10,000 pieces of gold.[40] In other rituals, practitioners obtain coins ranging from 5 to 100,000 in number.[41] Some of these rituals solely involve lengthy *mantra* recitations (8,000 times near a painted cloth[42] or a sacred image,[43] or 100,000 times near a *stūpa* containing the essence incantation of Dependent Origination).[44] In one ritual, a practitioner must recite continuously for one month near a painted cloth.[45] Other rituals involve fresh offerings or burnt offerings, from 8,000 to 100,000 in number. Examples of these rituals appear below:

> Having made a *stūpa* that measures a full span of the Sugata, and having burned incense, one should present an offering of 8,000 magnolia flowers and one will obtain a thousand [pieces of] gold.[46]
>
> One who has observed a purification vow should drink milk, or eat leaves, and recite 300,000 times near a *stūpa* containing relics. Then, on the eighth day or the fourteenth day of the waning moon, perform 8,000 burnt offerings

> of black sesame seeds and find 1,000 ounces of gold (Tib. *gser srang*; Skt. *kanaka tulā*).[47]
>
> On the fourteenth day of the waxing moon, having maintained a fasting vow for three nights, and having ignited a fire with *udumbara* wood, perform 8,000 burnt offerings of *udumbara* firewood pulverized with yogurt, honey, and butter. Find 500 gold and silver coins (*karṣāpaṇa*).[48]

A wide variety of fragrant flowers are used in the burnt offerings of prosperity rituals, including *arka* flowers,[49] *atimuktaka* flowers,[50] *karavīra* flowers pulverized with milk,[51] magnolia flowers,[52] (red) lotuses (*padma*), blue lotuses (*utpala*),[53] *priyaṅgu* essence,[54] sweet-smelling flowers,[55] and flowers that are not named, whether used alone[56] or pulverized with yogurt.[57]

Prosperity: Offerings to acquire a village

Rituals to acquire one or more villages generally require 100,000 or more *mantra* recitations,[58] 100,000 offerings of lotuses[59] or jasmine flowers,[60] and/or 100,000 burnt offerings of black sesame seeds, rice,[61] fresh butter,[62] or yogurt, honey, and butter combined in the presence of a *stūpa* with relics.[63] One ritual requires fasting:

> Having begun from the first day of the waxing moon, [a person who has] fasted for a day and a night, and entered a river that flows into the ocean, should offer 100,000 jasmine flowers. At the end [of those offerings], perform 100,000 burnt offerings of black sesame seeds. Find ten walled villages.[64]

Prosperity: Offerings to obtain a kingdom or sovereignty

Prosperity rituals for obtaining a kingdom require huge numbers of burnt offerings, recitations, food offerings, and flower offerings. Some rituals request up to 300,000 performances of burnt offerings.[65] Lotuses are the flower of choice, whether used in a river offering after fasting[66] or in burnt offerings pulverized with yogurt, honey, and butter.[67] More complex burnt offerings include white *apāmārga* pulverized with yogurt, honey, and butter in a fire of *bilvā* wood.[68] Even an old-fashioned household staple such as molasses can elicit attainment when:

> One recites 300,000 [times] in the presence of the painted cloth; then, performs 300,000 burnt offerings of molasses with firewood measuring one inch. [If] that painted cloth shakes, [and] whole bunches of flowers move, then, one will find a kingdom or alternatively, whatever one imagines.[69]

Some rituals even suggest a pinch of gold dust for success:

> Beginning from dawn or dusk as desired, with preliminary offerings performed each day in front of the image; then, having ignited a fire with *arka* wood, perform 8,000 burnt offerings of wood crushed with fragrant sesame oil and a pinch of gold dust. Obtain a kingdom within six months and a large kingdom within three years.[70]

Recitations to obtain a kingdom may last for six months in duration, sitting near a *stūpa* containing relics,[71] or may be up to 800,000 in number, if maintaining the proper diet, observances, and offerings:

> Having eaten alms or an oblation (*caru*), one who has observed a purification vow should recite 500,000 [times], and will obtain sovereignty over the earth. Having eaten cooked barley with milk, one should recite 800,000 times and offer 100,000 white lotuses, and one will obtain complete sovereignty.[72]

Subjugation rituals: Introduction (Tib. *dbang du 'gyur; dbang du byed*; Skt. *vaśīkara, vaśīkaraṇa*)

Subjugation rituals, performed to bring others under one's control, are the most frequently occurring category of rituals in this chapter (110 in number). Most subjugation rituals are performed to subjugate a king (27), a king's minister (7), a king's priest (2), or an earth-owner spirit (*sa'i bdag po*) (3). Perhaps the most powerful substance for subjugating is the earth containing a king's footprint:

> A tantric practitioner (*vidyādhara*) who has taken earth with a king's footprint, pulverized it with butter, and performed 500 to 800 burnt offerings, will bring the king under control as long as he lives, during all seasons.[73]

Some subjugation rituals require that practitioners pulverize a combination of plants and food items,[74] form them into an effigy,[75] chop it into pieces, and throw them into the fire as offerings. The examples below are performed during the summer, rainy season, and late winter.

> Having mixed together alkali (*sarjikā*), milk, green barley-corn ashes,[76] *vacā*,[77] chickpeas, Bengal beans (*caṇakāmāṣa*), and sesame, pulverize it with bodily water,[78] and produce an effigy of a king (*nṛpati*) [weighing] 30-*tulā*. Having ignited a fire with *āmra* wood, every day for one month, at dawn or dusk as desired, starting from the head, chop and chop it to pieces with the right hand, and perform 8,000 burnt offerings. One will bring a king (*rgyal po*) under control.[79]

> Having pulverized grain husks, barley husks,[80] *gavina*,[81] and sweet flag (*vacā*)[82] into one [mixture], and having created an effigy of an earth-owner spirit (*sa'i bdag po*)[83] with a measurement of 50 *tulā*, place the head in the western [direction], with its feet facing east, [and] starting from the head of the effigy, chop and chop it to pieces with a sharp sword using the right hand, and make 1,000 burnt offerings in a fire of *nimba* wood, every day, during a two-hour period according to one's wishes, for one month. It will bring a king (*rgyal po*) under control.[84]

Other rituals include the sacrifice of effigies without stating that they should be chopped up for the fire offering:

> Having pulverized [fruit of the] yellow myrobalan tree,[85] *āmalakī* fruit, *śribāsaka*,[86] olibanum,[87] and cow's butter, make [this mixture] into an effigy of a king (*nṛpati*). Having placed the head of the image in the west, as before, in a fire of *palāśa* (wood), perform 8,000 burnt offerings in the fire for a two-hour period as desired, every day for one month. In this way, one will always bring the king (*rgyal po*) under control as if a servant (*kiṃkara*).[88]
>
> Having combined myrobalan fruit (*vibhītaka*), barley, *tsi-ka-se* leaves[89] with roots, sesame, and white mustard, pulverized with cow's butter, make an effigy of a king (*rgyal po*) [weighing] 30 *tulā*, and display the head in the west, as before. Perform 8,000 burnt offerings every day for one month in a fire of *uḍumbara* wood. Without a doubt, one will bring the earth-owner spirit (*sa'i bdag po*) under control.[90]

In two of the four rituals mentioned above, there is a discrepancy between the effigy's identity and the target of the subjugation, whether a king or an earth-owner spirit.

Subjugation rituals using black mustard seeds, salt, poison, or blood appear in the TMK as well as other Indian tantric texts. Aleksandra Wenta discusses these materials along with additional features of Śaivite and Buddhist tantras that she has identified as "magical recipes."[91] Her research promotes the idea that "the tantras came into being through the reuse of textual fragments that circulated across sectarian boundaries as they were re-used and interspersed in the ritual literature of different groups."[92] These substances, as they appear in the TMK, are discussed below.

Subjugation with black mustard seeds (Tib. ske tshe, yungs kar nag po; *Skt.* rājikā, kṛṣṇasarṣapa*)*

All subjugation rituals using black mustard seeds require 8,000 burnt offerings for success. In some rituals, the seeds are crushed and formed into an effigy of the person one desires to control. Effigies made of mustard seeds are generally used to subjugate kings.

> Having created an effigy of a king with black mustard seeds and flowers, starting from the right foot, one should chop and chop it to pieces with a sharp weapon and perform 8,000 burnt offerings. Then, pour butter into the fire 800 times at the three junctures of the day for seven days. Having become the king's attendant for a "watch,"[93] a fortnight, or a month, one will bring [the king] under one's control.[94]

Sometimes, black mustard seeds are simply thrown into the fire with other materials:

> To exert control over the king's minister, [use] equal amounts of dust from the king's footprint and black mustard seeds, and perform 8,000 burnt offerings at the same time [of day] for a two-hour period for one month, according to one's wishes. This will bring [the king's minister] under control. In another ritual, perform 8,000 burnt offerings for one month, using black mustard seeds with shoots of *dūrvā* grass, and one will subjugate as before.[95]

At the end of another ritual to subjugate a king and his minister, the narrator adds, "whatever you say, they will do!"[96] Other subjugation rituals in this chapter use various substances with black mustard seeds.[97]

Subjugating with salt (Tib. **lan tshwa, rgyam tshwa,** *Skt.* **saindhava, lavaṇa;** *rock salt, sea salt)*

Subjugation rituals using salt effectively bring others under one's control. If the salt is formed into an effigy, it represents a king, an earth-owner spirit, or a man or woman whom the practitioner desires. Salt may be used alone or combined with other materials, depending upon the ritual, and used as burnt offerings that are usually 8,000 in number. In the ritual below, salt is used alone:

> Having made an effigy of a universal monarch (*cakravartin*) out of salt [weighing] 18 *tulā*, starting from the left foot, chop it to pieces with a sword and perform burnt offerings in the king's fire. Within one month, the king will come under one's control.[98]

In the first group of rituals, an effigy of a king is made of salt every day for one month, after which it is chopped to pieces and thrown into the fire with 8,000 burnt offerings. Depending upon the ritual, salt can be pulverized with the following ingredients: (1) red flowers;[99] (2) red sandalwood;[100] (3) *uśīra* root, *vālaka*, *sauvāsa*, and Ganges water;[101] or (4) cow products that have not fallen on the ground.[102]

> Example: Having mixed sea salt with cow products (*gavyam*) that have not fallen on the ground, and pulverized it with green barley-corn ashes and sky-water, make an effigy of a king [weighing] 30 *tulā* every day for one month, at dawn or dusk as desired. Starting from the right foot, chop and chop it to pieces with the right hand using a sharp sword, and having performed burnt offerings in a fire of *udumbara* wood, one will bring a king under control.[103]

In the second group of rituals, the practitioner forms an effigy of a king, which is not chopped to pieces, but still thrown into the fire during 8,000 burnt offerings. In this group, the salt is pulverized with: molasses, *amlaka* tree fruit,[104] and white mustard seeds;[105] barley, sesame seeds, molasses, and cow butter[106] or barley and wheat:

> Example: Having made an effigy with 30 *tulā* of sea salt, barley, and wheat crushed together, fill the mouth with three pungent substances,[107] and performed recitations over a steady[108] flame in a copper spoon. Pierce [the effigy] from beneath the foot, departing from the crown of the head. Then, having set it down on the right side of the head, and having cut *palāśa* leaves with the teeth of one's sword, perform 8,000 burnt offerings with the right hand in a fire of *khadira* wood for a two-hour period according to one's wishes. Within one month, one will bring the king under control as long as he lives.[109]

In the third group, the practitioner performs a subjugation ritual every day for one month, using salt to form an effigy of a man or a woman who is desired by the practitioner.

> Example: Having made an effigy out of salt, it is cut into pieces and burnt offerings are performed. Any man or woman who is desired will be brought under one's control.[110]
>
> A similar ritual is used to target a prostitute:
>
> To exert control over a common woman (that is, a prostitute), having made an image with salt, perform burnt offerings with the left hand. It will bring her under one's control.[111]

Subjugating with poison

Some rituals use black mustard seeds with poison in burnt offerings. One ritual is used to subjugate a person of the lowest occupational group (*śūdra*).[112]

> To exert control over all [from a] lesser [status group], having ignited a fire with firewood possessing thorns, [every day] for one month, [perform] burnt offerings of a combination of black mustard seeds, poison, and *nimba* [wood], having begun at dawn or dusk, as desired. Having performed 8,000 burnt offerings during a single [period of] time, it will bring that [*śūdra*] under control.[113]

Other rituals in this chapter concern healing the effects of poison or eliminating poison.

Subjugating with blood (Tib. **ske tshe,** *Skt.* **rājikā** *or* **kṛṣṇasarṣapa***)*

One ritual in the text uses blood to subjugate a family's lineage (*rigs brgyud*):

> Having taken the ashes of a burnt corpse from a charnel ground, [a person who has] maintained a fasting vow for a day and a night during the full moon, [should] extract a drop of blood from the ring finger and drawn an image [with it], and [then] having pressed down on it with the left foot, recite a thousand [times]. [The ritual] will exert power over one's family lineage.[114]

Subjugating with red substances (Tib. **dmar po***)*

Some rituals for subjugating kings and earth-owner spirits (*sa'i bdag po*) use red substances that are pulverized and formed into effigies, chopped to pieces, and thrown into the fire as burnt offerings. These substances include: red flowers (genus unspecified), red sandalwood,[115] red rice husks, and red oleander flowers.[116] Three examples with effigies appear below:

> Having produced an image with crushed red oleander flowers (*karavīra*), starting from the right foot, chop and chop it to pieces and perform 8,000 burnt offerings over a fire made with oleander firewood (*karavīra*). During each month, make an image [weighing] 30 to 36 *tulā*. After that, the king will come under one's control.[117]
>
> Having mixed salt and red flowers back and forth, pulverize and form them into an effigy of a body [weighing] 8 *tulā*. Starting from the right foot, chop it to pieces with a sharp weapon, and perform burnt offerings. Then, a carpenter [who] has performed [the ritual] in the same way every day for one month will bring an earth-owner spirit under one's control.[118]
>
> Having created an effigy [weighing] 25 *tulā* with equal amounts of red sandalwood crushed with rock salt, during a two-hour period in the early morning of each day, starting from the right foot, chop and chop [the effigy] to pieces with a sharp sword and perform 8,000 burnt offerings in a fire of red sandalwood. For this rite, pour sacrificial offerings [into the fire] with the right

hand. Within exactly one month, one will issue the king commands as if he were a servant.[119]

Subjugation of women

Some rituals in this chapter are used to bring a range of women under the practitioner's control. Some of these rituals use salt.[120] Others use effigies.[121] Most of these rituals include the number 8,000, or multiples thereof. In one ritual, the practitioner is instructed to perform 8,000 burnt offerings of sesame seeds,[122] or offer 800,000 flowers in front of Noble Avalokiteśvara.[123] To exert control over a maiden, one is instructed to worship Noble Avalokiteśvara with 8,000 *raṅga* flowers.[124] To exert control over a maidservant, one combines *puṃnāga* pistils, barley, wheat, and meat to perform 8,000 burnt offerings.[125] To exert control over a brahman woman, the practitioner performs 8,000 burnt offerings of shoots from the wood-apple tree (*bilvā*) in the presence of a painted cloth. Anyone who is seated in front of any woman in a charnel ground and performs 8,000 recitations will bring her under control.[126]

Attainments (Tib. *dngos grub*, Skt. *siddhi*)

The attainments of the rituals have been defined as "one of many supernatural powers acquired by practitioners (*siddhas*) as a result of their practice, their *sādhana*."[127] The word "*siddhi*" has been defined as magical accomplishment,[128] magical success,[129]and magical power.[130] Mkhas grub rje (1385–1438),[131] a chief disciple of Tsongkhapa (1357–1419), discusses *siddhis* according to different classifications. They can be divided into three groups: superior, middling, and lower. When classified according to their nature, superior *siddhis* include (achieving the state of a) *vidyādhara*, supernormal faculties (*abhijñā*),[132] and perfect comprehension of the scriptures. Middling *siddhis* include invisibility, vigor, and swift walking. Lower siddhis include subjugation, killing, and expelling hindrances (*bskrad*).[133] A practitioner's attainment reflects the level of service of the deity. For practitioners who do not serve with "proper exertion," a lower *siddhi* may result. If one serves well, a superior *siddhi* may be granted.[134]

In the "Extensive Prayer-Bead Ritual," attainments are acquired through the three types of worldly rituals, namely, (1) pacifying,[135] (2) increasing wealth or prosperity, and (3) subjugating. Attainments include healing illness and eliminating disease, subduing demons, removing blindness, obtaining elixir, invisibility, swift movement, and becoming a *vidyādhara*. The latter is referred to as "a supreme secret" (*mchog tu gsang ba*)[136] and is a superior attainment with superior powers, including obtaining the wish-fulfilling jewel,[137] traveling through the sky,[138] living for an eon,[139] traveling anywhere without obstacles,[140] attaining rebirth in the pure land of Sukhāvatī,[141] and recalling past lives.[142] White traces literary vestiges of archaic Siddha and Vidyādhara cults to mountain worship and protector deity cults. He also notes that practitioners of alchemy, *haṭha yoga*, and erotic rituals sought to transcend the human condition to become semi-divine Vidyādharas.[143] The TMK's ritual below delineates the powers of a *vidyādhara*, previously defined in the fifth-century *Amarakośa* as a class of demigods (*devayoni*).[144]

> If wishing to produce an animated corpse, having taken the undamaged limbs of the corpse to a charnel ground, or a wooden footbridge, or the juncture of four paths, and having worshipped all spirits (*bhūta*s) for one night with offering cakes, anoint a *maṇḍala* on the right side of the body of Mahādeva. Having bestowed offering cakes, bathed, and become adorned with ornaments, draw a *maṇḍala* using ashes. In the center of that [*maṇḍala*], place the [corpse's] head on a cushion in the east, and cover the body with a white cotton cloth. Remain mindful, and sit with legs crossed on top of that [corpse]. So long as [the corpse] bestows a jewel from its mouth, perform burnt offerings in its mouth with mustard seeds and sesame. Having taken that jewel from its mouth, one will become a curly-haired *vidyādhara* with the color of the rising sun, obtain a desirable form possessing the power of a thousand elephants, go to the realm of the gods, live for a great eon, and travel wherever one desires to go.[145]

A ritual with corpse worship in the *Mañjuśrī-mūla-kalpa* (26.20) has a similar result.[146] Herein, the practitioner is told to:

> procure an uninjured human corpse, secure its chest with four stakes of *khadira* wood and, sitting on it, offer into the fire powdered jewels. A wish-fulfilling gem will then appear at the tip of the corpse's tongue. If one seizes it, one will become a monarch of the *vidyādhara*s.[147]

Attainments of the fire offering (Tib. *sbyin sreg*, Skt. *homa*)

Many rituals throughout the Prayer-Bead Ritual mention three levels of success for the burnt offerings: warmth, smoke, and flames. Mkhas grub rje identifies these levels of success as "omens" for the types of *siddhi*s that will result from the ritual, namely, warmth (*uṣma*), which indicates lower *siddhi*s; rising smoke (*dhūma*), which indicates middling *siddhis*; and blazing (*jvalita*), which indicates superior *siddhis*.[148]

In the TMK, if the burnt offering achieves warmth, the practitioner may subjugate and/or achieve long life.[149] If the burnt offering raises smoke, the practitioner may achieve long life and/or invisibility.[150] If the burnt offering bursts into flames, the practitioner may achieve the state of a *vidyādhara*, become invisible, recall former births, travel through the sky, or live for an eon, and upon death transmigrate to the realm of Sukhāvatī.[151] In the example below, all three outcomes of the ritual are mentioned:

> Having bestowed offering cakes of various kinds in the presence of the painted cloth, perform a very extensive offering (*pūjā*). Having placed yellow pigment (*gorocana*) on lotus leaves, and having become seated with legs crossed, so long as the three kinds of attainments (*siddhi*) arise, one should recite [the mantra]. [If the offering] becomes warm, one will exert power over all sentient beings and live for 1,000 years. [If there is] rising smoke, one will live for 1,000 years, and come and go for 1,000 miles. One will become king of all that is accomplished, should be accomplished by mind, and produce food by means of mind. Then, [if the offering] bursts into flames, one will assume the form of a sixteen-year-old with curly hair–similar in color to the rising sun, live for the lifespan of an eon, and go wherever one desires, having become completely surrounded by many hundreds of thousands of *vidyādharas*.[152]

Attainments with "magic" pills (Tib. *ril bu*, Skt. *gulikā*)

Twenty-one rituals in this chapter feature pill production, a common ingredient of which is *guggulu* incense.[153] The primary results of pills include invisibility and long life (from 1,000 to 10,000 years).[154]

> Having taken yellow orpiment (*gorocana*) and made pills, wrap them with three metals (gold, silver, and copper). Then, having washed and donned white clothes, gone to a charnel ground, and performed an offering with perfume, incense, flowers, and so forth, bestow offering cakes to all elemental spirits (*bhūtas*). Having placed the pills in a skull cup (*kapālaḥ-puṭaḥ*), so long as one hears sounds of danger, one should recite. Do not be frightened.[155] Having distributed[156] [the pills] among friends, as well as having placed them in the mouth, one will become invisible and will live for 10,000 years.[157]

Other results of rituals with pills include finding gold, fulfilling one's desires, and subjugation.

Obstacles to attainment

Sometimes practitioners do not achieve attainments (*siddhi*). This may be due to an imperfectly performed ritual or the practitioner's status. As for the latter, there are many issues, which prevent attainment. The first concerns a deficiency on the part of the performer:

> Whether due to lacking a holy guru, or due to lacking ability, as it is said, "Although I have made an offering to the master (*ācārya*) of the *maṇḍala* and although I have become worthy of the gift of the holy guru, I myself still lack knowledge." [Hence,] there will be no realization, even by one with strong determination.[158]

Apart from lacking knowledge or a guru, the text states that rituals may fail if a practitioner has impaired faculties, a specific constitution that prevents a successful performance, or lacks access to the appropriate rituals.[159] Furthermore, any practitioner who experiences a breach in practice will be bereft of attainments:

> [This includes] one who speaks in a non-meritorious manner, [whether due to] broken ethics, or even due to monks (*bhikṣu*), or nuns (*bhikṣuṇī*), or male novices (*upāsaka*), or female novices (*upāsikā*), whose interval of training has [prematurely] ended [i.e., due to having become disqualified], or because one remains in a state of [moral] defeat [having violated bodhisattva and *pratimokṣa* vows], or because one is deprived of the mind of enlightenment (*bodhicitta*).[160]

Last, and perhaps the most concerning, are practitioners who *intentionally* display non-virtuous behaviors that disrespect the teacher, teachings, or tradition. This is mentioned in the text when a practitioner tramples upon and kicks a reliquary mound (*stūpa*), treads upon the shadow of a spiritual teacher, scorns a spiritual teacher (*ācārya*), the Mahāyāna, or all deities, shows hatred toward bodhisattvas, or *deliberately* performs [one or more crimes of] immediate retribution (*ānantarya*).[161] Regarding these non-virtuous behaviors, the text states:

> Any other ritual activities performed by those [persons] with these faults (*doṣa*) will not be correctly performed, because that [person] who lacks attainments (*siddhi*) has violated the ritual of that [tantra]. Anyone who commits these [violations] instantly destroys the attainments of that [ritual].[162]

Nevertheless, practitioners with the proper intentions who inadvertently err in the performance of the ritual may eventually attain *siddhi* through repeated attempts. A passage from the text states that if the ritual fails, try again:

"Having recited the *vidyā* for a little while, and having remained still for some time, moreover, if there are no attainments (*siddhi*s) of the time of accomplishment, it will happen [now]."[163]

Conclusion

A close reading of the TMK's chapter "The Extensive Ritual of Prayer Beads" elucidates how to achieve "magical" results of rituals and how to avoid unsuccessful performances. Magical attainments (*siddhi*) only result from the correct use of *vidyā*-mantras (spells) and materials that are naturally potent or empowered via incantation and/or perfectly performed rituals. Furthermore, rituals only succeed when ritual performers keep their commitments to the practices and display moral behavior, which respects teachers, teachings, and tradition.

> With the correct application of ritual activity,
> Undertaken with the cause of the secret mantra,
> Attainments that are nothing but fruitful
> Will be accomplished.[164]

When all the requirements are met, the practitioner can attain a miraculous accumulation of precious metals, coins, and land, miraculous powers of invisibility and flight, as well as the spiritual state of a *vidyādhara*, which increases one's physical powers and life span, and facilitates rebirth in Sukhāvatī.

Abbreviations

CK	Comparative Kangyur recension of the *Tārā-mūla-kalpa* [Comparative edition of various Tibetan Kangyur, largely based on the Derge (*sde dge*) Kangyur]
TMK	*Tārā-mūla-kalpa*
TPTMK	Stog Palace manuscript of the *Tārā-mūla-kalpa*
UB	Ulaan Bataar manuscript of the *Tārā-mūla-kalpa*

Notes

1 My sincere appreciation is extended to the Robert H. N. Ho Family Foundation for their support to carry out this research as a 2021–2 Grantee in Buddhist Studies; the editors of this volume, Aleksandra Wenta and Cameron McMullin Bailey, for making this project possible; Genla Lozang Jamspal, Ph.D. and Dr. Paul G. Hackett for their help in clarifying difficult Tibetan passages.

2 Bu ston added the TMK to the tantra section (*rgyud 'bum*) of the Bka' 'gyur and classified it as an "action-tantra" or *kriyātantra*. For further discussion, see Landesman (2020: 23–32).

3 TPTMK (394a-1 to 448a-3); CK (94, 225–318); UB (112, 369a-6 to 416b-8).

4 Skt. *Ūrdhvajaṭā-kalpa*, Tib. *ral pa g.yen brdzes kyi rtog pa*.

5 The colophon of this chapter (TPTMK, 448a-2 to 3) states: *byang chub sems dpa'i sde snod phal po che theg pa chen po'i mdo sde ral pa gyen brdzes kyi rtog pa las/ bgrang 'phreng srad bu'i cho ga'i le'u rab 'byams bcu gcig pa yongs su rdzogs so//*. "The eleventh extensive chapter of the ritual of prayer-bead thread from the Bodhisattvapiṭaka Avataṃsaka Mahāyāna Sūtra and the Ūrḍhavjaṭā-kalpa is completed."

6 All references following excerpts are from the Stog Palace recension of the TMK (TPTMK), unless specified otherwise.

7 Skt. *parvatarāja potala*, Tib. *ri'i rgyal po gru 'dzin*. The term *parvatarāja* is a name of the Himalayas.

8 In this opening section, the Bhagavān praises the ritual text of Ūrdhvajaṭā [Tārā] and its secret continuation tantra (Skt. *uttaratantra*, Tib. *rgyud phyi ma*) for benefiting many beings, making them happy, and showing compassion for those scorched by suffering (TPTMK 394a-3 to 4).

9 Encyclopedia Britannica, https://www.britannica.com/topic/magic-supernatural-phenomenon.

10 Brown (1997: 127).

11 The TPTMK (402b-4 to 5).

12 The TPTMK (402b-6 to 7).

13 Encyclopedia Britannica. https://www.britannica.com/topic/magic-supernatural-phenomenon.

14 Brown (1997: 124) quoting Malinowski (1935: 2: 233).

15 See Kinsley (1997: 58).

16 Lessing and Wayman ([1968]1983: 116, fn. 18) note that *mantra*s are associated with male deities and *vidyā*s with female deities.

17 In the TMK's chapter entitled "Ritual of Prayer Beads," it is the maṇḍala of Ūrdhvajaṭā.

18 TPTMK (394a-6 to 394b-2).

19 Gray (2019: 105–8) on “Mantras and Magic.”
20 The TPTMK (401a-7 to 401b-1).
21 The term *vidyādhara* refers to a female partner in tantric practices and a magician (Przyluski (1923: 306). It is further discussed in the section “Attainments.”
22 Brown (1997: 122).
23 [397a-2] A burnt offering of white mustard is for prosperity [rites]. Using manure of donkeys and camels, [instead of mustard], it will become [a] fierce [rite] (*abhicāra*).
24 TPTMK (445a-5 to 7).
25 TPTMK (413b-2, 420a-2, 424b-4, 442a-7, 444a-7, 445a-6).
26 TPTMK (413b-2, 444a-7, 445a-6).
27 TPTMK (442a-6 to 7).
28 TPTMK (427b-1): “Having recited 800 [times] over water, place it on one's limbs, [and] pacify disease.” TPTMK (434a-7): “Water mixed with salt, having been consecrated 800 times with mantras, will pacify all sharp pain.”
29 TPTMK (418b-1).
30 Sesame oil TPTMK (411b-5), *girikarṇikā* flowers TPTMK (438a-1).
31 TPTMK (419b-1 to 2).
32 TPTMK (424a-5 to 6).
33 TPTMK (424a-5) and CK (94, 277, 4) spelling is *durbha*, which appears to be a corruption of *dūrva*.
34 See pp. 47–49.
35 These include *apāmārga* wood (409a-7), *arka* wood (429b-7), *aśoka* wood (431b-6), *bilva* wood, milk-fruit tree wood, *nyagrodha* wood, *palakṣa* [*palāśa*?] wood (TP 445a-5; CK: 313, 6; UB: 414b-8), and *udumbara* wood (443a-2 to 3). See TPTMK (397a-1, 420a-4, 424b-4, 443a-3, 445a-5 to 6ff).
36 These include white mustard seeds (415a-7), black sesame seeds (408a-6, 419a-1), beans (420a-2 to 4), rice (408b-6), yogurt, honey, and butter (408a-4, 408a-5, 408b-4, 418a-3), sesame, thick rice porridge, peas or beans of the sub-Himalayan region, and so forth, crushed with yogurt, honey, and butter in a fire with wood from the milk-fruit tree (TPTMK 420a-2 to 4).
37 These include *guggulu* incense or pills, TPTMK (408b-2 to 3, 415a-7), saffron with fragrant sesame oil (TPTMK 411b-1), and *kunduru* incense (TPTMK 408b-3).
38 TPTMK (408b-3, 409a-7, 422b-2 to 3, 437a-6).
39 TPTMK (436a-7).
40 TPTMK (439b-6).
41 Tib. *dong tse*, Skt. *karṣāpaṇa*. According to Das (1983: 642), these are coins of lesser value, usually in gold, silver, or copper. Eighteen rituals in this chapter are performed for the attainment of coins.
42 TPTMK (434b-7).
43 TPTMK 435b-5).

44 TPTMK (435b-6).
45 TPTMK (436a-2 to 3).
46 TPTMK (437a-6 to 7).
47 TPTMK (418b-7 to 419a-1).
48 TPTMK (443a-2).
49 TPTMK (408a-3).
50 TPTMK (436a-6).
51 TPTMK (432a-1).
52 TPTMK (437a-7).
53 TPTMK (422b-2 to 3).
54 TPTMK (424a-6).
55 The attainment is 8,000 gold or silver coins in the TPTMK (434b-5 to 6).
56 TPTMK (408a-4, 431b-4 to 5).
57 TPTMK (429b-6).
58 TPTMK (421a-1).
59 TPTMK (424b-5).
60 TPTMK (409a-6).
61 TPTMK (424a-1).
62 TPTMK (423b-3, 430a-1).
63 TPTMK (410a-7 to 410b-1).
64 TPTMK (409a-5 to 6).
65 TPTMK (417b-7, 436b-5 to 7).
66 Fast for twenty-four hours on the seventh day of the waxing moon, enter a river flowing into the ocean, and offer 10,000 lotuses.
67 These must be performed 300,000 times to obtain a kingdom (TPTMK 417b-6 to 7).
68 TPTMK (436b-5 to 7).
69 TPTMK (410b-5 to 6).
70 TPTMK (411a-6 to 7).
71 TPTMK (436a-3).
72 TPTMK (424a-4 to 5).
73 TPTMK (401b-5 to 6).
74 The most common offering materials for subjugation rituals in this chapter include *nimba* seeds, sesame seeds, mustard seeds, beans, chickpeas, hot sesame oil, honey, yogurt, butter, flowers (jasmine, *arjuna, aśoka*), *dūrva* grass, *śāli* rice, dust from a king's footprint, and poison.
75 See Mumford (1989: 141, 149–57, 19) for a contemporary Buddhist exorcism ritual in which an effigy (*glud*) is used to trap and subdue demonic spirits.
76 Tib. *nas kyi 'gyur ba*, Skt. *yāva-kṣāra. The Monier-Williams Sanskrit Dictionary*, p. 847, gives the following definition: "an alkali prepared from the ashes of burnt green barley-corns."

77 Tib. *shu dag*. This is a medicinal herb or aromatic root.

78 Tib. *lus kyi chus*, Skt. *kāyika/śārīra-udaka*.

79 TPTMK (399b-5 to 400a-1).

80 Tib. *tshigs ma* means "husks, chaff, or residue." The Tibetan text (TPTMK 400a-4; CK 94, 236, l. 4) reads *tshigs*.

81 The Sanskrit word "*gavina*" appears to be a corruption in the text. It may be related to the Skt. *gava* or *gavī* (cow).

82 Tib. *shu dag*, a special medicine, in Negi (2005: vol. 15: p. 6902) or an aromatic root in Monier-Williams (1979: 912). This word is defined by 84000 Translating the Words of the Buddha: Glossary Definitions as "sweet flag, a medicinal plant." The definitions are found under the entry for "shu dag" at https://dictionary.christian-steinert.de

83 A *sa bdag* refers to the "owner" of a particular area of land, etc. Reference: oral communication with Rinchan Sonam (July 11, 2022). Samuel (1993: 162) defines *sa bdag* as " 'lords of the soil' who become irritated when someone 'wounds' the soil, their domain, through work, excavation, or building."

84 TPTMK (400a-4 to 6).

85 Tib. *arura,* in Das (1983: 1346), Negi (2005:16:7591); and https://dictionary.christian-steinert.de is the Tibetan translation of the Skt. *harītakī*, the yellow myrabalan tree.

86 TPTMK (400a-7). This spelling may be a corruption of the word *śrībhakṣa*, an auspicious food.

87 Skt. *kunduruka*. Olibanum is a tree product that has been referred to as an aromatic gum resin, sometimes called "Frankincense."

88 TPTMK (400a-7 to 400b-2).

89 Alternate readings from the CK (94, p. 236, l. 16) include *tsi ka seng, tsi ga seng, tsi ma seng.* This appears to be a corruption of the word "*tiktasāra*" or "*tiktaśāka*," a fragrant grass or herb, or a bitter herb.

90 TPTMK (400b-2 to 4).

91 See Wenta (forthcoming).

92 Ibid.

93 Tib. *thun*. A watch is a period of time defined as a three-hour period. See Das (1983: 580).

94 TPTMK (397a-2 to 4). In another ritual (TPTMK, 397b-7ff), blue lotuses are crushed with black mustard seeds to create an effigy.

95 TPTMK (403b-1 to 3).

96 TPTMK (409b-5).

97 Black sesame seeds are mixed with yogurt, honey, and butter to subjugate ministers (TPTMK: 403b-2), family priests (403b-5 to 6), kings (409b-5 to 6), those from the four occupational groups (*varṇa*) (422b-6 to 7), a person from a priestly class

(*brahman*), and from the warrior group (*kṣatriya*) (432b-3 to 4). Black sesame seeds are mixed with poison and *nimba* wood in a fire of thorny wood for a person of the lowest occupational group (*śūdra*) (404a-3 to 5), in a fire of *palāśa* wood for enemies (408b-5), or with *arka* wood to extinguish karmic obscurations (415b-3 to 4).

98 TPTMK (397a-4 to 5).

99 TPTMK (397b-3 to 4).

100 TPTMK (398a-7 to 398b-1).

101 TPTMK (399a-7 to 399b-3). Das (1983: 737) defines *nam mkha' chu bo* as a "heavenly river" and "epithet of the river Ganges."

102 TPTMK (398b-3 to 5).

103 TPTMK (400a-1 to 3).

104 Skt. *amla* means "sour" or "acidic," and is one of the six tastes (*rasa*).

105 TPTMK (400b-4 to 6).

106 TPTMK (400b-6 to 401a-1).

107 According to Negi (2005: 11:4807), *tsha ba gsum* = *trikaṭu*, meaning "three pungent substances." Apte ([1957] 1985: 789) identifies these as dry ginger, black pepper, and long pepper, sometimes referred to as *vyoṣa*. A related term is *kaṭutaila* for "white mustard" or "mustard oil." See Apte ([1957] 1985: 520). Another combination includes *tri-ūṣaṇaṃ*, which is made of black pepper and ginger.

108 The TPTMK reading (399a-5) *dhī-ra* is a transliteration of the Sanskrit term ("constant," "steady," "firm").

109 TPTMK (399a-4 to 7).

110 TPTMK (415b-1).

111 TPTMK (435b-1 to 2).

112 Another ritual (TPTMK, 412a-6) mixes burnt offerings with poison to subjugate "one who cannot be harmed by others."

113 TPTMK (404a-4 to 5).

114 TPTMK (437a-7 to 437b-1).

115 TPTMK (398b-1, 432a-7 to 432b-2).

116 TPTMK (397b-3) (397b-7 to 398a-2).

117 TPTMK (397b-2 to 3).

118 TPTMK (397b-3 to 4).

119 TPTMK (398a-7 to 398b-2).

120 TPTMK (415b-1, and 435b-1 to 4).

121 TPTMK (435b-3 to 4): "Having made an effigy out of pulverized *śāli* rice, perform burnt offerings and chop it to pieces. It will bring [a maiden] under one's control."

122 TPTMK (404a-6).

123 TPTMK (404b-5 to 6).

124 TPTMK (404a-7 to 404b-1).
125 TPTMK (435b-2 to 3).
126 TPTMK (404b-3 to 5).
127 White (2011: 11, 388, 313).
128 Samuel (1993: 423), ranging from ordinary, worldly goals to the ultimate goal of enlightenment.
129 Wayman (1984:148).
130 Kinsley (1997: 55–7).
131 Lessing and Wayman (1983: 11–12) discuss Mkhas grub rje as the author of the "Fundamentals of the Buddhist tantras" (*rgyud sde spyi rnam*) and other commentarial works. Also see https://treasuryoflives.org/biographies/view/Khedru bje-Gelek-Pelzang/8027.
132 Skt. *abhijñā* are faculties of a Buddha, which include: taking any form at will, hearing or seeing to any distance, penetrating others' thoughts, and knowing others' states.
133 Lessing and Wayman (1983: 202).
134 Ibid.: 203. Clough (2012: 79–87 in Jacobsen, K., ed. 2012) devotes much thought to the fifth-century Theravāda source *Visuddhimagga* (Path of Purification) by Buddhaghoṣa, wherein the word *siddhi* is referred to by the Pāli term *iddhi*. Clough (2012: 84–7 in Jacobsen, K., ed. 2012) defines *iddhi* as "supernormal ability" and reviews eight *iddhi*s in the *Visuddhimagga* as follows: the ability (1) to multiply, (2) to become invisible, (3) to pass through solid obstacles (walls, mountains), (4) to dive in and out of the ground, (5) to walk on water (as if on land), (6) to travel through the sky, (7) to touch and feel the sun and moon, and (8) to travel to the Brahmā-loka, that is, world realm of Brahmā.
135 Ibid.: 136. According to Mkhas grub rje (in Lessing and Wayman 1983: 136) pacifying rituals include requests to appease illness and offer protection.
136 TPTMK (401a-2).
137 TPTMK (406a-3, 409a-4).
138 Tib. *nam mkha' la 'gro*; TPTMK (419a-4 and 7, 424b-7, 426a-6).
139 TPTMK (407a-6, 409a-4, 420b-3, 420b-6, 425b-3, 427b-3, 428a-7, 428b-6, 429a-2, 430b-6, 434a-2, 440b-7, 441a-7).
140 TPTMK (407a-6).
141 TPTMK (407b-4, 433a-3).
142 TPTMK (408a-3).
143 White (1997: 86–91).
144 White (1996: 57, 373) and White (1997: 80–1) quote the *Amarakośa* (I.1.11).
145 TPTMK (428b-1 to 6). Dezső (2010: 392, 404–8) notes that practitioners (*sādhaka*) or "accomplished magicians" can obtain occult powers (*siddhi*s) from an animated corpse (*vetāla*), especially when a fire-sacrifice (*homa*) is performed

using the mouth of a corpse as fire-pit. The latter is observed in the TMK's ritual quoted above.

146 See Landesman (2020: 36–40) on the relationship between the *Tārā-mūla-kalpa* and the *Mañjuśrī-mūla-kalpa*, especially that the first fourteen chapters of these two texts share parallel passages. The English translation of *The Root Manual of the Rites of Mañjuśrī: Mañjuśrī-mūla-kalpa* (2020) is found at: https://read.84000.co/translation/toh543.html.

147 *The Root Manual of the Rites of Mañjuśrī: Mañjuśrī-mūla-kalpa* (2020) chapter 26:20. https://read.84000.co/translation/toh543.html.

148 Lessing and Wayman (1983: 202–3).

149 TPTMK (426a-4).

150 TPTMK (406b-4, 419a-3, 419a-7, 428a-7, 424b-6, 433a-2).

151 TPTMK (408a-3, 419a-7, 424b-7, 433a-2).

152 TPTMK (425a-7 to 425b-4).

153 TPTMK (408b-3, 412b-1, 414b-4, 415a-6, 419a-1 to 2, 423b-4).

154 TPTMK (412b-7, 434b-2, 438b-3, 440a-2, 440a-4, 440a-4 to 7).

155 I have relied upon the DTMK's (CK 94, p. 304, l. 6) reading *'jigs par mi 'gyur*, meaning "will not be frightened."

156 I have relied upon the DTMK's (CK 94, p. 304, l.6) reading *grogs rnams la bgos nas*, meaning "distributed."

157 TPTMK (439b-6 to 440a-2).

158 TPTMK (401a-5 to 6).

159 TPTMK (401a-4 to 5).

160 TPTMK (401a-7 to 401b-1).

161 TPTMK (401b-1 to 3).

162 TPTMK (401b-3 to 5).

163 TPTMK (401b-5).

164 TPTMK (447b-5 to 6).

References

Primary sources

Ral pa gyen brdzes kyi rtog pa chen po byang chub sems dpa' chen po'i rnam par 'phrul pa le'u rab 'byams las bcom ldan 'das ma 'phags pa sgrol ma'i rtsa ba'i rtog pa zhes bya ba, [DTMK/CK] (2006–9), in The *Bka'-'gyur (dpe bsdur ma)*, 93: 624–884 and 94: 3–510, Beijing: China Tibetology Research Center.

Ral pa gyen brdzes kyi rtog pa chen po byang chub sems dpa' chen po'i rnampar 'phrul pa le'u rab 'byams las bcom ldan 'das ma 'phags pa sgrol ma'i rtsa ba'i rtog pa zhes bya ba,

[TPTMK] (1978), in The Stog Palace Manuscript of the Tibetan Kanjur, 107: rgyud 'bum Ma (128b-5 to 532a-4), Leh: Sman rtsis Shesrig Dpem zod.

Ral pa gyen brdzes kyi rtog pa chen po byang chub sems dpa' chen po'i rnam par 'phrul pa le'u rab 'byams las bcom ldan 'das ma 'phags pa sgrol ma'i rtsa ba'i rtog pa zhes bya ba, [UB] ([1671] 2010) in Them spang ma manuscript of the Tibetan Kangyur (bka' 'gyur rgyal rtse'i them spang ma), 112: 1–497b, Ulaanbaatar, Mongolia: National Library of Mongolia, Tokyo: Digital preservation Society.

Tārā-mūla-kalpa [TMK]. [See *Ral pa gyen brdzes kyi rtog pa chen po*].

Secondary Sources

Apte, V. ([1957] 1985), *The Practical Sanskrit-English Dictionary*, Reprint: Kyoto: Rinsen Book Company.

Brown, M. (1997), "Thinking about Magic," in S. Glazier (ed.), *Anthropology of Religion: A Handbook*, 121–35, Westport, CT: Greenwood Press.

Clough, B. (2012), "The Cultivation of Yogic Powers in the Pāli Path Manuals of Theravada Buddhism," in K. Jacobsen (ed.), *Yoga Powers: Extraordinary Capacities Attained through Meditation and Concentration*, 77–96, Leiden: Brill.

Das, S. C. ([1902] 1983) *Tibetan-English Dictionary*, Reprint: Kyoto: Rinsen Book.

Dezső, C. (2010), "Encounters with Vetālas: Studies on Fabulous Creatures I," *Acta Orientalia Academiae Scientiarum Hungaricae* 63 (4): 391–426.

Encyclopedia Britannica, https://www.britannica.com/topic/magic-supernatural-phenomenon.

Gray, D. ([2007] 2019), *The Cakrasamvara Tantra (The Discourse of Śrī Heruka: Śrīherukābhidhāna)*, New York: American Institute of Buddhist Studies, Columbia University, Tibet House, and Wisdom Publications.

Jacobsen, K. (ed.) (2012), *Yoga Powers: Extraordinary Capacities Attained through Meditation and Concentration*, Leiden: Brill.

Kinsley, D. (1997), *Tantric Visions of the Divine Feminine*, Berkeley: University of California Press.

Landesman, S. (2020), *The Tārā Tantra*: Part 1 (The Root Text), New York: American Institute of Buddhist Studies, Columbia University, Tibet House, and Wisdom Publications.

Lessing, F., and A. Wayman ([1968] 1983), *Introduction to the Buddhist Tantric Systems*, Reprint: Delhi: Motilal Banarsidass.

Malinowski, B. (1935), *Coral Gardens and Their Magic*. 2 vols. New York: American Book Co.

Monier-Williams, M. ([1899] 1979), *A Sanskrit-English Dictionary*, [MW] Reprint: Oxford: Clarendon Press.

Mumford, S. R. (1989), *Himalayan Dialogue: Tibetan Lamas and Gurung Shamans in Nepal*, Madison: University of Wisconsin Press.
Negi, J. S. (2005), *Tibetan-Sanskrit Dictionary (16 vols.)*, Sarnath, Varanasi: Central Institute of Higher Tibetan Studies.
Przyluski, J. (1923), "Les Vidyārāja: Contribution a l'Histoire de la magie dans les Sectes Mahāyānistes," in *Bulletin de L'École Française d'Extréme Orient* 23: 301–18.
Samuel, G. (1993), *Civilized Shamans: Buddhism in Tibetan Societies*, Washington, DC: Smithsonian Institution Press.
The Noble Root Manual of the Rites of Mañjuśrī: Āryamañjuśrīmūlakalpa (2020) Dharma-chakra Translation Committee, translators, in 84000: Translating the Words of the Buddha. https://read.84000.co/translation/toh 543.html (accessed July 14, 2022)
Wayman, A. (1984), *Buddhist Insight*, Delhi: Motitlal Banarsidass.
Wenta, A. (forthcoming), *The Vajrabhairavatantra: A Study and Annotated Translation*. Studies in Indian and Tibetan Buddhism, Boston, MA: Wisdom Publications.
White, D. G. (1996), *The Alchemical Body: Siddha Traditions in Medieval India*, Chicago: University of Chicago Press.
White, D. G. (1997), "Mountains of Wisdom: On the Interface between Siddha and Vidyādhara Cults and the Siddha Orders in Medieval India," in *International Journal of Hindu Studies* 1 (1): 73–95.
White, D. G. (ed.) (2011), *Yoga in Practice*, Princeton, NJ: Princeton University Press.

3

The *Vajrabhairavatantra*: *Materia Magica* and Circulation of Tantric Magical Recipes

Aleksandra Wenta

The *Vajrabhairavatantra* is a seminal Buddhist *yogatantra*, dedicated to the Buffalo-headed tantric deity, Vajrabhairava (Tib. *rdo rje 'jigs byed*). This text consists of ritual procedures concerning Vajrabhairava that deal primarily with magical technology. As such, it may be regarded as a prime source of Buddhist aggressive magic (Skt. *abhicāra*, Tib. *mngon spyod*) that traditionally includes such rites as attracting, subjecting under one's will, paralyzing, killing, creating dissent, and driving away. Composed in India between the early and mid-eighth century, the *Vajrabhairavatantra* (VBhT) was translated into Tibetan[1] by Rwa lo tsā ba Rdo rje grags (b. 1016), the famous Vajrabhairava tantric master who used this text to fight his enemies and rivals (Cuevas 2015). Several Vajrabhairava lineages emerged in Tibet where the cult of Vajrabhairava became part of practice in all the prominent traditions of Tibetan Buddhism, especially the Sa skya and Dge lugs (Cuevas 2021: 149–53; Wenta forthcoming).

The magical recipes found in the VBhT share parallels with other early Śaiva and Buddhist tantras, such as the sixth- to eighth-century Śaiva *Guhyasūtra* of the *Niśvāsatattvasaṃhitā* (NTGS); the *Vīṇāśikhatantra* (VŚ), an early Śaiva text of the Vāmasrotas (Törzsök 2016: 137); and the eighth-century Buddhist action-tantra, the *Mañjuśriyamūlakalpa* (MMK). The parallel recipes do not only provide evidence of the shared magical technologies that crossed sectarian boundaries but also suggest adherence to the same conceptual framework or rationality that informed their semantic construction. It is argued that this rationality, rather than the reflection of the eponymous "other," located in the domain of the lower, folk superstitions had their provenance in "high" Brahmanical discourse as well as other literary traditions.

What is tantric "magic"?

In speaking of tantric "magical" recipes, I will be examining ritual procedures (Skt. *karma*, Tib. *las*) preserved in tantric texts. This does, of course, raise both theoretical and practical difficulties. On the theoretical level, one may ask whether ritual practices preserved in the tantras are indeed "magical," and if they are, then, what are the distinguishing features that make them so. On a more practical level, one may ask the question of how medieval "tantric" magical recipes really were tantric, and to what degree non-tantric magical technology has influenced tantric magic on the whole. One way of approaching the first issue is to find out if, and to what degree, the features through which we usually understand "magic" as an etic concept apply to tantric "magic" as well. The way to deal with the second issue would be to determine if the terminology, ideas, and "know-how" drawn from non-tantric magical practices were absorbed into tantric magical recipes. A positive answer would, then, constitute fairly good evidence that tantric "magic" (at least to some degree) has been influenced by magical practices found in earlier Sanskritic textual sources.

There are several arguments for and against the use of the etic term "magic" to describe ritual procedures in tantric texts. The ground for calling tantric recipes "magical" is the fact that the rituals investigated below follow the law of sympathy "like produces like," which, from the time of Frazer's classic definition (Frazer [1922] 1996: 12), infers that a person can "produce any effect he desires merely by imitating it." For example, a doll filled with thorns that represents the target causes harm to the target himself. Implicit in the principle of sympathy is the notion of correspondence, which is a belief that one can control something through something else. Tantric texts developed different taxonomies of correspondences that were based on the symbolic understanding of a culturally determined order of things that linked the natural/material and the social worlds in a cause-and-effect relationship. While these features can be decidedly regarded as arguments in favor of calling tantric recipes "magical," there are also other aspects that can serve as a counterpoint against using this term. The main counterargument derives from the fact that a distinction between religion—seen as "high," soteriologically oriented—and magic—viewed as "low," popular, and used for pragmatic purposes—often made in anthropology, is blurred in tantric context. The execution of tantric magical recipes belongs to the repertoire of the advanced practitioner. For instance, the VBhT refers to the mantra-master who has already performed the previous service (Skt. *kṛtapuraścaraṇa*)—the purification of the mantra by reciting it for a long time—, received initiation, and achieved the mastery of the mantra. In this context, magical results are regarded as attainments (Skt. *siddhi*s, Tib. *dngos grub*) and as such they are part and parcel of a religious practice (Skt. *sādhana*, Tib. *sgrub thabs*), which may also include other practices that fall under the category of religion, such as the invocation of the deity into the *maṇḍala*, visualization of the deity, and the worship of the deity with various substances. It may be the case that it is the deity himself who grants the practitioner various *siddhi*s.[2] The *siddhi*s are usually classified into three categories: low, intermediate, and highest.[3] Despite different classifications of the *siddhi*s, the early Śākta-Śaiva and Buddhist tantras seem to agree that the highest *siddhi* is connoted with the soteriologically oriented goals, such as obtaining awakening, liberation, or becoming a deity, whereas the low *siddhi*s include the category of aggressive magic (*abhicāra*), such as subjugating under one's will, paralyzing, creating dissent, and so on.

Another counterargument against the depiction of magic as a lower and pragmatically oriented type of ritual practice, apparent especially in tantric Buddhist context, is its ethical dimension. The employment of aggressive magic is not intended for personal gain, but in line with the Mahāyāna's (and tantric) concept of benefit for others (Skt. *parārtha*, Tib. *gzhan don*), it has an implicit altruistic purpose of helping other beings from harm inflicted on them by the evil doers, and liberating those who are "wicked" or "corrupted" from the evil *karma* that awaits them for their evil deeds. In this way, aggressive magic is incorporated as the means of liberation and the exercise of compassion.

Another point worth keeping in mind when discussing definitional issues of "magic" in tantric context, which also addresses the issue of influence of non-tantric magical traditions on the production of tantric "magic," is that the rituals discussed here adhere to the precise definition of what, in etic terms, is called "magic." Generally speaking, magical practices in India can be traced back to the *Atharvaveda*, also known as *Atharvāṅgirasaḥ* (Bloomfield 1899: 1). The text divides magical technologies into three distinct categories in accordance with the expected magical result. The rituals attributed to the sage Atharvan contain hymns for averting evil (Skt. *śānti*), promoting welfare (Skt. *puṣṭi*), and curative practices (Skt. *bheṣajāni*). The rituals attributed to the sage Aṅgirasa deal specifically with aggressive rites, called *āṅgirasa*, which in the *Kauśikasūtra* assumed the meaning of *abhicārikā*, literally, "to go against" also called fierce (Skt. *ghora*), directed against the enemies (ibid.: 8).[4] In tantric studies, the influence of the *Atharvaveda* upon the development of tantric magical practices has been examined from the perspective of both textual and social history, where an emphasis has been placed on the tantric officiating priests, called *rājaguru*s, "royal officiants" who subsumed the role of the Atharvavedic priests (Skt. *purohitas*) and employed a whole array of apotropaic ritual repertoire specifically designed to kill the enemies, protect the kingdom, and ensure victory in battle (Sanderson 2004, 2009).

An Atharvavedic influence on the production of the VBhT is detectable on the basis of some linguistic features. For instance, the VBhT (§37) betrays an Atharvavedic terminology when it uses the term *pratyaṅgirā* (Tib. *phyir ldog pa*) to refer to the magical recipes that rebound on the practitioner if he executes the procedures for a wrong purpose or with a wrong intention in mind. The passage reads as follows:

> If the yogin does otherwise out of cruelty for someone, then the magical procedure (*karma*), which is being set up by him, will rebound on him.[5]

The term *pratyaṅgirā* is not a common word in classical Sanskrit. On the other hand, in the *Āṅgirasakalpa* of the Oriyā Paippalāda we find mentions of the goddesses called *pratyaṅgirā*, who are worshipped precisely to turn back the hostile magic of another sorcerer (Sanderson 2007). Bloomfield (1899: 66) argues that the term *pratyaṅgirā*, employed in the *Ṛgvidhāna* (4.6.4; 8.3) with the meaning of counteractive sorcery, is a later systematization of the Atharvavedic concept of retaliative magic. The above example shows that the meaning and context in which the usage of the term *pratyaṅgirā* is attested in the VBhT goes back to the Atharvavedic tradition, where it is applied in a similar sense, which, in turn, supports the argument about the influence of the non-tantric magical practices on the production of tantric rituals.

The second influence on the development of the tantric magical recipes of the VBhT and other tantric texts may have been the Brahmanical ritual of *homa* (Tib. *sbyin sreg*). A considerable amount of magical recipes found in tantras belong to the category of vocative fire-offerings or *homa*, a type of ritual technology that seems to have been developed from the Vedic *homa* and the Indo-Iranian cult of fire (Payne 2016). The archaic ritual syntax, namely, the use of verb "one should offer as oblation" (Skt. *juhuyāt*, Tib. *sbyin sreg byas na*) for the performance of fire-offerings, as well as the technical vocabulary used to denote fire-pits, woods, ladles, and so on, bears this out (Goodall and Isaacson 2016: 20–2). Even though the *homa* recipes form a distinctive category of tantric ritual procedures and are often treated separately, they can also be adopted for a wide range of other *abhicāra* technologies or for the gain of magical *siddhi*s, and even initiation. It is certainly not unusual to find individual recipes for the *abhicāra*-related purposes containing *homa*-components, and existing alongside other "magical" technologies, such as the manipulation of different types of material objects, or the use of specifically tantric technologies, such as *yantra*s, *mantra*s, and so on. This shows the extent to which *homa* formed an important and constituent part of tantric magical recipes.

Circulation of tantric magical recipes

The term used for "magical recipes" in tantric texts is *karma*, literally "action" or "ritual" (with the Tibetan equivalent *las* having the same semantic range). This word, which appears already in the *Atharvaveda* to describe magical procedures of a similar kind, is also attested in early tantric Buddhist texts, such as the MMK, and the Śaiva NTGS. Unlike in the *Atharvaveda*, however, magical recipes found in early Buddhist and Śaiva texts are written in prose, which appears to be an early compositional model for writing magical recipes. The register in which the recipes are written carries characteristics of formulaic language, by which I mean the use of conventional forms of expressions typical for this kind of "magical" genre. At the most basic level, the recipes include a heading or a title, which explains what the recipe is good for (e.g., "if he wishes to cause dissent") followed by the directives on what to do (namely, ingredients and their manipulation) and the indicator that the recipe has ended. In many magical formulas, the very end of the recipe is accompanied by a declaration of its immediate efficacy, insisting that the outcome of the recipe will happen "immediately," "in an instant." Another common way of ending the recipe is indicated by the time-period within which the outcome of the recipe can be expected, usually three or seven days. Thus, we find such expressions as "in three days, the target will die." In other recipes, the end of the magical procedure is accompanied by the claim of assurance that the result of the *karma* will definitely come "without any doubt."

The comparison of the formal structure of magical recipes in the Śaiva and Buddhist tantras indicates that their production appears to have been determined by "literary" consideration. Thus, it is possible to assume that the writer or the copyist of tantric magical recipes was emulating the "template" of the magical recipe "genre" that circulated in that period. Indeed, the existence of the shared prescriptions suggests that magical recipes are embedded in the culture of circulation, where the same objects, the same substances are defined by their common semantic construction that cross boundaries, and therefore, defy fixation to a single religious location. Moreover, the circulation of tantric recipes can be seen as a process that took place both synchronically and diachronically. The latter allows perceiving how magical recipes changed through their circulation, for example, by adapting to different tantric cults.

Materiality of tantric magical recipes

The best part of the VBhT contains various magical recipes that are distinguished from other ritual procedures by their prescriptive core, which typically relies on the manipulation of a wide range of material objects or substances—grains, minerals, chemicals, plants, sweets, effigies, animals, and so on. These objects and substances were deemed efficacious to cause magical results, and as such they offer a proof for the existence of highly standardized *materia magica* that had been copied, recycled, and adopted into different tantric systems. The choice of these ingredients and materials as well as the techniques of manipulation was, by no means, arbitrary. On the contrary, they seem to be embedded in a certain worldview and semantic construction related to the order of things. When we talk about the order of things, the word "ontology" comes to mind. Conventionally, ontology refers either to the study of being or the relations between different concepts or categories of being(s). It is the latter meaning that becomes particularly useful in highlighting a kind of dependence of the conceptual on the material that occurs in magic. As Hildred Geertz (1975: 83) puts it, magical practices:

> are comprehensible within the framework of a historically particular view of the nature of reality, a culturally unique image of the way in which the universe works, that provides a hidden conceptual foundation for all of the specific diagnoses, prescriptions, and recipes [...]. The common linking element is not a psychological attitude but an ontology.

My aim in the following survey is to examine the available evidence for the recourse to different magical technologies in the VBhT and other early (and, in some case, later) tantric texts, and classify them on the basis of various material substances and objects they use. It is argued that the early tantric milieu had a very similar understanding of materiality and methods of its manipulation for magic purposes that was embedded in the specific semantic construction. This semantic construction transcended sectarian boundaries of "Buddhist" and "Śaiva" (Hindu) religious discourses and was connected to the "cultural image of the universe" that was seen as dominant at that time. Rather than the expression of "little" folk traditions, the semiotic construction of tantric magical recipes was deeply embedded in the Brahmanical worldview of elites.

Pungent mustard oil and "crow magic"

One of the common *abhicāra* substances used in early Śaiva and Buddhist tantras is pungent mustard oil (Skt. *kaṭutaila*, Tib. *tsha ba'i mar*). Already in the NTGS (10.15ab), pungent mustard oil is considered a powerful ingredient that guarantees successful annihilation of the enemies: "If he includes pungent mustard oil, there will be certain destruction of his enemies."[6] Exactly what makes mustard oil an agent of destruction is unclear. The Buddhist tantras seem to point to its pungent, acidic, foul smell[7] as the quality that makes mustard oil effective in *abhicārahoma*. Pungent mustard oil is semantically connected to the adjective *kaṭu* in a sense of "bitter," "acrid," "sharp," traditionally classified as one of the six tastes (Skt. *rasas*)[8] and not smells. *Kaṭu* is categorized as the hottest of all tastes and shares the quality of pungency with "three pungent substances" (Skt. *kaṭutraya*, Tib. *rtsa ba gsum*), namely, fresh ginger, hot pepper, and onion/garlic. Apart from its usage in *homa* sacrifice, mustard oil is also employed as a type of ointment applied on the body of a mantra-master before the start of any aggressive procedures. The reasons for this odd practice can perhaps partially be explained by looking at the general typology of smells in South Asian religion and culture, recently researched by McHugh (2012). McHugh's discussion highlights the existence of foul-smelling substances, such as urine and feces, which are considered impure and inauspicious (ibid.: 75); these substances are located on the opposite end of sweet-smelling substances like milk, honey, or lotus that are considered pure and auspicious. Of course, in tantric ritual, inauspicious energies need to be harnessed in order to make *abhicāra* potent. Anointing oneself with foul-smelling substances attracts negative, demonic energies through the law of sympathetic magic, "similar attracts similar." Moreover, the use of foul-smelling substances seems to be also directly connected to the efficacy of the magical procedure. The *Guhyasamāja* (14.51) provides a case in point, when it says:

> Having worn a garment, which is soaked in urine and feces, which is disgusting because of its appalling odor, he should then repeat the mantra until it dries up; as soon as it has dried up, the victim will die immediately.[9]

In this passage we may note the obvious agreement concerning the employment of foul-smelling substances in tantric magic found in Buddhist tantras. Pungent mustard oil, liquefied fat from a black crow, as well as urine and feces are listed as examples of foul-smelling substances that play an important role in making aggressive magic effective.

Another context in which pungent mustard oil appears in tantric texts is the cluster of driving away (Skt. *uccāṭana*, Tib. *skrod pa*) recipes connected with "crow-magic." In this regard, the recipes preserved in the Buddhist VBhT and the Śaiva *Vīṇāśikhatantra* show a remarkable degree of similarity with respect to contents and methods. Moreover, parallels of crow recipes are also found in later tantric scriptures, such as the Hindu *Tantrasārasaṃgraha* and the *Mantramahārṇava*. Before turning our attention to the analysis of these specific recipes, a brief examination of the main reasons behind the popularity of crow in tantric magic seems to be in order.

The semantic construction surrounding the crow draws together key religious meanings associated with impurity, death, and inauspiciousness. In the dharmaśāstric literature, the crow is generally considered impure, and contact with a crow or its leftovers brings defilement (*Baudhāyanadharmasūtra*, 3.6.5). The crow is regarded as a messenger of the god of death, Yama, who, as the epic Sanskrit literature tells us, granted the crow a special status as the only bird free of death by natural causes. According to the *Uttarakāṇḍa* of the *Rāmāyaṇa* (18.23–26, ed. Shah Premanand 1975), the crow was promised to live as long as humans do not kill it (see Zeiler 2013: 215). The crow's association with death is also conveyed through the belief that the bird embodies the soul of the departed ancestors. The ritual feeding of a crow with balls of rice plays a prominent part in ancestor worship practiced from antiquity to the present (Olivelle 1999: 289).[10] The sight of a crow is generally considered inauspicious and forebodes death and downfall. In folk literature, the crow is often portrayed as sitting on the neem tree, the bitter fruits of which it savors. The connection between the crow and the neem tree is prominent in tantric magic, which may have assimilated popular perceptions or imitated forms of folk literature.

Let us now turn to the first "crow recipe" that deals with the preparation of ash for the purpose of driving away:

> VBhT §22: Now, there is another procedure for driving away: [the mantra-master] having anointed himself with pungent mustard oil (*kaṭutaila*), and having taken hold of a nest of a crow in a neem-tree, burns that nest with a wood in the fire taken from the cremation ground and collects the ashes. The person on whose head [the ashes] are placed is driven away.
>
> *Vīṇāśikhatantra* (vv. 171–3, trans. Goudriaan 1985: 115): Having collected a crow who lived on a neem-tree, caught by a *śvapāka* (member of a despised

> group), he should sacrifice it in [a fire taken from] a pyre sprinkled with pungent mustard oil[11], while saying these [seed-syllables] *bīja*s in inverted order; being clothed in red with black hems, he should recite the five *bīja*s in inverted order for a thousand times over these ashes which he has sprinkled with poison and blood; the person whom he touches with these ashes will roam over the earth like a crow, hated by all people, even if he were equal to Indra.

Both passages from the VBhT and the VŚ give an almost identical recipe that focuses on the preparation of the ash. This recipe finds a close parallel with the late (nineteenth-century) *Dhūmavātītantra* of the *Mantramāharṇava*: "if one burns a crow in the fire of a cremation ground, takes her ashes, implies the mantra on this and throws it at the head of the opponent, he will be ruined immediately" (Zeiler 2013: 224). A very similar recipe is attested in another late tantra, probably fifteenth-century Śaiva *Tantrasārasaṃgraha* of Nārāyaṇa (17. 56cd-57ab, ed. Unithiri 2002, see Goudriaan 1978: 364), where "a performer should burn a crow in the fire of cremation ground, and saying the mantra, strew the ashes in the enemy's house into the eight directions." The similarity of these recipes, based on the magical principle of sympathy (in which the ash obtained from burning a crow has to come into direct contact with the target) may offer a proof for the existence of highly standardized tantric magical recipes that had been copied, recycled, and preserved in similar forms from the eighth to (at least) the nineteenth century.

One striking feature of the crow recipe given in the VŚ is the expression: "to wander aimlessly in the world like a crow" (Skt. *kākavad bhramate mahīm*, Tib. *bya rog bzhin sa kun tu 'khor*), which appears to be a figurative manner of referring to the outcome of the driving away of the human target. Such expression is found in a number of textual sources that employ crows for the purpose of driving. The VBhT (§21) mentions the same phrase as the outcome of another recipe involving a crow. The recipe instructs the adept to tighten on a crow's neck a piece of birch-bark picturing the wind-*maṇḍala* drawn with crow's blood and charcoal of the cremation ground, and then to set the crow free. Similarly, in the Śaiva *Svacchandatantra* (6.76), the expression "he wanders the earth like a crow" is used to signal the final result of the driving away recipe, which heavily relies on the use of crow's feathers, crow's blood, and so on.[12] The same is attested in the Buddhist MMK (chap. 41), where one is instructed to sacrifice into the fire a crow's feathers twenty-one times, which results in "wandering like a crow."[13] Finally, we have evidence from the late (fifteenth- to seventeenth-century) Hindu tantra *Phetkāriṇītantra* (13.35–38), where the same expression is attested as the result of driving away (Nihom 1987: 89).

The catchphrase "to wander like a crow" points to the phenomenon of "recycled phrasing" in magical recipes across tantric texts that do not only encompass the span of several centuries but are also embedded within the same ritual framework of driving away and "crow-magic." As we have seen above, this phrase is a figurative way of referring to driving away,[14] but it could also have a psychosomatic meaning. Kṣemarāja in his commentary on the *Svacchandatantra* (6.76, p. 350) gives the following explanation: "He is driven away in this way [means that] the enemy who is overpowered with a disease wanders in the world like a crow" (*sa itthamuccāṭitaḥ—bhramate kākavat pṛthvīṃ śatrur vyādhinipīḍitaḥ*). In the light of Kṣemarāja's explanation, it is plausible to argue that "to wander like a crow" corresponds to "feeling giddy or unsteady," especially on account of the fact that this meaning of the root *bhram* is attested in Sanskrit dictionaries.

The second cluster of "crow recipes" under investigation here presents us with a completely different model for the production of tantric magical recipes. This model breaks off with the previously described "standardized model" and shows the existence of tantric techniques that, although employing the same items intended for the same magical result, feature differing ways of manipulating these items in each particular case. In this regard, the VŚ gives a *homa*-recipe involving the collection of dry leaves of the neem tree, tips of banners, human hair, ashes from the cremation pyre, and feathers and tails of crows; these items have to be smeared with mustard oil, poison, and blood and offered into the fire with the wood collected by an outcaste.[15] This *homa* results in driving the enemy away in three days. The VBhT (§20) gives a recipe for making an ointment that is to be applied to the sandals, feet, head, or towel of any person whom one wishes to drive away. The preparation of the ointment goes through several stages. First, one has to smear an outcaste with mustard oil and make him climb the neem tree. Then, one gathers the mustard oil from the outcaste's body and burns it in the fire together with a black banner of Śiva; finally, one mixes the lampblack that remains from burning the banner with mustard oil gathered from the outcaste sitting on the neem tree, thereby obtaining the ointment.

Both recipes operate within the same framework of magical categories insofar that they acknowledge the special magical properties of a neem tree, mustard oil, banners, and an outcaste, which need to be magically manipulated to cause driving away. Nevertheless, the magical technology executed in both cases does not bear any similarities. The recipe from the VBhT makes use of an outcaste,[16] who appears to be a substitute for a crow: indeed, both are associated with the neem tree. In tantric magic, the crow is often linked to the neem tree—cf. the above-described expressions "crow in the neem tree" or "crow which lives on the neem tree," found also in folk literature. Furthermore, outcastes, crows, and dogs are often linked together in the dharmaśāstric literature[17] as embodiments of impurity and, therefore, it may be argued that within the framework of tantric magical technology heavily relying on the implementation of transgressive substances and objects, a crow and an outcaste can be regarded as substitutes. In addition, the VBhT seems to give special emphasis on the ritual connection between the neem tree and mustard oil that seem to be common also in other tantric[18] and non-tantric magical texts.[19] These examples show that the mixture of mustard oil and neem is used for a wide range of aggressive magical rites, not only for driving away. In the VBhT (chapters 2 and 6), however, these two substances are always linked with the cluster of crow recipes (six recipes in total) meant to cause driving away. Thus, with regard to the specific driving away cluster, the VBhT adheres to a fairly consistent ritual syntax.

The three sweets: Milk, honey, and ghee

The previous sections examined the use of a wrathful substance, namely, mustard oil, which is prominent in aggressive magic. There exists also the set of "peaceful" substances that are mainly used for the purpose of averting evil (Skt. *śānti*, Tib. *zhi ba*)[20] or reinvigoration after an illness (Skt. *puṣṭi*, Tib. *rgyas pa*).[21] To these substances belong milk (Skt. *dadhi*, Tib. *'o ma*), honey (Skt. *madhu*, Tib. *sbrang rtsi*), and ghee (Skt. *ghṛta*, Tib. *mar*). These substances are also sometimes referred to not by their individual names but by their collective name, that is, the "three sweets,"[22] or simply "the three." For example, the NTGS (10.96) refers to them by their collective name in the context of the ascetic observance of mastering the *vidyā* (i.e., the *mantra*):

> Having worshipped the god he should make the offering into the fire; consuming only milk for seven days, he should sacrifice into the fire at the three junctures a hundred summits of *udumbara* wood smeared with the three. In this way, he will be the one who has accomplished the ascetic observance of obtaining a power over [his] spell.[23]

The commentary *Uddyota* by Kṣemarāja to the Śaiva *Netratantra* (6.17b, ed. Śāstrī 1926) uses the phrase "anointed with the three sweets," namely milk, ghee, and honey. The context of the verse is the rite of invigoration, which occurs by doing *homa* with pills of *gugullu* incense smeared with three sweets: butter, milk, and sugar (*gugulludupagolikabhir ajakṣīrakṣaudraṃ*). The

Svacchandatantroddyota (vol. 3, *paṭala* 6, Shastri 1921–35, p. 158), by the same author, refers to the three sweets as "milk, sugar, and ghee." Buddhist tantric texts are also aware of the existence of the three sweets, but sometimes present them in different combinations. In the *Cakrasaṃvarapañjikā* of Bhavabhaṭṭa (v. 14, ed. Pandey 2002), we read that the three sweets are molasses, honey, and sugar (*trimadhuraṃ guḍa madhu śarkāra*). The continuity of their significance as curative substances is confirmed in contemporary Tibetan Buddhist ritual practice, where the three sweets (Tib. *mngar gsum*), namely, honey, sugar, and molasses, are added, for example, to the peaceful *torma* offering during the accomplishing medicine ritual (*sman sgrub*), widely practiced by Buddhists in Tibet (Garret et al. 2013: 498).

The second meaning of *puṣṭi* as the ritual effectuating prosperity is found in the NTGS and the *Sampuṭatantra*. The examples found in both texts seem to put special emphasis on the *udumbara* wood and the three sweets as the substances connected with creating wealth. The NTGS (10.127) gives the following recipe:

> If he offers into the fire 1008 times sticks of *udumbara* wood smeared with **milk, honey, and ghee**, he will immobilize a treasure. All obstacles will be paralyzed and the treasure will not move from that place. [Even better,] it will be obtained in his own place (author's emphasis).[24]

In the *Sampuṭatantra* (7.2.14) the three sweets are mentioned both collectively as well as individually:

> Next, if he wishes to cause prosperity: [he takes] a sesame, black lentil together with red unhusked rice or, alternatively, a barley, etc. .... They should be combined with **three sweets**, rice pudding cooked in ghee, **milk, honey, and ghee**, fennel, *bilva*-fruit, lotus-root, *nāgakesara* flowers and rice. Then, having lit the fire with the *udumbara* wood, sustaining the yoga with the deity in accordance with the ritual, facing north, established in meditative equipoise, he makes one thousand oblations at the three times of the day. Within seven days, he will become a very rich man (author's emphasis).[25]

The ritualistic employment of *udumbara* tree with its milky sap that brings nourishment and prosperity goes back to the Vedic texts and the Brāhmaṇas, where it is etymologically linked to the Sanskrit root *ūrj* meaning "strengthening liquid" (Minkowski 1989; Gerety 2016: 168). Its usage in tantric magical recipes appears to be in continuation with earlier Vedic understanding, where contact with the *udumbara* tree was thought to bestow strength and well-being even to the gods themselves.

The logic of archenemies

The efficacy of tantric magic was based not only on the employment of various magical technologies but also on imitating the basic principles that governed the natural and social worlds. In so doing, tantric magic sought to establish taxonomies of correspondences between various objects from the natural world and their analogous magical properties. One of those taxonomies of correspondences applied in the rite of creating dissent (Skt. *vidveṣaṇa*, Tib. *dbral ba*) was based on the logic of archenemies. The items procured from natural enemies catalyze conflict and, for that very reason, they are employed in sympathetic magic to produce the same result on the targeted people. The following groups of archenemies are listed in the VBhT: horse and buffalo, crow and owl, mongoose and snake, Brahmin and outcaste. In the grammatical tradition of India, these pairings were thought of as examples defining the rule of the *dvandva* compound, which Pāṇini's *Aṣṭādhyāyī* (2.4.9) describes as: "And between whom there is constant strife" (McGovern 2019: 67–8). The VBhT gives a procedure for causing dissension among them that is almost identical to those found in the NTGS and MMK.[26] The recipe involves collecting a fur of a mongoose and the slough of a snake, as follows:

> VBhT (§24): Next [the mantra-master writes the ten-letter mantra] on the rag of the cremation ground with the substances beginning with poison and encloses it with the name of the target. Having customized the *smaraṇa*[-mantra] and having got hold of a hair of a mongoose and a slough of a snake, he should put it [on the rag] and make a wick; in whosoever house he lights with it, there will be a fight among each other.
>
> NTGS (3.90cd–92ab): That person who enchants with ten thousand recitations the fur of a mongoose and a slough of a snake and offers them into the fire or burns them as incense. Or if they are placed in his house, garment, seat, or bed, if they are placed in this way, it will cause the two people to fall out with each other.
>
> MMK (41, p. 463): That person with whose name hairs of a mongoose, mustard seeds, and the slough of a snake are burnt as incense becomes hated by all the world. (trans. Goodall and Isaacson 2016: 25)

Another example of this logic is found in yet another parallel creating dissent recipe given in the VBhT and in a later Buddhist *yoginītantra*, the *Saṃvarodaya*, which makes use of the wings or nests of a crow and an owl for causing dissent.

> VBhT (§23): There is also another procedure for causing dissension: [the mantra-master] having combined together the wings of a crow and an owl, and a hair from a Brahmin and an outcast, he lits up the fire with a thorn-apple wood, making a fire free of smoke. Having gathered the ashes of that fire and having empowered [the ashes] by the recitation of the ten-letter mantra, he should place the ashes in between a man and a woman. They will fall out instantaneously.
>
> *Saṃvarodayatantra* (28.9–10): That which is called the rite of causing hostility [is as follows]: [the practitioner] who knows mantras should sacrifice nests of crows and owls mixed with sloughs together with leaves of the neem-tree in the fire of a thorn-apple plant one hundred and eight times; [as a consequence, the target] will be hated by the whole world and deserted by his friends and relatives. (trans. Tsuda 1970: 300 with minor modifications)

The topic of enmity between the crow and the owl is widely attested in various narrative literatures originated in India. Probably, the earliest reference is found in the Pāli Buddhist *Jātaka* story (no. 270), where the Buddha narrates the origins of hostility between these two species of birds (see Francis and Thomas 1916: 213–15). This theme is repeated in a number of scriptures, often in a military context. For example, in Book Nine of Kauṭilya's manual of statecraft, the *Arthaśāstra*, the enmity between the crow and the owl is mentioned while considering the proper time of marching into battle, where it is said "during the day, a crow kills an owl, while during the night an owl kills a crow" (Olivelle 2013: 350). The same martial setting is attested in the *Hitopadeśā*, where the dangers of marching into a war out of season is compared to the violence inflicted by an owl on the crow (Wilkins 1885: 248). This is yet another example in support of the argument that the semantic construction of tantric magical recipes aligned with the worldview found in the literary traditions of India had their established presence prior to the emergence of tantric sects.

Image-magic: Manipulation of dolls

Another common object used in magical recipes is the use of a doll (Skt. *pratimā*, *pratikṛti*, *kṛti*, *puttalikā*, *liṅga*). On the basis of the principle of sympathetic magic, "like produces like," a doll is created by a *mantrin* in the image of the target, and it is believed that whatever is done to a doll will happen to the target as well. The doll representing the target may be trampled upon, cut with a knife, filled with thorns, burnt, worshipped, or buried facedown. An analysis of the magical recipes using dolls found in the early Buddhist and Śaiva tantras shows the existence of common ritual procedures, that is, "things to be done to a doll." Moreover, the way in which the doll is manipulated does not seem to depend on the purpose of the rite, but rather on the general understanding of the various acts performed on the doll. For example, one procedure enacted on the doll is filling it with thorns.[27] This procedure resembles the magical systems of Europe, Asia, Africa, and Americas, where the humanoid "voodoo doll" is pierced with pins with the intention of inflicting harm (Flint et al. 1999: 71). Elizabeth Southerns, who lived in seventeenth-century England and was hanged in the 1612 Pendle Witch trails, advices: "The speediest way to take a man's life by witchcraft is to make a picture of clay, like unto the shape of the person whom they mean to kill," prick it with a thorn or pin to cause pain, burn the clay figure, and "thereupon by that means, the body shall die" (Lipscomb 2020: 9). In the early tantras, however, the purpose of such a procedure clearly differs across the texts. In the VBhT and *Guhyasamājatantra*, it is a part of the ritual that leads to killing. In the VŚ, the intended purpose is subjugation under one's will.

Another example is dismembering the doll, which does not always indicate killing but can also mean subjugation; nevertheless, the act consistently performed on the doll is dismembering, despite the different magical purposes for which it is executed. One such act is cutting the doll into parts and sacrificing those parts into the fire. The parallel recipes are found in the VBhT, NTGS, MMK, and VŚ.

> VBhT (§25): Then, if he who wishes to kill, [the mantra-master] **makes an image** [of a target] in feces and urine and smears the top of it with a powdered bone, and **then cuts it up repeatedly**. Then, naked, with hair disheveled, facing south, while in meditative union with the Buffalo-faced one, **he should offer that into the fire** taken from the cremation pyre **at midnight**; that person in whose name he offers that into the fire **will die instantly.** (authors's emphasis)

> NTGS (3.86cd–87): On the eighth of the dark fortnight **at midnight,** having worshipped He whose banner is the bull (i.e., Śiva), **having made a** male **figure** with salt or a woman if that is what he likes, and **having cut it up repeatedly by sacrificing that into the fire, at that instant [the victim] comes** immediately. He becomes a slave [subject to his will], or else [one may attract] a woman from one hundred miles. (authors's emphasis)

> MMK, chap. 55 (ed. Vaidya 1964, p. 526): Having made a doll with salt, **having cut it repeatedly**, he sacrifices it into the fire 8000 times. Whosoever he wants—a woman or a man—will become subjected to his will. (authors's emphasis)

> VŚ (268cd–269): **Having made an image** of salt, the clever man should speak the mantras over it for a hundred times and **sacrifice it in parts beginning with**

> **the feet, dividing it into eight hundred parts,** in due concentration during the three crucial points of the day, he will reduce the victim to a state of unfailing subjugation (author's emphasis). (trans. Goudriaan 1985: 125).

These recipes are interesting because of the way in which they combine relatively simple conceptions of figurative image-magic with the Brahmanical ritual of fire-offerings, and thus, they represent with particular clarity the mingling of magical and religious traditions.

Visualizing the target: "Camel-magic"

Apart from the use of material objects in tantric magic, we also find magical recipes that involve the visualization of the target. In some cases, visualizations can also accompany other ritual procedures that make use of material objects. For example, the VBhT (§19) gives a recipe for driving away in which both the image-magic and visualization are employed together, as follows:

> Next, if his wishes to drive away, the mantra-master should make [an image of a] camel with soil from the seven anthills. Having visualized on its back a wind-*maṇḍala* having the shape of a half-moon generated from the syllable YAṂ, he should visualize the target on the top of it. Having visualized the form of Yama holding a club in his hand on the top of that [target], he should think of [him] being struck with a club and being sent to the south. He puts the same wheel in his heart, having customized it with the name of the target in accordance with the prior procedure, [after which] he will be driven away in seven days, there is no doubt about this.

The above recipe is based on the understanding of correspondences existing between the camel, known in India for its speed, the wind, and the seed-syllable YAṂ, representing air in Brahmanical tradition,[28] all of which are envisioned in accordance with the principle of sympathetic magic as the agents of driving away. A parallel recipe is found in a number of textual sources, the first of which being the Śaiva-tantra *Kakṣapuṭa* (9.23), where a recipe for causing driving away that resembles the recipe of the VBhT reads as follows:

> Having meditated on an enemy mounted on a camel,[29] he who has become conversant with mantra should beat him with a stick. In 21 days he will cause the enemy to be expelled southwards from the land. [The mantra:] *oṃ hrīṃ* O [goddess] Vidyujjihvā, terrible like an owl, restrain, restrain, expel so and so, *hūṃ phaṭ*.

Both recipes given in the VBhT and the *Kakṣapuṭa* include the detail of the camel as the agent of driving away on which the target is mounted. Moreover, the target is to be visualized as being struck with a club and expelled southward. Nihom (1987: 76) shows that the *Kakṣapuṭa* recipe finds a parallel with the driving away recipe given in the *Yogaratnamālā* commentary (c. twelfth century) on the *Hevajratantra* (I.11.34, eds. Tripathi and Negi Lang 2006), where it is linked with the visualization of the Vajrayoginī. The recipe begins with the instruction on how to visualize Vajrayoginī emerging from the syllable I, blue in color and holding various implements. Then, one is directed to recite the Vajrayoginī-mantra *oṃ khaṃ svāhā* one hundred times. Afterward, the text illustrates the visualization procedure for driving away, as follows:

> He should recite the mantra *oṃ khaṃ svāhā* and visualize the target as naked, with his hair disheveled, blue in color, mounted on a camel,[30] fleeing towards the south struck by wrathful ones holding sticks; he should [then] begin the recitation of the mantra: *oṃ khaṃ*, O Vajrayoginī! Drive away so and so! *Khaṃ hūṃ hūṃ hūṃ phaṭ*. In seven nights, one surely drives him away.

The recipe shares with the VBhT and the *Kakṣapuṭatantra* the detail about the target being mounted on a camel. Like in the recipes of the VBhT and the *Kakṣapuṭa*, here too the target flees toward the south as he is being struck with a stick by wrathful beings. The aforementioned recipe is interesting because it shows the adoption of the same driving away recipe into the cult of the Vajrayoginī. The basic magical core of the recipe, namely visualization of the target mounted on a camel and the target being beaten with sticks and driven toward the inauspicious south direction, remains the same; what changes is tantric "packaging," that is, the mantras, the deity, and the visualization of the deity prior to the execution of the recipe. This example from the *Yogaratnamālā* provides evidence for the process of creativity in adopting magical recipes into different tantric systems.

Another example of the same process of creativity comes from the c. eleventh- to twelfth-century *Saṃvarodayatantra*. The first part of the *uccāṭana* recipe deals with the drawing of a *yantra* customized with the seed-syllables *hūṃ phaṭ* and the name of the target on the rag taken from the cremation ground that is to be placed in the skull-vessels. Then, one is instructed to visualize the *yantra* being buried in the funeral pyre, which has the form of the tantric deity Heruka. The second part of the recipe contains many details, which correspond to those found in the recipe of the VBhT, as follows:

> He should imagine in front the character *yaṃ* which is existing in the middle of [the *maṇḍala* of] wind, having the shape of a bow, riding on a camel, being blue

> in color and being sent to the south, being led away by a host of wrathful [deities] and being always distraught. He should incessantly recite the mantra connected to the characters *Hūṃ phaṭ*, for whomsoever the rite may be practiced, it drives away [the *sādhya*] from that very moment. (trans. Tsuda 1970: 259).

Similarly to the *Yogaratnamālā*'s adoption of this recipe for the cult of Vajrayoginī, here the recipe is linked to the cult of Heruka, where the correspondence between the camel, the wind, and the seed-syllable YAṂ with its air symbolism that goes back to the Vedic tradition is again brought to the forefront. Thus, the *Saṃvarodaya* constitutes yet another example of the process of creative adoption of magical recipes into various Buddhist tantric cults.

Conclusion

The analysis of tantric magical recipes revealed that the choice of the substances and the objects as well as methods of their manipulation operated on the basis of sympathy that linked the natural and the social worlds through the taxonomies of correspondences. These equivalences were aligned with a particular worldview that informed the semantic construction of the recipes' contents. Their meaning, however, rather than shaped by the folk beliefs of "little traditions" had their provenance in the established cultural and literary tropes that were also found in the dominant Brahmanical ideology and discourse. Moreover, the magical recipes of tantric milieu were embedded in the culture of circulation that crossed sectarian boundaries. One form of circulation was the adoption of recipes as a type of magical "genre." The other form of circulation was a reuse of magical recipes that can be taken as an indication of their capacity to adapt not only to heterogeneous religious traditions but also to various cults within homogeneous religious tradition. The presence of the same magical recipes across the fixed sectarian identities, across different tantric cults, and across time suggests shared understanding of magic and its practices. Although manipulation of material objects and substances played an important part in the technology of tantric magic, there were also other ritual techniques utilized to practice magic, such as visualization and Brahmanical ritual of *homa*. The range of methods applied in tantric recipes investigated here points to a considerable degree of fluidity and adaptability characterizing the performance of magic. Studying tantric practices through the lens of magical recipes does not only offer a possibility of examining these resilient rituals in their inter- and intracultural settings but also cross-culturally. This remains a desideratum for future generations of tantric scholars interested in the study of this virtually unexplored aspect of tantric traditions.

Notes

1 For the Tibetan translation, see Siklós (1996).

2 This model is attested in chapter one of the VBhT (§10), and in chapter forty-five of the Śākta tantra, the *Picumata-Brahmayāmalatantra*.

3 For an analysis of *siddhi*-classification in the Śaiva tantric traditions, see Vasudeva (2012).

4 The *abhicāra* category further expanded into six *karmas* (*ākarṣaṇa*, *vaśīkaraṇa*, *stambhana*, *māraṇa*, *vidveṣaṇa*, and *uccāṭana*); these constitute the so-called "six acts" (*ṣaṭkarmāṇi*). Additional categories were eventually added, for example, *jvara* or *unmādana*.

5 All the VBhT's passages are based on a critical edition of the text prepared by Wenta (forthcoming).

6 *kaṭutailasamāyuktaḥ śatrunāśaṃ bhavet dhruvaṃ.*

7 The Buddhist *Susiddhikara* (Giebel 2001: 169) refers to mustard oil as a powerful ingredient for the *abhicāra*, together with liquefied fat from a black crow and any foul-smelling oil.

8 *Kaṭu* is one of the six *rasas* or tastes in Āyurvedic literature (along with *madhura* "sweet," *amla* "sour," *lavaṇa* "salty," *tikta* "bitter," *kaṣāya* "astringent") and are also found in Buddhism (see, e.g., *Dharmasaṅgraha*, section 36, trans. Ānandajoti 2017).

9 GS_(14.51, p. 68): *viṇmūtrārdragataṃ vastraṃ pūtigandhajugupsitam/ prāvṛtya mantram āvartec chuṣyate mriyate kṣaṇāt//.*

10 *vayasāṃ piṇḍaṃ dadyāt/ vayasāṃ hi pitaraḥ pratimayā carantī iti vijñāyate/* "He should give a lump of rice to crows, for it is stated: 'ancestors roam about in the guise of crows.'" (*Baudhāyanadharmasūtra* 2.15.4, trans. Olivelle 1999: 289).

11 Goudriaan (1985: 115) translates *taila* as "sesamum oil," which may not be correct taking into account the ritual syntax of a crow and neem tree.

12 See *Svacchandatantra* 6.72–76.

13 *kākapakṣāṇām ekaviṃśatyāhutiṃ juhuyāt sadyaḥ kākavad bhramati/*. MMK, chap. 41, p. 358.

14 I disagree with Nihom (1987: 89–90), who thinks that *kākavat bhramate* refers to the practitioner performing the hostile magical rite.

15 See VŚ 165–167 (p. 74). My translation slightly differs from that of Goudriaan, who translates *kaṭutailaviṣaṃ raktaṃ tenāloḍya* as "pound *kaṭutaila*, *viṣa* and *rakta*

together," which does not make sense in this context since the verb "*aloḍya*" is used commonly in the magical recipe for the act of smearing/anointing.

16 The use of humans in tantric magic is not uncommon, but they usually occur in possession rituals for the purpose of predicting the future. See, for example, Orofino (1994).

17 For example, the *Vasiṣṭhadharmasūtra* (11.9–13) states that crows' and dogs' food should be thrown on the ground for the outcasts, thereby emphasizing their lowest social status and their connection with impurity.

18 The NTGS (10.90) confirms the magical efficacy brought about by the combination of mustard oil and neem tree for driving away. The VŚ (197cd–199ab, p. 75) connects us again with the topic of crow-magic, where the magical efficacy of crow, neem tree, and mustard oil for the purpose of creating dissent is highlighted.

19 This association is further confirmed in the *Āsurīkalpa* of the *Atharavedapariśiṣṭas* (Magoun 1889: 176) in the *homa*-recipe meant for killing.

20 See, for example, VBhT (Siklós 1996: 45), VŚ (vv. 181–2, trans. Goudriaan 1985: 116).

21 The employment of the same three sweets for peaceful purposes and for gaining prosperity is also attested in the early *Tāramūlakalpa*'s *Continuation Tantra* (see Landesman's contribution in this volume).

22 The same nomenclature features in the Rnying ma recipes investigated in Brown's contribution to this volume.

23 *Devaṃ pūjyāgnau juhuyāt audumbarasamidhānāṃ* ***tryaktānāṃ*** *sahasraṃ tṛsandhyaṃ kṣīrāśī sapta dinānī juhuyāt. Cīrṇavidyāvrato bhavati.*

24 *Audumbarasamidhānāṃ* ***dadhimadhughṛtā****ktānām aṣṭasahasraṃ juhuyāt nidhistambhī bhavati. Sarve vighnāś ca stambhitā nidhisthānān na calate. Svasthāne ca gṛhyate.*

25 For the Tibetan text of the *Sampuṭa*, see *Yang dag par sbyor ba zhes bya ba'i rgyud chen po*, ff. 252–3.

26 The appearance of the same recipe in the NTGS and MMK has been already mentioned in Goodall and Isaacson (2016: 25–6).

27 See VBhT (§16), GS (15.79cd–80, p.77), and VŚ (270–271ab, p. 79).

28 Sanderson (1994, n. 35) shows that the *bījas yaṃ, raṃ, vaṃ, laṃ* in Buddhist *sādhanas* correspond to those found in Vaiṣṇava and Śaiva tantric traditions. He further argues that these are Brahmanical in origin. Heilijgers-Seelen (1994: 20) demonstrates that the four syllables are indeed attested in the *Yogatattva-Upaniṣad* (84ff.), where *ya* represents air presided over by Īśvara.

29 Trans. Nihom (1987: 76), slightly modified. I disagree with Nihom, who translates *uṣṭrā* as a buffalo.

30 My emendation of *daṃṣṭrāyudhaṃ* to *uṣṭrārūḍhaṃ* is supported by the Tibetan version of the *Yogaratnamālā*, which reads *rnga mo* "camel" instead of "wild boar."

Furthermore, the Tibetan version of the text makes it clear that the color blue classifies the camel on which the target is mounted and not the target himself: "*rnga mo sngon po la zhon pa bsams la*."

References

Primary sources

Baudhāyanadharmasūtra. See P. Olivelle (1999), *Dharmasūtras: The Law Codes of Āpastamba, Gautama, Baudhāyana and Vasiṣṭha*. Delhi: Motilal Banarsidass.

Cakrasaṃvarapañjikā of Bhavabhaṭṭa J. Shastri Pandey (ed.) (2002), Rare Buddhist Texts Series 26. Sarnath, Varanasi: Central Institute of Higher Tibetan Studies.

Dharmasaṅgraha. See B. Ānandajoti (trans.) (2017), The Dharma Collection (Dharma-Saṅgrahah). Ebook: https://www.ancient-buddhist-texts.net/English-Texts/Dharma-Collection/index.htm.

Guhyasamājatantra (GS) Y. Matsunaga (ed.) (1978), Osaka: Toho Shuppan, Inc.

Guhyasūtra of the *Niśvāsatattvasaṃhitā* (NTGS). NAK Ms. 1–227, NGMPP Reel No. A 41/14. Palm-leaf ms. Devanāgari transcript by D. Goodall. The chapter and verse numeration used in this paper is based on D. Goodall's transcript. I thank Prof. A. Sanderson for giving me this transcript.

Hevajratantram with *Yogaratnamālāpañjikā* of Mahāpaṇḍitācārya Kṛṣṇapāda (ed.) (2006), Prof. R. S. Tripathi and Dr. T. Sain Negi Lang. Sanskrit and Hindi. Sarnath and Varanasi: Central Institute of Higher Tibetan Studies, 2006.

Mañjuśriyamūlakalpa (MMK). *Āryamañjuśrīmūlakalpa* P. L. Vaidya (ed.) (1964), Buddhist Sanskrit Texts 18. Darbhanga: Mithila Institute, 1964. For the Tibetan translation, see *Jam dpal gyi rtsa ba'i rgyud* Toh. 543, Derge Kangyur vol. 88 (rgyud 'bum, na), folios 105.a–351.a.

Netratantra with the commentary (*Netroddyota*) of Rājānaka Kṣemarāja. M. Kaul Śāstrī (ed.) (1926 and 1939), Bombay: KSTS 46, 59.

Picumata-Brahmayāmala. NAK 1-363, NGMPP A 42/6: palm-leaf; Newari script; AD 1052. Transcript by S. Hatley.

Sampuṭatantra (*Yang dag par sbyor ba zhes bya ba'i rgyud chen po*) (1976–9). Delhi Karmapae Chodhey Gyalwae Sungran Partun Khang Delhi.

Saṃvarodayatantra. See S. Tsuda (1970). *The Saṃvarodaya-tantra. Selected chapters.* Ph.D. diss. Australian National University (unpublished).

Svacchandatantra with the commentary (*Svacchandoddyota*) of Rājānaka Kṣemarāja. (ed.) (1921–35), M. Kaul Shastri. Bombay: KSTS 31, 38, 44, 48, 51, 53, 56.

Tantrasārasaṃgraha of Nārāyaṇa with Mantravimrsinī commentary by Svarṇagrāma Vāsudeva, Part 1 and 2. N. V. P. Unithiri (ed.) (2002). Calicut: University of Calicut.

Uttarakāṇḍa Rāmāyaṇa. See U. Shah Premanand. (1975). *Uttarakāṇḍa: The Seventh Book of the Vālmīki-Rāmāyaṇa, the National Epic of India*. Critical Edition. Baroda: Oriental Institute.

Vajrabhairavatantra. See B. Siklós (1996). *The Vajrabhairava Tantras: Tibetan and Mongolian Versions, English Translation and Annotations*. Tring: The Institute of Buddhist Studies. See also Wenta (forthcoming).

Vīṇāśikhatantra. See T. Goudriaan (ed. and trans.) (1985), *The Vīṇāśikhatantra: A Śaiva Tantra of the Left Current*, Delhi: Motilal Banarsidass.

Secondary sources

Bloomfield, M. (1899), *The Atharvaveda*, Strassburg: Verlag von Karl J. Trübner.

Cuevas, B. J. (2015), *Ra Yeshé Sengé: The All-Pervading Melodious Drumbeat: The Life of Ra Lotsawa*, New York: Penguin Classics.

Cuevas, B. J. (2021), *The Rwa pod and Other "Lost" Works of Rwa lo tsā ba's Vajrabhairava Tradition: A Catalogue of Recently Acquired Tibetan Manuscripts from Mongolia and Khams and Their Significance*. WSTB 101, Wien: Arbeitskreis für Tibetische und Buddhistische Studien Universität Wien.

Flint, W., R. Gordon, G. Luck, and D. Ogden (1999), *Witchcraft and Magic in Europe, Vol. 2. Ancient Greece and Rome*, London: The Athlone Press.

Francis, H. T., and E. J. Thomas (1916), *Jātaka Tales: Selected and Edited with Introduction and Notes*, Cambridge: Cambridge University Press.

Frazer, G. J. Sir. ([1922] 1996), *The Golden Bough*, New York: Touchstone.

Garrett, F., A. Erlich, N. Field, B. Hazelton, and M. King (2013), "Narratives of Hospitality and Feeding in Tibetan Ritual," *Journal of the American Academy of Religion* 81 (2): 491–515.

Geertz, H. (1975), "An Anthropology of Religion and Magic I," *Journal of Interdisciplinary History* 6 (1): 71–89.

Gerety, F. M. M. (2016), "Tree-Hugger: The Sāmavedic Rite of Audumbarī," in F. M. Ferrari and T. W. P. Dähnhardt (eds.), *Roots of Wisdom, Branches of Devotion: Plant Life in South Asian Traditions*, 165–92, Sheffield: Equinox.

Giebel, R. (2001), *Two Esoteric Sutras*, Berkeley: Numata Center for Buddhist Translation and Research.

Goodall, D. and H. Isaacson (2016), "On the Shared 'Ritual Syntax' of the Early Tantric Traditions," in D. Goodall and H. Isaacson (eds.), *Tantric Studies: Fruits of a Franco-German Project on Early Tantra*, 1–76, Pondicherry: EFEO/IFP/Asien-Afrika Institut Universität Hamburg.

Goudriaan, T. (1978), *Māyā Divine and Human*, Delhi: Motilal Banarsidass.

Heilijgers-Seelen, D. (1994), *The System of Five Cakras in Kubjikāmatatantra 14–16*, Groningen: Egbert Forsten.

Lipscomb, S. (2020), *A History of Magic, Witchcraft & the Occult*, Dewey: DK Publishing.
Magoun, H. W. (1889), "The Āsurī-kalpa: A Witchcraft of the Atharva-Veda," *American Journal of Philology* 10 (2): 165–97.
McGovern, N. (2019), *The Snake and the Mongoose: The Emergence of Identity in Early Indian Religion*, New York: Oxford University Press.
McHugh, J. (2012), *Sandalwood and Carrion: Smell in Indian Religion and Culture*, Oxford: Oxford University Press.
Minkowski, Ch. (1989), "The Udumbara and Its Ritual Significance," *Wiener Zeitschrift für die Kunde Südasiens* 33: 5–24.
Nihom, M. (1987), "On Buffalos, Pigs, Camels, and Crows," *Wiener Zeitschrift für die Kunde Südasiens* 31: 75–109.
Olivelle, P. (2013), *King, Governance, and Law in Ancient India. Kauṭilya's Arthaśāstra*, New York: Oxford University Press.
Orofino, G. (1994), "Divination with Mirrors. Observations on a simile found in the Kālacakra Literature," in P. Kvaerne (ed.), *Tibetan Studies: Proceedings of the 6th Seminar of the International Association for Tibetan Studies, Fagernes 1992, vol. 2*, 612–28, Oslo: The Institute for Comparative Research in Human Culture.
Payne R. K. (2016), "Homa: Tantric Fire Ritual," in *Oxford Research Encyclopedia*. Online publication https://oxfordre.com/religion/view/10.1093/acrefore/9780199340378.001.0001/acrefore- 9780199340378-e-82?rskey=1gIWHM&result=6 (accessed May 18, 2017).
Sanderson, A. (1994), "Vajrayāna: Origin and Function," in *Buddhism into the Year 2000: International Conference Proceedings*, 89–102, Bangkok: Dhammakaya Foundation.
Sanderson, A. (2004), "Religion and the State: Śaiva Officiants in the Territory of the King's Brahmanical Chaplain," *Indo-Iranian Journal* 47: 229–300.
Sanderson, A. (2007), "Atharvavedins in Tantric Territory: The Āṅgirasakalpa Texts of the Oriya Paippalādins and their Connection with the Trika and the Kālīkula, with critical editions of the Parājapavidhi, the Parāmantravidhi, and the *Bhadrakālīman travidhiprakaraṇa," in A. Griffiths and A. Schmiedchen (eds.), *The Atharvaveda and Its Paippalāda Śākhā: Historical and Philological Papers on a Vedic Traditions*, 195–311, Aachen: Shaker Verlag. Geisteskultur Indiens: Texte und Studien, 11, Indologica Halensis.
Sanderson, A. (2009), "The Śaiva Age: The Rise and Dominance of Śaivism during the Early Medieval Period," in S. Einoo (ed.), *Genesis and Development of Tantrism*, 41–350, Tokyo: Institute of Oriental Culture, University of Tokyo: Institute of Oriental Culture Special Series 23.
Törzsök, J. (2016), "The Emergence of the Alphabet Goddess Mātṛkā in Early Śaiva Tantras," in D. Goodall and H. Isaacson (eds.), *Tantric Studies: Fruits of a Franco-German Collaboration on Early Tantra*, 135–56, Pondichéry: EFEO, Institut français de Pondichéry (IFP). Asien-Afrika-Institut, Universität Hamburg.

Vasudeva, S. (2012), "Powers and Identities: Yoga Powers and the Tantric Śaiva Traditions," in A. Jacobsen (ed.), *Yoga Powers: Extraordinary Capacities Attained Through Meditation and Concentration*, 265–302, Leiden: Brill.

Wenta, A. (forthcoming). *The Vajrabhairavatantra: A Study and Annotated Translation.* Studies in Indian and Tibetan Buddhism, Boston, MA: Wisdom Publications.

Wenta, A. (forthcoming). *A Critical Edition of the Vajrabhairavatantra (Sanskrit and Tibetan Texts) with Kumāracandra's commentary (Vajrabhairavatantrapañjikā)*, Peking: Research Institute of Sanskrit Manuscripts and Buddhist Literature, Peking University.

Wilkins, Ch. (1885), *Hitopadeśā, Fables and Proverbs from the Sanskrit*, London: George Routledge.

Zeiler, X. (2013), "Dark Shades of Power: The Crow in Hindu and Tantric Religious Traditions," *Religions of South Asia* 7: 212–29.

4

The Magic That Lies within Prayer: On Patterns of Magicity and Resolute Aspirations (*smon lam*)

Rolf Scheuermann

Introduction

It may surprise the reader how a piece on a Tibetan Buddhist prayer practice such as *smon lam* prayers or resolute aspirations (Skt. *praṇidhāna*), a standard Buddhist practice, managed to sneak into a volume on Tibetan magic. Indeed, this appears to be a random choice at first glance as this practice is not commonly associated with magic, which makes them a perfect fit for the questions addressed in this chapter.

"*Magic*" is a heavily loaded word that, just like the term *meditation*, can refer to a plethora of very distinct phenomena and induces various reactions depending on the recipients' backgrounds. This holds true for what has been labeled as "Buddhist Magic"[1] just as well as for many very different phenomena that occur in other cultural contexts. As this chapter intends to show, the analytical category of magic is quite problematic. It may indeed inflict harm on the analytical process as it excludes certain practices, particularly those labeled as religion. Thus, this study intends to examine an alternative approach by focusing on "patterns of magicity" as proposed by Bernd-Christian Otto and Michael Stausberg.[2] Applying this concept to the particular (Tibetan) Buddhist prayer practice of resolute aspirations will facilitate the examination of whether patterns of magicity may be observed in practices not generally coined as "magic."

What is (Tibetan) Buddhist magic?

So what is magic? Leaving the Tibetan context aside, magic has sometimes been considered a counterpart to science, for example, by Edward Burnett Tylor[3] or James G. Frazer,[4] or formal religion by Émile Durkheim[5] or Hubert and Mauss.[6] Hence, it is viewed by many as belonging to the realm of superstition. The situation is, however, a bit more complex than that. While magic and science are often considered mutually exclusive, the boundaries between magic and formal religion may not always be so clear-cut. Still, Clarke's famous Third Law states: "Any sufficiently advanced technology is indistinguishable from magic."[7]

Of course, the underlying idea behind the Third Law, formulated by the famous science fiction author, Arthur C. Clarke, is that our technological capabilities of today may seem magical to people of former times. In medieval times, the idea that iron birds fly through the air would have sounded too fantastic to be anything else but magic. On the flip side, a glance into the history of science reveals that many theories accepted by the ancients, such as Galen's *four humors* that played a dominant role in medicine for over a thousand years, appear to us today like some form of magical medicine based on superstition. We should not consider this bias as pertaining only to the ancient people. Even today, the boundaries between science and the realm of "superstition" are fluid, as the example of *technical analysis*—a widespread technique to forecast the developments of stock prices—shows. This practice, focusing on patterns seen on stock market charts, led Burton Malkiel to state "that under scientific scrutiny, chart reading must share a pedestal with alchemy."[8]

This chapter does not attempt to offer a precise and elaborate definition of what "magic" in the context of (Tibetan) Buddhism is or is not. This would be very challenging, as scholarly debates to arrive at a definition of magic have been carried on in different fields for a long time. This difficulty prompted Owen Davies to state that "defining 'magic' is a maddening task."[9] While observing magical protective techniques, Ernesto de Martino cautions us not to construct an artificial "magical world" by examining isolated practices outside of their cultural contexts:

> When we isolate magical protective techniques from the concrete cultural context in which they carry out a protective function and we compare them to other, similar techniques present in other cultural contexts, in order to end up by showing a type of "magical world" that in such a fictitious isolation

> has never existed **as a cultural fact**. The historical sense of magic's protective techniques lies in the values that such techniques reveal, grafting themselves onto the critical moments of a certain regime of existence, and it is therefore manifested only if we consider these techniques as a **moment** of a perceptible cultural dynamic within a *single* civilization, a *particular* society, a *certain* period (original emphasis).[10]

There is no single Tibetan term that corresponds to the English "magic." This adds to the difficulty when considering Tibetan Buddhist magic. The word "magic" occurs in the context of translations for different Tibetan religious concepts, such as, for example, *ngan sngags*, sometimes referred to as "black magic" (i.e., magic that involves the use of evil mantras), *mthu*, which has also been rendered into English as "(black) magic," *sgyu ma* or "magical illusion," *sgyu 'phrul* or "magical manifestation," *rdzu 'phrul* or "magical powers/magical emanation," and *cho 'phrul* or "magical display." It is noteworthy that at least *mthu*, *rdzu 'phrul,* and *cho 'phrul* can occur as qualities acquired along the Buddhist path and are hence used in formulations such as *sangs rgyas kyi mthu* or "the magical powers of the Buddha," *sangs rgyas kyi rdzu 'phrul* or "the magical emanation of the Buddha," and *sangs rgyas kyi cho 'phrul* or "the magical display of the Buddha." This exemplifies that a clear delineation between religion and magic is not easy.

Nevertheless, reluctance in discussing the definition of the phenomena under examination here is no option either, as it would leave us behind confused. Phenomena coined as "magic" may be described as approaches to influence circumstances through invisible or supernatural powers, often with the help of rituals, substances, and spells. However, this may apply only to some of the Tibetan phenomena mentioned above, but not to all. In general, I subscribe to Bernd-Christian Otto and Michael Stausberg's viewpoint that magic is a critical category of distinction that "distinguishes things, practices or ways of thinking from others, including religion, rationality and science."[11]

Sam van Schaik's working definition of Buddhist magic in his recent publication *Buddhist Magic* is a meritorious and courageous first attempt. It is one of the most mature definitions of Buddhist magic that currently exists. Still, some reservations regarding his approach need to be voiced. His definition is rather lengthy, but its main points could be summarized as follows.
Buddhist magic comprises of rituals:

(1) that focus on this-worldly aims and not so much on the ultimate aim of Buddhism, that is, enlightenment (therefore, excluding standard Buddhist

practices that focus, for example, on the accumulation and the transfer of merit),[12]

(2) that have a swift and clear relationship between ritual and result (excluding magical powers that arise from meditation after long periods of practice), and[13]

(3) that are based on practices laid out in books of spells with a focus on activities such as healing, protecting, divining, enchanting, cursing, summoning, finding treasures, clairvoyance, clairaudience, and invisibility.[14]

Van Schaik's working definition of Buddhist magic is, of course, logocentric and disregards the domain of popular religion. It is influenced by Wittgenstein's concept of family resemblance[15] and in the end lists some features that, for him, are characteristic of the definition of Buddhist magic. Overall, his approach is very nuanced and it is particularly laudable that he takes great care not to follow Durkheim's distinction between magic and religion. He explicitly rejects such an approach by stating that "rather than reviving the idea that magic stands in opposition to religion, we can see it as having a specific role in the wider context of Buddhist practice."[16] Still, by restricting his definition of Buddhist magic to rituals "performed for 'this-worldly ends', in which the ultimate aim of Buddhism is only very indirectly linked to the practice,"[17] he establishes a distinction between Buddhist practices that are more directly linked to the goal of Buddhist soteriology and Buddhist magical practices that are merely indirectly linked to it.

His observation that "magic might be a thread running through Buddhist practice"[18] is a viewpoint I fully subscribe to, but it should be broadened. It should include both practices focused on this-worldly ends as well as those focused directly on the ultimate aim of Buddhism, that is, Buddhahood, such as selecting one's individual *yi dam* deity during the process of an empowerment by means of divination.[19] This becomes even clearer if we examine the agents that engage in "Buddhist magic." It holds true in the case of Buddhist diviners, too, where we notice a substantial overlap, as many diviners are also Buddhist religious figures. Hence, the delineation between general (Tibetan) Buddhist religious practice and magic is not clear-cut but rather fluid.

Furthermore, as pointed out by Bernd-Christian Otto and Michael Stausberg, applying the ideologically loaded label "magic" to phenomena in the context of non-Western traditions may be considered ethnocentric: "In the belief that one is discovering 'magic' 'out there', one may, in fact, end up with just universalizing one's own Western categories and background assumptions."[20] Hence, any attempt to define "Buddhist magic" remains indeed a maddening task, but what could be an alternative?

Patterns of magicity

In their discussion of what magic is or is not, Bernd-Christian Otto and Michael Stausberg introduce the analytical categories of "patterns of magicity," which they explain as follows:

> Instead of instinctively interpreting the occurrence of a limited number of features from our catalogue as evidence for the existence of a family-like concept, we suggest splitting the extended tribal family into a number of nuclear families. Instead of instances of "magic," we suggest speaking of patterns of magicity. … "Patterns of magicity" do not automatically involve "MAGIC" (as the supreme meta-category), nor are they "magic" (as referring to ontological features), but they are a way of dealing with cross-culturally attested observations. "Magicity" acknowledges the fact that they were traditionally assigned to the overall category "MAGIC" in which we have stopped believing.[21]

In other words, magic is a conceptually constructed label that creates a dichotomy of phenomena classified as magic vis-à-vis other religious practices that are not. For many, classifying a phenomenon as belonging to the realm of magic involves the connotation that we are dealing with a form of superstitious practice outside the realm of formal religion. Given the implications that go along with such a judgment, it seems preferable to investigate individual and cross-culturally identifiable "patterns of magicity" that may be found either within or outside of formal religion, within or outside of formal Buddhist practice, or even within or outside of science. The benefit of such an approach is compelling: one can investigate patterns of magicity in Buddhist practice without attaching the heavily loaded label "magic" to the entire category. Hence, it spares us all the reflexes to differentiate between certain techniques that include patterns of magicity from others. This is particularly useful when dealing with standard Buddhist practices that include such patterns, but where such an association with the category of magic is unwanted.

Some patterns of magicity suggested by Otto and Stausberg relate, for example, to the categories of efficacies of words (M_{WOR}), signs (M_{SIG}), objects (M_{OBJ}), and places (M_{PLA}), the idea that it is possible to control other peoples' desires (M_{DES}), harms (M_{HAR}), or the ascription of miraculous capabilities to individuals (M_{MIR}) as well as the evaluation of ritual activities (M_{EVA}).[22]

What is *smon lam* or resolute aspirations?

The Tibetan term *smon lam* has often been used either in a transliterated form as *monlam* in English or translated as "wishing prayers," even though a more literal rendering of the Tibetan would be "paths of aspirations." Edgerton's *Buddhist Hybrid Sanskrit Dictionary* translates the underlying Sanskrit term *praṇidhāna* as "ardent desire," "earnest wish," or "vow."[23] As such, the term relates to vow-like aspirations with a long-term perspective. Resolute aspirations are deeply rooted in Mahāyāna soteriology and should be regarded in the context of the spiritual career of a Bodhisattva that lasts throughout many consecutive lifetimes. In this sense, resolute aspirations are not simple prayers involving wishes, but are aspirations designed to focus and shape an individual's development, while practicing the two accumulations throughout many lifetimes until Buddhahood. Their important status within the Mahāyāna soteriology is underlined by the fact that resolute aspirations are listed as the eighth item in the set of ten *pāramitās*. The *Āryākṣayamatiparipṛcchānāma-Mahāyānasūtra* (Toh. 89), for example, gives the following short description of the ten *pāramitās* mastered on the different bodhisattva stages:

> Son of a noble family, Bodhisattvas residing at the first bodhisattva stage, master the *pāramitā* of giving.
>
> At the second bodhisattva stage, they master the *pāramitā* of ethics.
>
> At the third stage, they master the *pāramitā* of patience.
>
> At the fourth stage, they master the *pāramitā* of joyful effort.
>
> At the fifth stage, they master the *pāramitā* of concentrative meditation.
>
> At the sixth stage, they master the *pāramitā* of higher knowledge.
>
> At the seventh stage, they tread upon the *pāramitā* of skillful means.
>
> At the eighth stage, they master the *pāramitā* of resolute aspirations.
>
> At the ninth stage, they master the *pāramitā* of strength.
>
> At the tenth stage, they master the *pāramitā* of wisdom.[24]

Associated liturgical texts often contain various utopian and dystopian narratives. Practices that focus on aspirations to take rebirth in the Pure Land of a Buddha are frequent, but an aspect of this technique also takes the particular form of Buddhist "worlding" practice. The latter aims at gaining the ability to form a Pure Land due to the merit of vigorous religious training throughout many eons in conjunction with continuous resolute aspirations. Many Tibetan Buddhist practitioners strongly believe in the self-transformative power of the formulae of these prayers.

Being a standard Mahāyāna practice, the literary genre of resolute aspirations encompasses many well-known texts that originate directly from the *sūtra*s or Indian *śāstra*s, such as the *Āryabhadracaryāpraṇidhānarāja* or the *King of Resolute Aspirations of Samantabhadra* (Toh. 4377) of the *Gaṇḍavyūha-Sūtra*,[25] the **Maitreyapraṇidhāna* (Toh. 4378),[26] which is a part of the *Maitreyaparipṛcc hā*,[27] a short *sūtra* that forms chapter forty-two of the *Ratnakūṭa* Collection, and the famous tenth chapter of the *Bodhicaryāvatāra* of Śāntideva (Toh. 4383).

The Tibetan literary tradition has also produced many independent liturgical texts that belong to the category of resolute aspirations, as well as commentaries and supplements to texts of Indian origin. In Tibet, resolute aspiration prayers are an integral part of the daily liturgies of monasteries and individual practitioners. The practice is also widely known because of the resolute aspirations festivals where resolute aspirations are chanted communally during large gatherings, such as the *smon lam chen mo* institutionalized by Tsong khapa pa in 1409 in Lhasa, which was also of enormous political importance. Numerous such festivals still take place around the world today, especially in Bodhgayā, India.[28] I have had the opportunity to attend several of these festivals since the late 1990s. Such a large gathering with thousands of participants generates a special atmosphere, revealing a sense of magic that lies within prayer. This may be due to the communal rhythmic chanting that induces a trance-like state, but the specific location and setting may add to it as well. Of course, during the current Covid-19 pandemic, associated festivals were increasingly held digitally, just like academic conferences.

Patterns of magicity and resolute aspirations

Resolute aspirations as an apotropaic practice

The practice of resolute aspirations appears as an apotropaic practice in divination texts and, in this way, is associated with the pattern of the magicity of words mentioned above. One example is a dice divination[29] manual by the Buddhist luminary ’Jam mgon Mi pham rgya mtsho (1846–1912). This particular divination involves a six-sided die that carries on each side one of the six syllables of the mantra associated with the deity Mañjuśrī, namely, [*oṃ*] *a ra pa tsa na dhīḥ* (Skt. *oṃ arapacana dhīḥ*). In this manual, the result of *pa-tsa*, which corresponds to rolling first a 3 and then a 5 on a six-sided die, is generally considered negative. Since it forebodes illness, this result suggests explicitly reciting, among others, the *Gaṇḍavyūha-Sūtra* or the *King of Resolute Aspirations of Samantabhadra*, which is the latter part of the *sūtra*. It states:

> Concerning illness: there is a disease [that causes an impairment of the circulation] of *prāṇa*, the function of movement, or the *nāḍīs*. To counter that which prevents your well-being, you should offer *gtor ma* to the elemental spirits, engage in the three-fold [*gtor ma*] ritual as much as possible, recite the *Gaṇḍavyūha-Sūtra*, the *King of Resolute Aspirations of Samantabhadra*, practice animal release, the *Ritual of the Four Maṇḍalas* [*of Tāra*] or train yourself in [the practice of] *Acala*.[30]

Of course, van Schaik explicitly excluded practices, like the *sūtra* recitations or resolute aspirations, in his definition of Buddhist magic:

> It is true that meritorious Buddhist activities such as recitation of scriptures and offerings at shrines are also considered effective for healing the sick and achieving other worldly aims, but this is different from the application of specific rituals by specialists, based on a book of spells.[31]

However, considering that the practices prescribed here are apotropaic practices used to remedy acute health issues, a more nuanced approach seems advisable. Ideally, one would not be required to label the entire practice as “magic,” but could still recognize the efficacy of words in the sense of a pattern of magicity (M_{WOR}). This goes along with Otto and Stausberg’s argument in the context of “word efficacy,” that “since the ‘patterns of magicity’ proposed here step back from the larger category of ‘MAGIC’, they also render irrelevant the historical but also scholarly disputes over whether a specific rite using efficacious words is actually ‘religious’ or ‘magical.’ ”[32]

By looking at verses such as the following, from the tenth chapter of Śāntideva’s *Bodhicaryāvatāra* on the *Transfer of Merit* (also known as the *Resolute Aspirations of the Bodhicaryāvatāra* (*spyod ’jug smon lam*), it becomes evident why resolute aspirations were sometimes included into a corpus of apotropaic practices:

> 4. As many hells as there are in the worldly realms, may the living beings in them be pleased by the pleasures of happiness in the Sukhāvatī paradise!

5. May those tormented by cold find warmth! May those tormented by heat be cooled by oceans of water pouring down from the great cloud of the Bodhisattvas![33]

Numerous further verses take a similar direction, focusing on lists of desirable items from either a Buddhist or a worldly perspective, or both. Very often, concrete problems are mentioned, and the result that would be desired in their place is formulated as an aspiration. In the following verse, also from Chapter Ten of the *Bodhicaryāvatāra*, there is even an explicit connection to the pattern of the magicity of words, which includes the aspiration that healing spells may be effective:

40. May also the healing plants be potent, the spells of the mutterers effective! May the Ḍākinī witches, the Rākṣasa demons, and other harmful beings be filled with compassion![34]

Resolute aspirations and the power of "words of truth"

A further aspect of the magicity of words found within resolute aspirations concerns the power attributed to the wording of resolute aspirations itself. The following quotation from the *Bhadracaryāpraṇidhānarāja* stems from the section on the benefits of the practice:

Whoever recites these resolute aspirations of Samantabhadra,
will thereby renounce negative rebirths,
shun negative friends,
and will swiftly come to see [the Buddha] Amitābha.[35]

This verse gives us an idea of the power attributed to reciting these words that goes beyond simple wishes. This becomes particularly obvious if we relate this passage and the ones before from the tenth chapter of the *Bodhicaryāvatāra* to the concept of *words of truth* (Skt. *satyavacana*, Tib. *bden tshig*). The latter is a widespread notion in Buddhism that Buddhas and Bodhisattvas are capable of uttering words of truth. The *Princeton Dictionary of Buddhism* even mentions that words of truths are "a solemn declaration or oath in which the truth inherent in its words generates magical or protective powers."[36] In an essay for the Rubin Museum, Donald Lopez further explains that, apart from being understood as merely saying facts, words of truth are considered to have "a particular power—indeed a magical power."[37]

Hence, words of truth refer to the ability of Buddhas and Bodhisattvas to utter statements with certainty that these words are either factually accurate or have the power to turn the meaning of these words into a reality. The latter may pertain to speech acts such as predictions regarding the future, offering protection, or directly influencing reality by other means.

Words of truth also play a role in resolute aspirations. Most of these prayers are words spoken by a capable being, such as the Buddha, a Bodhisattva, or a revered Buddhist master of a Tibetan tradition. The importance of the concept of words of truth for resolute aspirations is attested by a significant number of texts that belong to the category of resolute aspirations that contain the term "words of truth" in their title. A prominent example is *Words of Truth* or *Bden tshig smon lam* authored in 1960 by the Fourteenth Dalai Lama, Bstan 'dzin rgya mtsho (1935–), shortly after being exiled.[38] This short text invokes both the power of the words of truth of previous Buddhas and Bodhisattvas as well as the Dalai Lama's own power of words of truth to overcome oppression and restore peace and Buddhism in Tibet.[39]

Resolute aspirations, location, and setting

There are also further factors considered conducive regarding resolute aspirations, such as the location and setting. Practicing resolute aspirations at holy places like Bodhgayā or Lumbini positively influences the outcome and connects the practice to the pattern of magicity of places (M_{PLA}). Likewise, the presence of particular objects such as statues and *stūpa*s filled with relics of Buddhas and Bodhisattvas is also commonly seen as an essential support for the efficacy of the practice. It is related to the pattern of magicity of the efficacy of objects (M_{OBJ}) and also ascribes miraculous capabilities to Buddhas and Bodhisattvas, namely, the pattern of magicity of miraculous capabilities (M_{MIR}). The latter is also visible in the idea that practicing in the presence of exceptional individuals, along with a large gathering of people, further improves the outcome of the practice. The reason for this is because of the capability of Buddhas and Bodhisattvas to utter words of truth.

The following quotation from a teaching given by the contemporary Karma bka' brgyud scholar Mkhan po Chos grags bstan 'phel during a resolute aspirations gathering in Bodhgayā in 1996 reflects these different aspects:

> It is said that the benefit of a large number of people doing aspiration prayers together is the merit, each individual accumulates through doing this practice,

> is obtained by each and every individual of the group. In the sutra "A Wall of Flowers," it is said that whatever aspiration prayer is made near a stupa containing one of the Buddha's relics, will be answered. Nagarjuna, the Indian Buddhist master said that if one makes aspiration prayers together with a highly developed Bodhisattva, the resulting prayer is so powerful that one can avert famine, for example, and natural disasters, and remove evil karma of all kinds. That is why every year groups of Tibetan Buddhists, representing the four schools of Tibetan Buddhism, come together to do these aspiration prayers in various holy places in India. The two main persons making those aspiration prayers in 1996 were His Holiness, the 17th Karmapa, Thaye Dorje and Kunzig Shamar Rinpoche. Both are great bodhisattvas, progressing throughout the ten bhumis. Reciting this prayer just once with two such individuals has more effect than performing it a million times on one's own. For centuries this has not been possible, but now we are lucky enough to have this opportunity![40]

In brief, this short passage of the teaching explains that each participant will accumulate the same merit as the entirety of all participants combined. Furthermore, reciting resolute aspirations together with highly realized individuals will benefit one's own religious practice to a large extent because of their capacity to support others by means of blessing (M_{MIR}). It also mentions the extraordinary powers of particular objects filled with relics (M_{OBJ}) and the holy place of Bodhgayā (M_{PLA}).

A pattern of magicity not mentioned by Otto and Stausberg, which, nevertheless, certainly plays a role in the context of resolute aspirations, as well as many other Buddhist rituals, is the pattern of magicity of special times (M_{TIM}). Hence, it is considered highly beneficial to engage in specific activities on certain days (or particular times of the day) that are either determined by astrology or because of their association with important events in the life of the Buddha. These may include not only the four great Buddhist festival days (*dus chen bzhi*) but also certain days associated with revered Buddhist masters. This is reflected, for example, by the title of the recent anthology of resolute aspirations, "Honoring the 49th Day of the Mahaparinirvana of His Holiness Kyabje Dodrupchen Rinpoche."[41] While the result of the merit accrued by the practice of resolute aspirations in such a fashion may manifest in a distant future, there is no doubt that the merit is obtained right away. Hence, there is even the swift and clear relationship between ritual and result that van Schaik formulated in the second point of his working definition of Buddhist magic.[42]

The *dhāraṇī* of accomplishing resolute aspirations

Even if one were to argue for a clear-cut separation between magic and Buddhist religion, the example of the *dhāraṇī* for accomplishing the resolute aspirations (*smon lam 'grub pa'i gzungs*) shows that such a viewpoint is not tenable. The *dhāraṇī* consists of the following short Sanskrit formulation that is commonly recited in Tibetan transliteration after the recitation of resolute aspirations: *tadyathā pañcendriyāvabodhanīye svāhā*. It is found in most anthologies of resolute aspirations toward the end, but has also been inserted directly into the text of some of the aspirations. Its purpose is clearly defined by its Tibetan name, the *dhāraṇī* of accomplishing resolute aspirations: it is a kind of spell that is meant to wield a positive influence on the recitation in that it safeguards that all aspirations will be fulfilled as they have been made and that the merit accumulated through the practice will be multiplied. Hence, there is a clear relation to the pattern of magicity of the efficacy of words (M_{WOR}), which further indicates that the separation between magic and religion may be an artificial construction.

Conclusion

The intent of this chapter was not to redefine resolute aspirations as a magical practice or to depict the entirety of Tibetan Buddhist religious practice as belonging to the realm of magic or superstition. On the contrary, the aim of using such a standard Mahāyāna practice, like resolute aspirations, as an example for examining patterns of magicity was precisely to show that it is very problematic to allocate certain practices to the realm of magic. It creates an artificial separation into practices that are "magic," vis-à-vis those considered more purely religious.

At the outset of this study, I have expressed my doubts whether such an examination would be of any benefit, and whether it could potentially lead to any results whatsoever, assuming that there were certainly no patterns of magicity to be found in a simple prayer practice like resolute aspirations. In the end, identifying several of the proposed patterns of magicity, for example, the patterns of magicity of the efficacies of words (M_{WOR}), places (M_{PLA}), objects (M_{OBJ}), and the ascription of miraculous capabilities (M_{MIR}), convinced me of the usability of such an approach. It was also possible to identify an additional pattern of magicity, the efficacy of special times (M_{TIM}) that had not been explicitly mentioned by Otto and Stausberg, but will certainly reoccur in other cultural contexts.

Using Otto and Stausberg's proposition to step back from the problematic analytical category of magic and instead examine patterns of magicity prevents us from having to distinguish and define practices that belong to the realm of magic from others that clearly do not. This allows us to look at distinct phenomena such as amulets, books of spells, or resolute aspirations in their own right, without attaching the heavily loaded label of magic to them. In this respect, it is of no importance at all whether a specific practice is labeled as magic or religion by an external observer or someone from within the tradition. It, therefore, becomes irrelevant whether the object of our examination would commonly be subjected to a mutually exclusive distinction, such as the distinction between magic and religion (or science). This also pertains to more fluid distinctions between Buddhist practices with a focus on achieving worldly aims and those with a focus on other-worldly aims.

Hence, the notion of patterns of magicity allows us to identify, examine, and compare cross-cultural concepts generally defined as part of the category of "magic" in their own right, but does not limit our observation to these. Instead, it allows us to extend our field of observation to standard religious practices not traditionally classified as "magic." Given that there is an overlap of practices within Buddhism that are either labeled as "Buddhist practices" or "magic," this is a noteworthy aspect and confirms the value of such an approach for the field of Tibetan Studies.

Notes

1 For instance, van Schaik (2020).
2 Otto and Stausberg (2013: 10–13).
3 Tylor ([1871] 2013).
4 Frazer ([1922] 2013).
5 Durkheim ([1912] 2013).
6 Mauss and Hubert ([1902/3] 2013).
7 Clarke (1990: 207).
8 Malkiel (2007: 144).
9 Owen Davies (2012: 1).
10 De Martino ([1969] 2015: 113–14).
11 Otto and Stausberg (2013: 1).
12 van Schaik (2020: 40).
13 Ibid.: 40–1.

14 Ibid.: 41.
15 Wittgenstein ([1953] 2009).
16 van Schaik (2020: 8).
17 Ibid.: 40.
18 van Schaik (2020: 167).
19 Dotson (2017: 541).
20 Otto and Stausberg (2013: 6).
21 Ibid.: 10–11.
22 Ibid.: 11.
23 Edgerton (1970, vol. 2: 360).
24 *'Phags pa blo gros mi zad pas zhus pa zhes bya ba theg pa chen po'i mdo*, *Bka' 'gyur*, Sde dge, vol. 44 [BDRC MW22084_0089]: 180a3–6: *rigs kyi bu de la byang chub sems dpa'i sa dang po la gnas pa'i byang chub sems dpa' ni sbyin pa'i pha rol tu phyin pa gnon to | | byang chub sems dpa'i sa gnyis pa la ni tshul khrims kyi pha rol tu phyin pa gnon to | | sa gsum pa la ni bzod pa'i pha rol tu phyin pa gnon to | | sa bzhi pa la ni brtson 'grus kyi pha rol tu phyin pa gnon to | | sa lnga pa la ni bsam gtan gyi pha rol tu phyin pa gnon to | | sa drug pa la ni shes rab kyi pha rol tu phyin pa gnon to | | sa bdun pa la ni thabs la mkhas pa'i pha rol tu phyin pa gnon to | | sa brgyad pa la ni smon lam gyi pha rol tu phyin pa gnon to | | sa dgu pa la ni stobs kyi pha rol tu phyin pa gnon to | | sa bcu pa la ni ye shes kyi pha rol tu phyin pa gnon to | |*.
25 *Shin tu rgyas pa chen po'i mdo sangs rgyas phal po che zhes bya ba las sdong pos brgyan pa'i le'u ste bzhi bcu rtsa lnga pa'o*, *Bka' 'gyur*, *Sde dge*, vol. 37 [BDRC MW22084_0044]: 274b – vol. 38: 363a.
26 *'Phags pa byams pa'i smon lam*, *Bka' 'gyur*, *Sde dge*, vol. 101 [BDRC MW22084_1096]: 266a–267a.
27 *'Phags pa byams pas zhus pa zhes bya ba theg pa chen po'i mdo*, *Bka' 'gyur*, *Sde dge*, vol. 44 [BDRC MW22084_0086]: 104b–116b.
28 Buffetrille (2012: 193–4).
29 On the topic of dice divination in Tibetan Buddhism, see Dotson (2019), Dotson (2021), and Sobisch (2019).
30 'Ju mi pham 'jam dbyangs rnam rgyal rgya mtsho, *Rigs sngags kyi rgyal po a ra pa tsa la brten nas blang dor brtag pa 'jam dpal dgyes pa'i zhal lung*, vol. 5 [BDRC MW23468_7EC3A7]: 371,1–2 [*pa-tsa*]: *nad ni rlung dang g.yo byed rtsa rgyus kyi nad yin | bde ba mi ster bas 'byung gtor dang cha gsum grangs mang | sdong rgyan mdo | bzang spyod | 'chi bslu | maṇḍala bzhi chog sogs bya | mi g.yo ba'i bsnyen pa dgos |* . The manual has also been discussed in Scheuermann (2018: 125–7), in the context of predictions related to death.
31 van Schaik (2020: 40).
32 Otto and Stausberg (2013: 11).

33 English translation by Steinkellner and Peck-Kubaczek (2019: 103). *yāvanto nārakāḥ kecid vidyante lokadhātuṣu |sukhāvatī sukhāmodair modantāṃ teṣu dehinaḥ ||4| śītārtāḥ prāpnuvantūṣṇam uṣṇārtāḥ santu śītalāḥ | bodhisattvamahāmeghasaṃbhavair jalasāgaraiḥ ||5|| 'jig rten khams na dmyal ba dag | | gang dag ji snyed yod pa rnams | |de dag tu ni lus can rnams | | bde can bde bas dga' bar shog | | grang bas nyam thag dro thob shog | | byang chub sems dpa'i sprin chen las | |byung ba'i chu bo mtha' yas kyis | | tsha bas nyam thag bsil bar shog* | | Source: https://www2.hf.uio.no/polyglotta/index.php?page=fulltext&view=fulltext&vid=1120&cid=841279&mid=1940332.

34 English translation by Steinkellner and Peck-Kubaczek (2019: 106). Source: *śaktā bhavantu cauṣadhyo mantrāḥ siddhantu jāpinām |bhavantu karuṇāviṣṭā ḍākinīrākṣasādayaḥ ||40|| sman rnams mthu daṅ ldan pa dang | | gsang sngags bzlas brjod grub par shog | |mkha' 'gro srin po la sogs pa | | snying rje'i sems dang ldan gyur cig* | |. Source: https://www2.hf.uio.no/polyglotta/index.php?page=fulltext&view=fulltext&vid=1120&cid=841305&mid=1940358.

35 *Bka' 'gyur, Sde dge*, BDRC, W22048, vol. 101 [MW22084_10959]: 529, 6–7: *gang gis bzang spyod smon lam 'di btab pas | | des ni ngan song thams cad spangs par 'gyur | | des ni grogs po ngan pa spangs pa yin | | snang ba mtha' yas de yang de myur mthong* | | .

36 Buswell and Lopez (2014: 789).

37 Lopez (2022).

38 Tenzin Gyatso (1993). Further examples are the *Kun mkhyen thub pa'i bstan pa rgyas pa'i smon lam drang srong lha yi bden tshig ces bya ba* (BDRC MW1KG12986_229D5E) by the second Rdzong gsar mkhyen brtse 'Jam dbyangs chos kyi blo gros (1893–1959) or the *Bden tshig 'grub pa'i pra ṇi dha rnam mkhyen grog 'jug ces bya ba* (BDRC MW23685_7B8E7E) by Rig 'dzin 'jigs med gling pa (1730–1798).

39 Cf. Cabezón (1996: 307).

40 Mkhan po Chos grags bstan 'phel 1996.

41 Pearcey (2022).

42 van Schaik (2020: 40–1).

References

Tibetan language sources

***

'Jam dbyangs chos kyi blo gros, Rdzong gsar mkhyen brtse II (2012), "Kun mkhyen thub pa'i bstan pa rgyas pa'i smon lam drang srong lha yi bden tshig," in K. Labrang (ed.), *Gsung 'bum 'jam dbyangs chos kyi blo gros*, Bir: Khyentse Labrang, vol. 12: 273–5 (BDRC MW1KG12986_229D5E).

'Ju mi pham 'jam dbyangs rnam rgyal rgya mtsho (1984–1993), "Rigs sngags kyi rgyal po a ra pa tsa la brten nas blang dor brtag pa 'jam dpal dgyes pa'i zhal lung," in L. Ngodrup and S. Drimey (eds.), *Gsung 'bum mi pham rgya mtsho*, Paro: Lama Ngodrup and Sherab Drimey, vol. 5: 349–98 (BDRC MW23468_7EC3A7).

Rig 'dzin 'jigs med gling pa (2001), "Bden tshig 'grub pa'i pra ṇi dha rnam mkhyen grong 'jug," in Seng brag sprul sku (ed.), *'Don cha nyer mkho phan bde'i bum bzang*, vol. 6, 'Brug sgar dpe mdzod khang: 382–5 (BDRC MW23685_7B8E7E).

Sde dge-Edition of the Tibetan Tripiṭaka = *Bka' 'gyur dang bstan 'gyur* (1976–85), Delhi: Delhi Karmapae Chodhey Gyalwae Sungrab Partun Khang (BDRC W22084 and W23703).

Secondary sources

Buffetrille, K. (2012), "Low Tricks and High Stakes Surrounding a Holy Place in Eastern Nepal. The Halesi-Māratika Caves," in K. Buffetrille (ed.), *Revisiting Rituals in a Changing Tibetan World*, 163–207, Leiden: Brill (Brill's Tibetan Studies Library, 31).

Buswell, R. E., D. S. Lopez, and J. Ahn (2017), *The Princeton Dictionary of Buddhism*, Princeton, NJ: Princeton University Press.

Cabezón, J. I. (1996), "Buddhist Principles in the Tibetan Liberation Movement," in C. S. Queen and S. B. King (eds.), *Engaged Buddhism: Buddhist Liberation Movements in Asia*, 295–320, Albany: State University of New York Press.

Clarke, A. C. (1990), *Astounding Days. A Science Fictional Autobiography*, New York: Bantam Books (Bantam Spectra).

Davies, O. (2012), *Magic. A Very Short Introduction*, Oxford: Oxford University Press (Very short introductions, 299).

Dotson, B. (2017), "On 'Personal Protective Deities' ('go ba'i lha) and the Old Tibetan Verb 'go," in *Bulletin of the School of Oriental and African Studies, University of London* 80 (3): 525–45.

Dotson, B. (2019), "Three Dice, Four Faces, and Sixty-Four Combinations: Early Tibetan Dice Divination by the Numbers," in P. H. Maurer, D. Rossi, and R. Scheuermann (eds.), *Glimpses of Tibetan Divination: Past and Present*, 11–48, Leiden: Brill (Prognostication in History, 2).

Dotson, B., C. A. Cook, and L. Zhao (2021), *Dice and Gods on the Silk Road: Chinese Buddhist Dice Divination in Transcultural Context*, Leiden: Brill (Prognostication in History, 7).

De Martino, E. (1959) / Zinn, D. L. (trans.) (2015), *Magic: A Theory from the South. Translated by Dorothy Louise Zinn*, Chicago: HAU Books.

Durkheim, É. (2013), "The Elementary Forms of Religious Life," in B.-C. Otto and M. Stausberg (eds.), *Defining Magic. A Reader*, 111–23, Sheffield: Equinox (Critical Categories in the Study of Religion).

Edgerton, F. (1970), *Buddhist Hybrid Sanskrit Grammar and Dictionary*, Reprint, Delhi: Motilal Banarsidass.

Frazer, J. G. (2013), "The Gold Bough," in B.-C. Otto and M. Stausberg (eds.), *Defining Magic. A Reader*, 81–96, Sheffield: Equinox (Critical Categories in the Study of Religion).

Gyatso, T. (Dalai Lama XIV.) (1993), *Words of Truth. A Prayer for Peace in Tibet and Compassion in the World*, Boston, MA: Wisdom Publications.

Lopez, D. (2022), *The Power of Truth*, New York: Rubin Museum of Art, online: https://rubinmuseum.org/spiral/the-power-of-truth, last checked on December 30, 2022.

Malkiel, B. G. (2007), *A Random Walk Down Wall Street: The Time-tested Strategy for Successful Investing*, New York: Norton [rev. and updated].

Maurer, P. H., D. Rossi, and R. Scheuermann (eds.) (2019), *Glimpses of Tibetan Divination: Past and Present*, Leiden: Brill (Prognostication in History, 2).

Mauss, M., and H. Hubert (2013), "A General Theory of Magic," in B.-C. Otto and M. Stausberg (eds.), *Defining Magic. A Reader*, 97–110, Sheffield: Equinox (Critical Categories in the Study of Religion).

Mkhan po Chos grags bstan 'phel (1996), *Purpose of Kagyu Monlam*, online: https://www.kagyumonlamchenmo.org/purpose-of-kagyu-monlam/, last checked on July 5, 2022.

Otto, B. C., and M. Stausberg (eds.) (2013), *Defining Magic. A Reader*, Sheffield: Equinox (Critical Categories in the Study of Religion).

Otto, B. C., and M. Stausberg (2013), "General Introduction," in B.-C. Otto and M. Stausberg (eds.), *Defining Magic. A Reader*, 1–13, Sheffield: Equinox (Critical Categories in the Study of Religion).

Pearcey, A. (ed.) (2022), *Honoring the 49th Day of the Mahaparinirvana of His Holiness Kyabje Dodrupchen Rinpoche. Monlam Prayers*, online: https://www.pemakilaya.org/wp-content/uploads/2022/03/CONSECRATION-4_Aspiration-Prayers-22may19-FINAL_HHDR-monlam-14mar22.pdf, last checked on December 30, 2022.

Queen, C. S., and S. B. King (eds.) (1996), *Engaged Buddhism. Buddhist Liberation Movements in Asia*, Albany: State University of New York Press.

Śāntideva/Steinkellner, E., and C. Peck-Kubaczek (trans.) (2019), *Śāntideva's Bodhicaryāvatāra. A Translation by Ernst Steinkellner, and Cynthia Peck-Kubaczek. An extract from the book Buddha Mind – Christ Mind. A Christian Commentary on the Bodhicaryāvatāra*, Vienna: Austrian Academy of Sciences, online: https://www.oeaw.ac.at/fileadmin/Institute/IKGA/PDF/digitales/Steinkellner_and_Peck-Kubaczek_2019.pdf, last checked on December 29, 2022.

Scheuermann, R. (2018), "'One Will Quickly Die!' – Predictions of Death in Three Tibetan Buddhist Divination Manuals," in A. P. Bagliani, M. Lackner, and F. Pregadio (eds.), *Longevity and Immortality. Europe – Islam – Asia*, 113–30,

Firenze: Sismel Edizioni del Galluzzo (Micrologus – Nature, Sciences and Medieval Societies, 16).

Schmidt-Leukel, P., E. Steinkellner, and C. Peck-Kubaczek (2019), *Buddha Mind – Christ Mind. A Christian Commentary on the Bodhicaryāvatāra*, Leuven: Peeters (Christian commentaries on Non-Christian Sacred Texts, 9).

Sobisch, J. U. (2019), *Divining with Achi and Tārā: Comparative Remarks on Tibetan Dice and Mālā Divination: Tools, Poetry, Structures, and Ritual Dimensions. Translated and Introduced by Jan-Ulrich Sobisch. With Contributions by Solvej H. Nielsen*, Leiden: Brill (Prognostication in History, 1.

Tylor, E. B. (2013), "Primitive Culture," in B.-C. Otto and M. Stausberg (eds.), *Defining Magic. A Reader*, 71–80, Sheffield: Equinox (Critical Categories in the Study of Religion).

van Schaik, S. (2020), *Buddhist Magic. Divination, Healing, and Enchantment through the Ages*, Boulder, CO: Shambhala Publications.

Wittgenstein, L. ([1953] 2009), *Philosophische Untersuchungen. Philosophical investigations*, G. E. M. Anscombe, P. M. S. Hacker and Joachim Schulte (trans.), Chichester: Wiley-Blackwell.

5

The *Yogin*'s Familiars: Protector Deities as Magical Guides

Cameron M. Bailey

Introduction

Despite decades of contact with the relevant materials, Western scholars are still grappling with the most basic questions about magic in Buddhist and Tibetan cultural contexts, including whether the term "magic" is even appropriate or relevant to the field at all. Elsewhere I have argued that not only is magic an appropriate categorical term in Buddhism, and specifically Tibetan Buddhism, but it is also vitally necessary in understanding the soteriological paradigm of the tradition.[1] So as not to rehash this general issue here, and for the sake of my current argument, I will simply define "magic" as *the ritual manipulation of non-obvious sympathetic bonds to produce an obvious supernormal effect.* This definition is based largely on the emic understanding of magic within the Western esoteric tradition that has some parallels to Buddhist understandings of magic (Skt. *māyā* or Tib. *'phrul*, usually translated literally as "illusion"), which often associate the generation of supernormal effects with the correct realization of interdependent origination (Bailey 2020: 545–6).

Here I intend to discuss specific subtypes of magical practices that are explicitly distinguished in European esotericism and implicitly exist in Buddhist magic as well, so-called "demonic" magic, in which nonhuman, potentially if not overtly malevolent beings are commanded to carry out a particular magical action. I am especially concerned with focusing on what I interpret as a further subtype of demonic magic, which is here referred to as "familiar magic" (my own heuristic) in which the agency of the demon, not the magician, is primary and magic is not forced upon the nonhuman being but taught *by* them to their human pupil. I examine this phenomenon specifically in the narrative and ritual context of the eighteenth-century Tibetan Buddhist master Sle lung Bzhad pa'i rdo rje (1697–1740) and his relationship with his personal protector goddess, Lha gcig Nyi ma gzhon nu.

Demonic magic

Before turning to Sle lung and his texts, however, it is necessary to ground my examination within a theoretical framework and an understanding of demonic magic and spirit familiars. Following medieval European convention, the practice of magic can be divided into two main categories: natural magic and demonic magic. "Demonic magic invokes evil spirits and rests upon a network of religious beliefs and practices, while natural magic exploits "occult" powers within nature and is essentially a branch of medieval science" (Kieckhefer 2022: 1). These two types of magic are not necessarily always separate, and a single spell can employ both or merge them together in interesting ways. However, ideally speaking there is an obvious distinction between their methods, which I will attempt to explain briefly.

Generally, natural magic is what would most likely come to mind for both scholars and laypeople upon hearing the word "magic": special preparation and deployment of material objects or substances, usually with the enhancement of spoken words of power, to achieve some kind of "natural," if supernormal, effect. In the Indian magical tradition, exemplified in such early classic texts as the *Atharvaveda*, natural magic is the combination of *dravya* (substance), *mantra* (words of power), and *karma* (action), that is, doing something with a particular substance after it is empowered by the mantra. Thus, there is an automatic or mechanistic quality to natural magic, which in antiquity and medieval to early-modern Europe was seen as an extension of natural philosophy. The "occult" qualities that were exploited in natural magical practices were often determined (or supposedly determined) by at least basic observation of and rudimentary experimentation with various material substances including plant and animal matter, minerals, and so forth. This has led some modern scholars to think of natural magic as a kind of pseudo- or proto science, as well as essentially an extension of medicine.

Demonic magic, on the other hand, purportedly operates by invoking a nonhuman entity as a critical intermediary in the magical act. Thus, rather than producing the magical effect directly, as in natural magic, the magician instead forces a demonic assistant to do it for him or her. The term "demonic" is misleading here, however, both in the European Christian and Buddhist contexts. In the European context many practitioners of magic would not have understood their work to be directed toward demonic beings. Devout Christian magicians would commonly invoke angels, while necromancy sought to summon the (usually morally ambiguous) spirits of the dead. The fifteenth-century Catholic priest Marsilio Ficino (1433–1499), for instance, is renowned for his study and use of rituals to harness the power of the spirits of the planets. However, mainstream anti-magic commentators, especially by the time of the early modern period, condemned such practices as a crime against God since it was necessarily dealing with demons, regardless of what or who the practitioner thought he was invoking. This anti-magic view eventually dominated European and by extension American discourse on the topic, permeated popular culture, and strongly influenced academic, especially anthropological, understandings of "magic" as being specifically opposed to religion rather than a natural part or even the perfection of religion as figures such as Ficino, Agrippa, and John Dee would have understood it.[2]

Similarly, in the Buddhist context, the antireligious and immutably morally evil connotations of demons and by extension the stereotype of demonic magic are not appropriate or applicable. Therefore, in order to avoid terminological confusion or bias, I here and elsewhere have used the pre-Christian Greek *daemon* to capture the morally ambivalent and malleable quality of these nonhuman beings as they exist in Buddhist (and European, for that matter) discourse.[3] To be clear, from now on when I use the word *daemon*, I generally mean it in a morally neutral sense, or potentially in a positive sense, as in the Platonic tradition where *daemons* were sometimes regarded as necessary intermediaries between humans and the gods. The dual nature of *daemons* is perhaps best articulated in Iamblichus' Neoplatonic theology where "daemons alienate the soul from divinity [but] they also outline the path to recover it" (Shaw 2016: 177).

Particularly in the Tibetan Buddhist context these nonhuman beings are often overtly malevolent, but since they are commonly employed as protector deities with an apotropaic function, to call them "demons" in a normative Christian sense is inappropriate. As we shall see, they often have a vital, positive, intermediary function between human practitioners and cosmologically higher deities somewhat reminiscent of the Neoplatonist system. Also, following Carolyn Graves-Brown's use of the term *daemon* in the ancient Egyptian context, I generally use the term *daemon* to refer to "active beings, liminal, divine, lesser than the 'great' gods, [who] did not have cult centres and could be either malevolent or benevolent" (Graves-Brown 2018: 13). That said, as she goes on to point out, "the daemons of one period may have been greater gods in another" (ibid.: 15). Also, I will occasionally refer to higher cult deities as *daemons* if they are understood to be in some sense of the same "species" as and have power over a great retinue of *daemons*. In other words, they could be classified as something of a "*daemon* lord." Therefore, in the Buddhist context "*daemonic* magic," as I am using the phrase, refers specifically to magic that relies on the intercession of unenlightened *laukika*, or worldly, *daemons* as opposed to the invocation of enlightened *lokottara*, or transcendent, buddhas and bodhisattvas. In the Neoplatonic tradition that strongly influenced European magic, these two metaphysically distinct types of deities were known as hypercosmic (transcendent) and encosmic (worldly). The magic that I will be discussing here is thus usually concerned with the invocation of *daemons* and encosmic deities.[4]

Turning to some arguable examples of *daemonic* magic in Buddhism, the *Śrāvakayāna rakṣā*, or "protection," genre provides an early case study for this kind of practice in the Buddhist tradition.[5] This popular genre of apotropaic text is exemplified by the *Āṭānāṭiya Sutta* in the *Dīgha Nikāya* in which the Guardian King of the North Vessavaṇa (Skt. Vaiśravaṇa) and overlord of the *yakkhas* (Skt. *yakṣa*) present a list of powerful *yakkhas* to be called upon by monks for protection in times of need (Walshe 1995: 471–8). A much clearer example of *daemonic* magic, however, is found in the *Bhūtaḍāmara Tantra*, classified as a *Kriyā Tantra* and a veritable grimoire of Buddhist *daemonic* magic. This text is far more obviously "magical" than the *Āṭānāṭiya Sutta*, in the technical sense that it offers many more concrete supernormal rewards than simply generic protection, and in the Durkheimian sense in that it is easy to interpret the text and its practices as, in a sense, "anti-religious." Here, the encosmic deities are not respectfully invoked through petition and prayer but are violently and brutally subdued and coerced to grant the *yogin* various boons. One short passage will suffice to exemplify the ruthless nature of this magic:

> If he wants to attain mastery in the practice of the goddess Umā, he should step on [an effigy of] her with his left foot and recite the mantra ten thousand times. Umā will then arrive in person and present all precious substances, including the elixir of long life. She will become his wife. If he is not successful, he should smear her effigy with poison and blood. Stepping on the effigy with his left foot, he should recite the mantra of Great Wrath, "*Oṁ*, kill kill! *Vajra*-kill so-and-so! *Hūṁ hūṁ, phaṭ*!" He should recite his wrathful mantra one thousand and eight times. By merely reciting it, the head of the target will burst and they will wither

and die. The practitioner should employ this wrathful mantra in all acts of killing.[6]

As the *Bhūtaḍāmara Tantra* exemplifies, with the development of tantric Buddhism came the increasing popularity of ritual and narrative literature focused on the subjugation and deployment of encosmic deities as guardians and assistants. Even those translocally popular enlightened protectors like Mahākāla and Śrī Devī have historically been depicted with the appearance and demeanor of dangerous worldly deities, with vast retinues of dangerous *daemons* that have been effectively press-ganged into serving as Buddhist protectors. Across the Buddhist world but especially in Tibet these beings were and still are regularly invoked not only for generic apotropaic protection but also for specific magical boons, for example, being directly used in warfare to slay armies or whole villages, called on to find buried treasure, cure disease, or control the weather.

All this is of course well known, but one aspect of Tibetan Buddhist *daemonic* magic that is underappreciated is the cases, documented frequently in hagiobiographical literature especially, where encosmic protector deities are depicted less as *daemonic* servitors to be exploited and more as spiritual guides, friends, and even lovers to the *yogins* and *yoginis* who encountered them not in the context of stilted ritual procedures but in vital, lived interactions. In this respect, Buddhist protector deities seemed to have functioned in much the same way as the familiar spirits of witches and so-called "cunning folk" in the vernacular religion of medieval and early modern Europe, particularly in the British Isles.

Comparing protector deities to "familiar spirits" may seem wildly inappropriate given the common understanding of a witch's familiar spirit, usually depicted in popular media as merely some kind of supernaturally gifted animal like a raven or a toad that acts in the capacity of a special pet, or at best a magical assistant. A closer examination of folklore and witchcraft trial records, however, reveals numerous stories depicting familiar spirits that run the metaphysical gamut, ranging from talking animals and mischievous imps, to sinister ghosts, fairy royalty, angels, and even beings claiming to be the Devil himself (Wilby 2005: 3). For my purposes here, the most important aspect of the purported witch/familiar relationship, however, which is mentioned in numerous trial record accounts, is that the witch typically did not exploit and coerce magical boons from their *daemonic* familiar, as is so often the case in elite, literate magical rituals. Rather, the *daemon* familiar often had most of the agency in the relationship, appearing to their witch at will, giving commands (rather than vice versa), and most importantly teaching the witch magical techniques and practices that were rarely if ever codified in writing.[7]

There are, of course, quite a few well-known examples from Buddhist literature of the hypercosmic or *lokottara* deities acting as spiritual guides, such as Maitreya's instruction of Asaṅga, or Mañjuśrī's explanation of Prāsaṅgika-Mādhyamaka to Tsong kha pa. But what interests me here are not examples of buddhas and high-level bodhisattvas providing instruction on the finer points of emptiness philosophy, but protector deities teaching magic spells to their *yogin* interlocutors, like a *daemon* familiar would teach a witch.

Buddhist familiars

Interestingly, and related to the implicit monism pervasive in Mahāyāna Buddhist thought, such mentorships (for lack of a better term) by apparently encosmic *daemons* are doctrinally enshrined in Mahāyāna scripture. Often involving female deities, there are a number of memorable episodes in popular *sūtras* where apparently worldly goddesses function as critical spiritual guides for the Buddha's disciples, such as in the *Vimalakīrti Sūtra* where a minor house goddess understands the Dharma better than Śāriputra, the foremost disciple in wisdom, and instructs him in the emptiness teachings (Thurman 1976: 58–63). Or in the *Gaṇḍavyūha Sūtra* where Sudhana is guided by a series of goddesses, including a group of ten goddesses of the night led by one Vāsantī who possibly served as the inspiration for the goddess Tārā in the later Indo-Tibetan tantric Buddhist tradition (Landesman 2020: 33–5).

With the advent of Vajrayāna Buddhism there came a greater emphasis on taming and apotheosizing, and thus interacting with, *daemons*, particularly the fierce goddesses generally referred to as *ḍākinī*s who in many legends and hagio-biographical stories from the Indo-Tibetan Buddhist tradition function as messengers, teachers, companions, and lovers to their *yogin* disciples. Accounts of (especially female) encosmic *daemons* acting as spiritual guides pervade later Tibetan literature, such as one fascinating story from Milarepa's collection of spiritual songs that features a *srin mo* ("ogress") *daemon*, identified as an encosmic disciple of the Rnying ma (Old School) teachings of Padmasambhava, who is nevertheless by her nature unable to control her cravings for flesh and blood, and is thus given to attacking people. Despite this, in a long dialogue punctuated by an exchange of spiritual songs of realization, the *daemoness* gives Milarepa specific and key Mahāmudra instructions on how to properly relate to disturbances of the mind of which her presence is indicative (Tsang nyon Heruka 2016: 43–58).

Closer in theme to the examples I specifically want to highlight, however, there are also cases recorded in Tibetan Buddhist literature of protector deities giving practitioners specific instruction in magical ritual. That is, the encosmic deity or *daemon* explains to the *yogin* how to perform a magical ritual, specifically recalling a witch's relationship with their familiar *daemon*. For instance, in an autobiographical account the nineteenth-century Rnying ma master Bdud 'joms gling pa (1835–1904) reports visionary encounters with Lha chen Dbang phyug chen po, the Tibetan protector form of the Indian god Mahādeva, or Śiva. Like encosmic deities in general, Buddhism, particularly the tantric Buddhism of Tibet, has a complicated history with Śiva who is often demonized as effectively a satanic figure and paradigmatic enemy of the Dharma, who replaces Māra as the lord of all encosmic deities and *daemons*, and who is consequently the foremost obstructor of spiritual liberation. But on the other hand, given the nondualist bent of Mahāyāna and particularly Vajrayāna Buddhist doctrine, especially in the Rnying ma tradition of Tibetan Buddhism, Śiva became a popular dharma protector, sometimes considered enlightened despite his commonly recognized status as the overlord of all encosmic deities.[8] For Bdud 'joms gling pa specifically he seems to have functioned as something of a tutelary deity, and the Rnying ma master wrote that during one extended meditation retreat in which he invoked Lha chen, the deity taught him a black magic[9] spell for blinding his enemies.

Bdud 'joms gling pa reported that in 1871 a red *ḍākinī* appeared to him to advise that he move his place of meditation retreat to a small valley known to be the abode of a powerful *gnod sbyin* (Skt. *yakṣa*) *daemon*. Due to its wrathful presence, the *ḍākinī* explained, Bdud 'joms gling pa would be able to accomplish wrathful (magical) activities and consequently be able to subdue an enemy of the Dharma. Following this advice, he went to the valley in question and began practicing the liturgical rituals and meditation on Lha chen (Śiva) who appeared to him to teach him a particular magic spell.

> I went to Lower Nyamang Valley on the first day of the first month, and stayed there performing the practice of Lhachen Wangchuk Chenpo, Magnificent Ruler Deity. I remained in sealed retreat from the fifteenth day of the first month through the fifteenth day of the second month. During that period, Lhachen openly gave me a five-syllable mantra that, when recited, was a sharp iron hook incantation capable of extracting eyes. By reciting it for ten days with the practical instructions, that [unnamed] enemy of the doctrine became blind. I gained renown for that power. (Traktung Dudjom Lingpa 2011: 125)

Thus, here we have an example of the *yogin* drawing on the powers of worldly deities, to the point of receiving direct instruction from them, which includes a magical spell that is used to cause harm to an enemy. Thus, Śiva effectively functions as a witch's familiar to Bdud 'joms gling pa by being a theologically controversial deity (many Buddhist sources denounce him as an unenlightened enemy of the dharma) who teaches the practitioner magical secrets. Other similar examples could be discussed but this brief survey will suffice to understand the cultural and religious matrix and the theological basis of the materials I mainly wish to focus on here – the magical practices purportedly taught to Sle lung Bzhad pa'i rdo rje by his personal protector deity, Lha gcig Nyi ma gzhon nu (Youthful Sun Lady).

The Laughing Vajra[10] and the Youthful Sun

The Fifth Sle lung Rinpoche (1697–1740), a Dge lugs reincarnate lama with a strong Rnying ma background and sympathies, was a controversial religious teacher who wielded notable political influence in the courts of multiple rulers, including two effective kings of central Tibet, in the early eighteenth century. He has been compared to Rasputin (Pomplun 2006: 41) and was known, among other things, for his vast knowledge and extensive command over the ritual propitiation of a host of protector deities, with the potentially sinister reputation that implies. Among his extensive bibliography are collections of magical rituals, several of which are part of a massive sixteen-volume cycle of texts related to his main meditational deity, Gsang ba ye shes mkha' 'gro or "Secret Gnosis Ḍākinī," essentially a special treasure-revealed Rnying ma form of Vajrayoginī (Bailey 2020: 539–42). Another, much larger grimoire compiled by Sle lung focuses specifically on magically invoking the Rnying ma protector Rdo rje legs pa, whom Sle lung writes that on at least one occasion he propitiated with "red offerings," by offering the blood of a black goat at a glacier where Rdo rje legs pa was believed to reside (Baker 2004: 461).

Sle lung is now perhaps best known for his collection of myths and legends related to dozens of protector deities, drawn from mostly Rnying ma canonical sources, entitled *The Liberation Stories of the Ocean of Oath-Bound Protectors* (*Dam can bstan srung rgya mtsho'i rnam par thar pa*). This book functions almost as an encyclopedic and theogonic guide to Tibet's protector deities (with a strong Rnying ma bias) and begins with the most cosmologically powerful protectors (Śiva and his immediate children Mahākāla and Śrī Devī), then proceeds to cover more and more localized, or encosmic, protectors including lake-dwelling serpent deities and mountain gods. Sle lung is careful to argue along the way that the apparently "lower" and "unenlightened" protectors are in fact just docetic forms of the hypercosmic deities. Śiva, for example, he defends as being the combined essence of the thousand buddhas of our current fortunate eon, despite appearing to be (in disguise) the paradigmatically unenlightened worldly god. Countering unnamed critics who seemed to have rejected the worship of encosmic deities like Śiva, Sle lung acts as an apologist for their cults and argues an essentially monist metaphysics and theology where all *daemons* are ultimately buddhas.[11]

One deity that is not discussed at all in the *Ocean of Oathbound* text (and only briefly mentioned in the opening prayer) is Sle lung's personally most important protector, Lha gcig Nyi ma gzhon nu. Her absence from Sle lung's protector *magnum opus* may at first seem curious but given her obscurity and apparent lack of scriptural basis beyond Sle lung's own visionary experiences, this is not surprising. Nyi ma gzhon nu, in fact, does not appear in the historical record before Sle lung and was likely an epiphany originating with him, appearing to Sle lung in a series of visionary and revelatory experiences probably beginning in the late 1720s. If her cult did predate Sle lung, given the dearth of textual evidence it is very likely she was an obscure local deity, outside the purview of centralized religious authority. However, she quickly rose to more widespread fame for purportedly helping the Seventh Dalai Lama to overcome an illness through Sle lung's intercession. She was and still is recognized as an oracular deity, claimed to possess human women and speak prophecies through them. According to Sle lung, the goddess regularly possessed his wife Rdo rje skyabs rje, and it appears from some of Sle lung's writings that the ontological distinction between his wife and protector was blurred at best; in typical Buddhist metaphysical language Sle lung identified Rdo rje skyabs rje as an "emanation" of the goddess. Today, since the time of the Seventh Dalai Lama who likely "adopted" and integrated her into official liturgy, Nyi ma gzhon nu is enshrined as one of the protectors at Gnas chung Monastery where she is identified as the deity of the land on which the monastery is built, an interesting case of the social mobility of deities (Bell 2021: 125). Still, publicly speaking, she is effectively known as a *sa bdag* ("earth lord") or a *lokapāla* and is thus firmly in the category of a worldly protector or an encosmic *daemon*.

To Sle lung, however, she was much more than that. Typical of Sle lung's theological agenda related to protector deities in general that recurs often in his writings, he did not see Nyi ma gzhon nu as merely an encosmic local deity but as an ultimately enlightened manifestation or even combination of all enlightened beings. More specifically, he identified her as the protector form of his meditation deity, Gsang ba ye shes. But beyond Sle lung's esoteric practices and secret biographical accounts, I know of no other context where Nyi ma gzhon nu was recognized as such. Like the witch or cunning folk's familiar, Nyi ma gzhon nu seems to have been of central personal import to Sle lung while being at best a marginal figure in the community at large. Similar to the "encounter narrative" in witchcraft lore and testimony, in multiple other recorded instances Nyi ma gzhon nu appeared in person or spoke to Sle lung through an oracle giving him instructions on a number of topics, including how to subdue and employ other (lesser) encosmic deities as protectors.

Furthermore, according to Sle lung's accounts, many of his visions of Nyi ma gzhon nu (and other protector deities) were not deliberately generated or sought, but apparently occurred spontaneously at the instigation of the deity. This again recalls the witch–familiar relationship (and sharply contrasts with elite demonic magic rituals where the *daemon* is always explicitly summoned) where the familiar *daemon* was usually said to appear, at least initially, at their own will outside of the witch's control (Wilby 2005: 60). Witches were often said, however, to have been taught rituals for later summoning their familiars at will to perform magical acts when needed (ibid.: 78), much like the "pure vision" practices Nyi ma gzhon nu is said to have taught Sle lung, which we will examine below. Whether we interpret these secret biographical accounts as narrative fictions or as accurate reports of altered states of consciousness, or something else, it seems clear that, on some level at least, Nyi ma gzhon nu was phenomenologically very real to Sle lung, and it would not be far-fetched to say that the goddess functioned as his most important spiritual guide in the latter part of his life.

Comparing Sle lung to a European witch or cunning person, at least initially, seems to be a strained similarity at best. What is socially significant about the latter is that they appear to have usually been relatively poor and uneducated, often illiterate. As stated above, our knowledge of their magical activities comes almost entirely from trial and interrogation records written about them rather than their own writings. Sle lung, on the other hand, was highly educated and literate, and very much engaged in literarily elite demonic magic which, as I have noted, is typically characterized by the tendency to command *daemons* and employ them as servitors. Furthermore, Sle lung was very much socially a part of the centralized, politically powerful ecclesiastic Dge lugs religious hierarchy, in some ways the very opposite social situation of the subaltern witches. And yet,

Sle lung was, especially in the latter part of his life, a controversial and marginal figure vis-à-vis Tibet's religious establishment.

Much of Sle lung's personal emphasis and involvement with specifically Rnying ma lineages and practices came in the wake of anti-Rnying ma persecution, primarily by the invading Dzungar Mongolians from 1717 to 1720, which saw purges of Rnying ma practitioners from the primarily Dge lugs political ecclesiastic establishment and full-on pogroms targeting Rnying ma teachers for execution and monasteries for destruction. By the time he died in 1740, Sle lung had become something of a pariah, and in a twentieth-century treatise written by one of the current Dalai Lama's most respected teachers, it is claimed that Sle lung was in fact killed by a Dge lugs protector deity for the crime of degrading the pure Dge lugs teachings by mixing them with Rnying ma practices and leading monks astray with the improper practice of sexual yoga and the consumption of alcohol. This account describes Sle lung thus:

> Previously at Olka Lelung there was one named Jedrung Lozang Trinley also known as Shepay Dorje, a great being renowned to be the Lhodrag Mahasiddha Lekyi Dorje's emanation. He studied at Ngari Tratsang in the early part of his life and became a great scholar. He kept the Lhodrag ear-whispered lineage teachings and Chakrasamvara as his innermost essence practice. He had attained realizations at quite a high level and cultivated pure view and action of the Geden [Dge lugs pa] lineage. At one point he began practicing a secret wisdom teaching in accordance with a Mindrol Ling treasure text and began emphasizing it in his teachings to his many disciples, both lay and ordained. In the name of offering the wisdom consort and offering nectar, he and all the disciples gathered many young women around them and enjoyed drinking intoxicants without restraint, singing and dancing. They started many monks of Sera and Drepung, lamas, tulkus and geshes into consort practice. With such actions as these they threw proper Tantric conduct into disarray, perverting it. (Kyabje Trijang Dorje Chang 1967: 112–13)

While I know of no condemnation of Sle lung's claims and practices regarding Nyi ma gzhon nu specifically, the major part of his infamy among the religious establishment was due to his lack of sexual discipline while being technically a fully ordained monk, something in which this oracle deity of his (apparently illicit) wife was very much involved. In fact, as we shall see below, Nyi ma gzhon nu is credited with instructing Sle lung in at least some of the sexual yoga practices for which he was later condemned. In one secret biographical account dated to late 1730 or early 1731, Sle lung discusses a visionary encounter with Nyi ma gzhon nu that he had while "sporting" (*'jug rnam rol*) with four female disciples, including his wife Rdo rje skyabs rje. After drinking beer and making love to them in the main hall of his personal temple, Sle lung reports that at dawn, in a blissful state of mental clarity, Nyi ma gzhon nu appeared to him and taught him a pure vision (*dag sngang*) ritual practice focused on her called "*The Combined Essence of the Three Roots of the Single Deity*" (*Lha gcig gi dril sgrub rtsa gsum thig le*).[12] In this practice, Nyi ma gzhon nu is to be visualized as containing an elaborate body *maṇḍala* of a pantheon's worth of other, more well-known hypercosmic deities, from the popular and well-established enlightened protector Dmag zor rgyal mo to various forms of Guru Rinpoche Padmasambhava. Sle lung understood Nyi ma gzhon nu to be the "essence" of all of them. It is hard to imagine that the Dge lugs establishment in central Tibet, in which Sle lung was educated as a boy and recognized as a reincarnate lama, would have sanctioned such practices.

It is interesting and perhaps notable that in the three Tibetan examples of *daemonic* familiars we have examined so far—Milarepa, Bdud 'joms gling pa, and Sle lung—all experienced a degree of social marginalization and liminality that one is tempted to compare to the social pressures that (as argued by Wilby) may have also contributed to the visionary experiences of British witches. However, my point here is not to argue some sort of universal link between social stress and visionary experience, but rather merely to use the witch/familiar relationship as a heuristic paradigm to highlight aspects of the protector/*yogin* relationship that are understudied in scholarship and usually completely ignored in normative presentations of Tibetan Buddhism, namely, the attributed role of protectors as teachers of magic. As such, in what space remains I now turn my attention to three magical practices or rituals that Sle lung claims were taught to him by Nyi ma gzhon nu, all three of which Sle lung classifies as received "pure vision" practices, a common mode of revelation in the Rnying ma school especially.

Three magic practices of Nyi ma gzhon nu

The first practice is a *bcud len* technique, rather than a ritual as such. *Bcud len* or "extracting the essence" is a well-established if not widely taught tantric yogic method for consuming and digesting, as sustenance, material substances or energy that ordinary people could not. It is usually meant to allow *yogin*s who may not have easy access to (or who may not want to eat) ordinary food to sustain themselves on something else, such as stones or sunlight. In Sle lung's case, in a text entitled *Lha gcig nyi ma gzhon nus dag snang du stsal ba'i thabs* *kyi lam mchog nyi zla'i bcud len dang brgyad 'debs* (*The Supreme Path of Skillful Means Given through the Pure Vision of Lha gcig nyi ma gzhon nu: The Sun and Moon Essence Extraction and the Eight Supplements*), the goal of the practice is not primarily to provide sustenance but to describe, in great detail, methods of sexual yoga during which the partners self-visualize as deities and generate bliss to the extent that Sle lung claims this is a method for achieving enlightenment through sexual intercourse.[13]

The extent to which this practice can be said to be "magical" in the sense that I defined it above is somewhat debatable. However, the actual "essence extraction" part of the practice refers to the consumption of a mixture of male and female sexual fluids empowered through the process of deity yoga, the consumption of which is held to have an arguably magical effect of "removing any kind of obscuration," which is to say it is held to be supremely purificatory. Notably, the female partner in this practice is meant to be specifically visualized as Nyi ma gzhon nu herself. Sle lung also describes admixtures of various natural substances, mostly plant extracts like cumin, sesame oil, and ginger, but also including rendered fat from various animals such as a vulture, sparrow, and donkey that are to be smeared on the body, particularly the genitals, to enhance sexual bliss and prevent disease, a potential example of natural magic.

Another magical technique purportedly taught to Sle lung by Nyi ma gzhon nu focuses on the blessing and empowerment of hot springs water to endow it with healing properties. Sle lung himself frequented hot springs due to medical issues and this practice was likely meant to aid his treatment. The main part of the ritual focuses on the worship of Nyi ma gzhon nu in the form of a *nāga,* an aquatic serpent *daemon*, with a vast retinue of various other *daemons*:

> She is a beautiful *nāginī,* pale blue in color. She is flirtatious and extremely desirous. From the pot of nectar in her hands emanates a feast of ambrosial medicine. She wears blue silk clothes. She is adorned with many precious ornaments. She has a blue water ox as a steed and is surrounded by 100,000 *sa bdag*, *nāga*s, and *gnyan daemons.* With light rays from the seed syllable the *nāga* kings with their retinues are invited from the ten directions.[14]

After invoking this special form of Nyi ma gzhon nu, the ritualized visualization proceeds with the protector goddess transforming into the meditation deity Gsang ba ye shes, who then transforms into Padmasambhava himself who is prayed to for the actual blessing and medicinal enhancement of the water, which is the purpose of the ritual.

> At the time of the arising of diseases which destroy the illusory bodies of sentient beings, if you are afflicted by diseases of overwhelming suffering, pray without doubt or hesitation. Inseparable from the supreme healer of Orgyan, obstacles to one's lifespan will be cleared away. I supplicate Orgyan Padmasmabhava.[15]

This practice is an interesting variation on the typical structure of a "demonic magic" ritual, for rather than the lower encosmic deities being directly invoked to create the magical effect, they are instead used as a gateway to invoke the higher, hypercosmic deities, in this case Gsang ba ye shes, and then Padmasambhava who is the ultimate source of the blessing.

The final, and perhaps the most obviously "magical," ritual taught to Sle lung by Nyi ma gzhon nu that I wish to examine here is a relatively complex, two-tiered practice for enhancing or generating material wealth, very simply titled *Dag snang lha gcig nyi ma gzhon nu'i nor sgrub bzhugs, The Pure Vision Wealth Ritual of Nyi ma gzhon nu*. It is two-tiered in the sense that there are effectively two versions of the practice, one which depends upon material components (which is to say, elements of natural magic) and one which relies entirely on the *yogin*'s innate mental focus. In the first, and implied lesser, case, the instruction states that the practitioner is first supposed to find a pretty stone that has come from a "wholesome natural power place where the eight classes abide."[16] The "eight classes" here refer to the standard eight types of encosmic *daemons* in Buddhist cosmology, and by making this the first material object necessary to accomplish the spell, essentially its base component, the implication is that the spell draws on, and even depends on, the innate power of these worldly *daemons*.

Such power, or "soul" (Tib. *bla*), objects are quite typical in Tibetan cults of protectors, especially encosmic deities, and denotes how they are in some sense bound to, or innate within, the material universe. Interestingly, and in a perhaps connected occurrence, in another secret biographical account related to Nyi ma gzhon nu dated less than three weeks after the revelation of the wealth ritual (both occurring in the third month of the Iron Dog Year, which corresponds to the late spring of 1730), the goddess is said to have spontaneously appeared to Sle lung in a vision and told him where to find the soul stone of a king of the *btsan*, a type of *daemon* typically associated with violence and war. It is described as a "dark red stone [that] is the life-force abode of the *btsan*. You will find a wrathful face projecting out of it. It is essential to not have any doubt. You will gain many benefits from it. Afterwards it will be a support for [magical] accomplishment."[17]

Perhaps just such a stone (or, more likely, a much smaller version) was considered necessary for the accomplishment of the wealth ritual specifically.

In any case, after the stone is collected the *yogin* is instructed to cleanse it and, with a mixture of animal bile, lac dye, and *sindura* powder, draw (presumably on the stone itself) the sixteen auspicious substances and signs[18] and images of various jewels, thus establishing a sympathetic bond with the kinds of material substances and wealth that the *yogin* is hoping to gather. Next, the practitioner is told to wrap the stone up in silk and place it inside a *ga'u*, or amulet box, which becomes the object of focus for the rest of the ritual. The *yogin* then surrounds the amulet with various offerings such as grain, medicines, jewels, and so forth. Just as it takes money to make money, so the adage goes, again the purpose here seems to be to create a sympathetic bond with the material goods that the practitioner is attempting to increase.

Next, the *yogin* performs deity yoga and visualizes Nyi ma gzhon nu in the form of a *yakṣī*, a manifestation befitting the purpose of the magical effect being generated. In the case of the hot springs practice, since that was intended to bless a water source, she appeared in the form of a *nāginī*, a type of *daemon* associated with water. In the case of the wealth ritual, she appears in the form of a type of *daemon* known for being guardians of wealth and treasure:

> On top of a jeweled throne, is the lady of wealth, *yakṣī* Gzhon nu ma, golden colored smiling radiantly. She holds a bejeweled chest with both hands. Having opened [the box] it sends forth whatever one wishes. It produces silk and jeweled ornaments. She abides in power, in a half-cross-legged posture. She is surrounded by a hundred thousand wealth gods, radiant like a hundred thousand suns, golden rays of light emanating from her body in the midst of a sky treasury of prosperity.[19]

The *yogin* then recites several mantras, in particular invoking "ratna dha ki" the jewel *ḍākinī* and praying for all the wealth in the universe to descend upon him.

> "From the heaps of all the wealth of the three worlds bestow it upon me. Cause a great rain of all desirable things and fulfill the wishes of the mind." Light rays radiate from the goddess and bring back all the food, wealth, and possessions of all gods, demons, and men. Those are bestowed without delay.[20]

The text specifies that this ritual, in particular the mantra recitation, is meant to be done repeatedly, four times daily for at least a week and up to three weeks, and at the end of the process the visualized goddess and her retinue of wealth *daemons* are dissolved into the amulet. The amulet is then meant to be placed inside a storehouse where material goods are kept, with the implication being that the now-empowered amulet will magically multiply or increase the amount of wealth one has.

Despite this ritual being a pure vision revelation, there is nothing particularly unique about its structure or details, except perhaps the inclusion of Nyi ma gzhon nu as the main deity of invocation. Clearly, the ritual is based on earlier, very similar, even almost identical wealth practices in the Tibetan Buddhist tradition. For example, in a large collection of short magic spells in Sle lung's massive cycle of texts focused on Gsang ba ye shes (the *Gsang ba ye shes chos skor* or GYCK), entitled *Las tshogs ci 'dod rgyan shar* (*A Collection of Activities That Brings Whatever Is Desired*), there is a spell for accumulating wealth that is extremely similar and is likely to have served as a direct inspiration for the Nyi ma gzhon nu wealth ritual. *Collection of Activities* is in fact Sle lung's redaction of a much earlier text entitled *Yon tan gyi rgyud bstan pa'i srog shing* (*The Tantra of Qualities, the Life-Pillar of the Teachings*) from a famous fourteenth-century cycle of treasure revelations called the *Bla ma dgongs pa 'dus* revealed by Sangs rgyas gling pa (1340–1396) but, as with most Rnying ma treasure teachings, is said to have been originally taught by Padmasambhava in the eighth century.[21] The seventeenth spell (out of ninety-two) in *Collection of Activities* reads thus:

> If you wish to accumulate wealth, after writing the root mantra[22] and the names of whatever food, wealth, and enjoyments you desire on a piece of paper write "*pā sham ku ru hoh*" with vermillion [ink], infused with perfume and *sindhura* powder and put it inside a casket of precious substances, filled with various grains, medicinal plants, silk brocade, and precious jewels. Imagine that oneself clearly [visualized as] the meditational deity summons the masters of food and wealth and all luxuries and after the root mantra recite "*sarwa ba su siddhi pā sham ku ru ma ma hring hring*." Having practiced thus for three days, carry the casket on your body and you will summon wealth.[23]

The basic goal of the practice, producing an amulet empowered by deities with power over wealth surrounded by offerings of the types of substances the *yogin* wants to multiply, is the same. The main, though relatively minor, differences are the mantras, and the fact that the box is meant to be worn on one's person instead of placed in a storehouse.

Unusually, there is also a second, much simpler, if perhaps practically more difficult, version of this practice that Sle lung describes in a few lines. This version eschews any material support and even any formalized ritual at all. Rather, the *yogin* is simply called on to keep constant awareness of Nyi ma gzhon nu and view all of existence as her *maṇḍala* while maintaining a steady stream of mantras and prayers. There is no time requirement specified, but essentially this requires the practitioner to always maintain tantric pure vision. This is implied to be sufficient to summon all the material wealth that the *yogin* may need, although this practice is barely ritual magic as it is typically understood, but more like a technique for cultivating innate magical abilities or miracle powers.

Conclusion

Emma Wilby in her study of witchcraft familiars in the British Isles ultimately argues that this phenomenon should be viewed in the context of cross-cultural shamanic practices common in (usually) preliterate cultures. She argues in convincing detail that the witch/familiar relationship as described in trial and interrogation records closely matches the anthropological accounts of the interactions between shamans and their spirit guides and tutelary deities from indigenous tribes all over the world (Wilby 2005: 128–59). While much has been said about the potential "shamanic substrate" of Indo-Tibetan Buddhism,[24] and it is tempting to read Sle lung's relationship with Nyi ma gzhon nu through this conceptual framework, I want to make clear that I do not intend to make such a sweeping universalist claim here.

However, it is notable and particularly pertinent to this discussion that Tibetan Buddhism is geographically and culturally adjacent to the shamanic societies of northern Asia, specifically Tibet's Turko-Mongol neighbors, who settled in parts of northern and eastern Tibet in especially the thirteenth and fourteenth centuries. The rituals and stories of these northern Asian cultures feature shamans with spirit guides who are often portrayed as being of the opposite sex. In a recent study of the Gesar epic, which itself in its earliest form may be an importation from northern Asia, Solomon FitzHerbert has noted the motif of shamanic familiar *daemons* that heavily feature in the Gesar *legendarium*. He highlights Ma ne ne, Gesar's special female protector and divine "aunt" who is a particularly important and active character in the story (FitzHerbert 2022: 105–6). Sle lung's relationship with Nyi ma gzhon nu can easily be similarly read as part of this same northern and central Asian shamanic complex, a case of a shaman and his female spirit guide codified in elite ritual and autobiographical literature.[25] The problematic reification of the concept of "shamanism" aside, to the degree that "magic" is an appropriate methodological and hermeneutical category in the study of Tibetan Buddhism, the term "familiar" should be as well.

Sle lung and Nyi ma gzhon nu's example also highlights a second point that is no less important, in that it blurs or outright demolishes the simplistic binary of elite versus preliterate magic. The witch/familiar or shaman/spirit guide relationship in which the *daemon* has primary agency and takes the role of mentor and teacher is not necessarily in sociocultural opposition or hermetically sealed off from the more elite, literate ritual summoning of *daemons* as servitors. Sle lung's writings make clear that, just as with the theological categories of *laukika* (encosmic) and *lokottara* (hypercosmic), these two types of *daemonic* magic can merge, blend, and coexist in interesting ways.

Notes

1 See Bailey (2020).
2 See Spoto (2014).
3 Probably the closest Tibetan word that captures the sense of *daemon* is *dregs pa*, usually translated as "haughty ones" and consistently refers to arrogant worldly spirit beings who must be tamed and are gathered in the retinues of higher protector deities.
4 Throughout I translate *lokottara* as "hypercosmic" and *laukika* as "encosmic" as I believe these terms capture these cosmological meanings more precisely and technically than "transcendent" or "worldly." *Daemons,* by definition, are usually encosmic.
5 See Skilling (1992).
6 Dharmachakra Translation Committee (2020), verse 11:5.
7 See Wilby (2005), especially pages 46–76.
8 On this complicated, shifting Tibetan Buddhist theology of Śiva, see Bailey (2019).
9 "Black" magic here is meant in the technical, not pejorative sense, to mean aggressive tantric magic.
10 The literal meaning of Sle lung's tantric name, Bzhad pa'i rdo rje.
11 See Bailey (2019).
12 The account of Sle lung's vision and revelation of this practice is found in Sle lung's *gsung 'bum* (abbreviated henceforth as "BRGB") vol. 12, pp. 301–305. The actual ritual manual for the practice itself is found in the same volume, pp. 241–61.
13 For a detailed description of the practice see Oliphant (2015: 167–9).
14 BRGB vol 12, p. 281 *klu mo mdzes 'dzum mdog sngo bsangs/ sgeg cing chags nyams lhag par rgyas/ phyag gnyis bdud rtsi'i bum pa nas/ nad sel bdud rtsi'i dga' ston 'gyed/ na bza' chu dar sngon po gsol/ rin chen du ma'i rgyan gyis spras/ chibs su chu glang sngon po chibs/ sa bdag klu gnyan 'bum gyis bskor/ thugs srog 'od kyis phyogs bcu nas/ klu rgyal 'khor bcas spyan drangs gyur/.*

15 BRGB vol. 12, pp. 281–2 *sems can sgyu lus 'jig pa'i nad byung tshe: mi bzod sdug bsngal nad kyis nyen pa na: yid gnyis the tshom med par gsol ba 'debs: o rgyan sman gyi bla dang dbyer med pas: tshe zad ma yin bar chad nges par sel: o rgyan pad+ma [282] 'byung gnas la gsol ba 'debs.*

16 BRGB vol. 13, p. 64 *dkar phyags skyong ba'i sde brgyad mthu bo che gnas pa'i sa nas rdo yid du 'ong ba zhig blangs te.*

17 BRGB vol. 9. p. 188 *btsan gyi srog gnas rdo dmar smug/ khro zhal dod pa rnyed pa yod/ the tshom ma byed blang ba gces/ de yis khyod kyi don mang po/ slad mar sgrub pa'i rten 'brel yod.*

18 *Bkra shis rdzas rtags*. This standard Buddhist grouping refers technically to the eight auspicious substances including a mirror, yoghurt, medicinal grass, mustard seeds, etc., and the eight symbols of good fortune, including the parasol, lotus, endless knot, etc. See Dagyab (1995: 17–64).

19 BRGB vol. 13, p. 65 *rin po che yi khri steng du/ nor bdag gnod sbyin gzhon nu ma/ gser mdog 'dzum ba'i mdangs dang ldan/ lag gnyis rin chen sgrom bu'i kha/ phye nas ci 'dod 'gyed bar mdzad/ dar dang rat+na'i rgyan mdzes/ skyil krung phyed ba'i stabs kyis bzhugs/ nor lha 'bum gyi 'khor gyis bskor/ nyi ma 'bum gyi gzi brjid can/ sku las 'od zer ser bo 'phro/ nam mkha' mdzod kyi longs sbyod dbus.*

20 BRGB vol. 13, p. 65–66 *srid* [66] *pa gsum gyi longs spyod rnams/ thams cad bsdus nas bdag la stsol/ 'dod dgu'i char chen 'bebs pa dang/ yid kyi re ba bskang bar mdzod/ lha mo'i sku las 'od zer 'phros/ lha 'dre mi gsum thams cad kyi/ zas nor longs sbyod thams cad bkug/ thogs pa med par stsal bar gyur.*

21 For more on this particular "grimoire" text in Sle lung's Gsang ba ye shes collection, see Bailey (2020).

22 In this context this probably refers to Gsang ba ye shes's root mantra.

23 GYCK vol. 12, pp. 14–15 *bcu bdun pa nor 'gugs par 'dod na/ shog bur rtsa sngags kyi bsham du zas nor longs spyad gang 'dod kyi ming bris pa'i mthar pā sham ku ru hoh zhes mtshal gyis bris par* [15] *dri bzang dang sindhu ras sbags pa rin po che'i za ma tog gi nang du bcug par 'bru sna/ sman sna dar zab/ rin po che rnams kyis bltems/ rang yi dam du gsal bas zas nor gyi bdag po dang longs spyod rnams bkug par bsams la rtsa sngags kyi mthar/ sarwa ba su siddhi pā sham ku ru/ ma ma hring hring/ zhes zhag gsum du bsgrubs nas za ma tog lus la bcangs pas nor 'du bar 'gyuro/.*

24 Most notably, Geoffrey Samuel's *Civilized Shamans* (1993) has tackled this controversial topic in detail.

25 Also notable in this context is the fact that Sle lung was one of the earliest Tibetan Buddhist figures to promote the cult of King Gesar as a Dharma protector, and among his collected works is a *dag sngang* (pure vision revelation) text describing a theogony of Gesar and his elder brothers, which functions as a preface for the ritual propitiation of Gesar (Dag snang ge sar gyi gtam rgyud le'u (BRGB vol. 12, pp. 1–9)). My thanks to Solomon George FitzHerbert for originally bringing this text to my attention.

References

Primary sources

BRGB: 'Ol dga' rje drung 03 bzhad pa'i rdo rje (1983–5). Gsung 'bum bzhad pa'i rdo rje. 13 vols. Sman rtsis shes rig spen dzod 115–27. Leh: T. Sonam & D.l. Tashigang. Accessed October 1, 2022. http://purl.bdrc.io/resource/MW22130. [BDRC bdr:MW22130]

GYCK: 'Ol dga' rje drung 03 bzhad pa'i rdo rje (1974–6). Mkha' 'gro gsang ba ye shes kyi chos skor. 16 vols. New Delhi: Sanje Dorje. Accessed October 1, 2022. http://purl.bdrc.io/resource/MW9209. [BDRC bdr:MW9209]

Secondary sources

Agrippa, H. C. (2021), *Three Books of Occult Philosophy* (E. Purdue, trans.), Rochester, VT: Inner Traditions.

Bailey, C. (2017), "A Feast for Scholars: The Life and Works of Sle lung Bzhad pa'i rdo rje." Ph.D. diss. Oxford University.

Bailey, C. (2019), "The Progenitor of all Dharma Protectors: Buddhist Śaivism in Lelung Zhepe Dorje's Ocean of Oath-Bound Protectors," *Bojo Sasang* 54: 179–237.

Bailey, C. (2020), "The Magic of Secret Gnosis: A Theoretical Analysis of a Tibetan Buddhist 'Grimoire,'" *Journal of the Korean Association of Buddhist Studies* 93: 535–70.

Baker, I. (2004), *The Heart of the World: A Journey to the Last Secret Place*, New York: Penguin Press.

Bell, Ch. (2021), *The Dalai Lama and the Nechung Oracle*, Oxford: Oxford University Press.

Dagyab, L. S. (1995), *Buddhist Symbols in Tibetan Culture: An Investigation of the Nine Best-Known Groups of Symbols*, Somerville, MA: Wisdom Publications.

Dharmacakra Translation Committee (trans.) (2020). *The Great Sovereign Bhūtaḍāmara Tantra*. 84000: Translating the Words of the Buddha. Current version v 1.0.5 (2022). Generated by 84000 Reading Room v2.11.0. Accessed October 1, 2022.

FitzHerbert, S. G. (2022), "Gesar's Familiars: Revisiting Shamanism as a Hermeneutic for Understanding the Structure, Motifs and History of the Tibetan Gesar Epic," in M. T. Kapstein and C. Ramble (eds.), *The Many Faces of King Gesar: Tibetan and Central Asian Studies in Homage to Rolf A. Stein*, 90–132, Leiden: Brill.

Graves-Brown, C. (2018), *Daemons and Spirits in Ancient Egypt*, Cardiff: University of Wales Press.

Kiechkhefer, R. (2022), *Magic in the Middle Ages* (3rd ed.), Cambridge: Cambridge University Press.

Kyabje Trijang Dorje Chang (1967), *Music Delighting the Ocean of Protectors: An Account Expressing the Realizations of the Wonderful Three Secrets of the Emanated Great Dharma King Mighty Dorje Shugden, Supreme Protector of Conqueror Manjusri Tsongkhapa's Teachings*. http://www.dorjeshugden.com/articles/musicdelighting.pdf. Accessed October 23, 2013.

Landesman, S. A. (2020). *The Tārā Tantra: Tārā's Fundamental Ritual Text* Tārā-mūla-kalpa, Somerville, MA: Wisdom Publications.

Oliphant, Ch. J. (2015), "'Extracting the Essence': Bcud len in the Tibetan Literary Tradition.'" Ph.D. diss. Oxford University.

Pomplun, R. T. (2006). "Ippolito Desideri, S.J. on Padmasambhava's Prophecies and the Persecution of the Rnying ma, 1717–1720," in B. J. Cuevas and K. R. Schaeffer (eds.), *Power, Politics, and the Reinvention of Tradition: Tibet in the Seventeenth and Eighteenth Centuries*, 33–46, Leiden: Brill.

Samuel, G. (1993), *Civilized Shamans: Buddhism in Tibetan Societies*, Washington, DC: Smithsonian Institution Press.

Shaw, G. (2016), "*Demon est Deus Inversus:* Honoring the Daemonic in Iamblichean Theurgy," *Gnosis: Journal of Gnostic Studies* 1: 177–95.

Skilling, P. (1992), "The *Rakṣā* Literature of the *Śrāvakayāna*," *Journal of the Pali Text Society* 16: 109–82.

Spoto, S. (2014), "A Brief History of the Use of Spirits in European Occultism," *Abraxas Journal* 5: 16–25.

Thurman, R. A. F. (trans.) (1976), *The Holy Teaching of Vimalakirti: A Mahayana Scripture*, University Park: Pennsylvania State University Press.

Traktung Dudjom Lingpa (2011), *A Clear Mirror: The Visionary Autobiography of a Tibetan Master* (Chönyi Drolma (Anne Holland), trans.), Hong Kong: Rangjung Yeshe Publications.

Tsang nyon Heruka (2016), *The Hundred Thousand Songs of Milarepa* (Christopher Stagg, trans.), Boulder, CO: Shambhala.

Walshe, M. (trans.) (1995), *The Long Discourses of the Buddha: A Translation of the Dīgha Nikāya*, Boston, MA: Wisdom.

Wilby, E. (2005), *Cunning Folk and Familiar Spirits: Shamanistic Visionary Traditions in Early Modern British Witchcraft and Magic*, Brighton: Sussex Academic Press.

6

Emic Perspectives on the Transubstantiation of Words in Tibetan-Script Textual Amulets

Valentina Punzi

Introduction: A definition of magic open to emic perspectives

Magic is a contested category in its theoretical definitions as well as in its transcultural applicability to the study of a variety of phenomena across the world from ancient times to today. With the long history of its use in anthropological discourse as well as in textual studies, it has been scrutinized from distinct analytical angles. Starting with the theoretical formulations of cultural evolutionism in the late nineteenth century, magic has been continuously subjected to translating, reframing, and interpreting.[1] However, while the meaning and the role of both ancient and contemporary "magic practices" remain extensively debated in academic writing, the emic meta-level reflections of those undertaking them—usually specialized members of the community acting within a ritual context—still remain largely overshadowed, when not altogether substituted, by the use of scholarly jargon and etic theorizing.

How can emic perspectives enter into dialogue with the prevailingly Western-led ethnocentric effort to enhance a cross-cultural theoretical understanding of magic? In the introduction to *The Anthropology of Magic*, Susan Greenwood describes her double path toward the acquisition of knowledge "as a practitioner of magic as well as an anthropologist" (Greenwood 2009: 1). This simultaneous insider–outsider perspective lays the ground for a transformative personal experience, which enables the author to reconceptualize magic as "an analytical category as well as a valuable source of knowledge" (ibid.). However, while this statement highlights the position of an academically trained practitioner of magic, the self-reflexive voices of the majority of magic practitioners often don't afford the same prominence in the ethnographic accounts concerning their practices but remain constrained within the outsiders' interpretative frameworks. In contrast to this approach, a vision of magic from within opens up the opportunity to understand magic phenomena in the terms of those who practice it and thus helps us reflect upon what makes magic an enduring way of being in the world for certain individuals and communities. Similar to academically trained researchers, magic practitioners master a body of specialized knowledge while also consciously reflecting on it. By being in direct conversation with contemporary practitioners and including their "insider" perspectives, not only the emic understandings and deployments of magic gain visibility, but a more respectful approach that is inclined toward epistemological openness can also emerge. Even without undertaking the arduous path to become a practitioner of magic, we should aim to contribute to building a "bridge of communication" (Greenwood 2013: 200) between academic communities and the ritual specialists whose magic practices we declare to study. By drawing on indigenous notions and conceptualizations of magic, we can elaborate more solid cross-cultural interpretations, thus creating a circular process of signification that echoes back and forth between emic and etic (Frankfurter 2019: 6). This is a necessary step toward forming a cross-cultural theorization of magic phenomena, which can only take shape after concepts of magic, for example, agents, objects, and performances, are situated into the respective historical and geographic coordinates of their emergence.

The study of magic in Tibetan Studies

In contemporary Tibetan Studies, valuing magic as an analytical category, and specifically taking an emic approach to it, is at once a challenging and rewarding task.

First, there is a general resistance to qualify certain cultural and religious phenomena that take place in Tibetan communities as pertaining to magic. The limited interest for the study of magic in Tibetan Buddhism overall rests upon a unidimensional and negative understanding of the concept. Based on a hierarchical approach between religion and magic—according to which, magic is a set of unorganized primitive practices—Buddhism in general has been portrayed and studied as a rational religion. Accordingly, the "magic components" in the lived experience of Buddhism are considered the surviving traces of pre-Buddhist beliefs and practices.[2] On the one hand, the predilection for the textual-philological study of the vast corpus of Tibetan Buddhist canonical scriptures and philosophical traditions further consolidated such an approach and didn't favor the development of a research interest toward the more mundane goals that magic and its practitioners aim to accomplish. On the other hand, the later emerging body of ethnography-based studies has acknowledged the presence of magic practices, but rarely engaged with the content of Buddhist texts (van Schaik 2020: 5). Second, the debate on magic that evolved both in Anthropology and Religious Studies has resulted in a pluralized understanding of the category, which so far has only been limitedly reflected in the study of Tibetan Buddhism.[3] Finally, by rejecting magic and what is perceived as its embarrassing reputation vis-à-vis religion, the scholarly community secures distance from a mystified image of Tibet, which was first fueled by Western travelers and explorers in the late nineteenth century and continues to be nurtured in popular culture through different new age–blended versions (Lopez [1998] 2018). The above circumstances concurred to deprive magic of the opportunity to be taken seriously in Tibetan Studies.[4]

Most recently, however, Sam van Schaik argued for the utility of applying the transcultural analytical lens of magic to the textual study of a Tibetan Buddhist book of spells. Found in Dunhuang and dating back more than one thousand years, the book covers a variety of magic ritual usages from healing humans and animals to weather control, from fertility to fortune-telling. While recognizing the challenges and limitations of any attempt to establish a "grand theory of magic," van Schaik proposed to look for the shared characteristics of different traditions that are labeled as magic, which in Wittgensteinian terms constitute a field of family resemblance (van Schaik 2020: 40–1). This is an approach worth exploring that echoes the pursuit of "patterns of magicity" (Otto and Stausberg 2013). The latter is described by the authors as a "way to deal with cross-culturally attested observations," which helps to achieve a more nuanced and yet systematic comparison of phenomena without evoking the generic macro-category of magic (ibid.: 10–11). By exposing the Western ethnocentrism that so far has underpinned the proliferation of unreflexive definitions of magic, both van Schaik's and Otto and Stausberg's non-essentialist approaches contribute to the development of an emically sensitive ethnographic documentation of "magic practices." In what follows, I apply this approach to the crafting of Tibetan textual amulets.

Tibetan textual amulets

Made of different materials and usually worn around the neck or carried on the body, amulets have been pervasively used across time by people of different social statuses and economic backgrounds to address a variety of needs. While the particular functions assigned to amulets differ across traditions and cultural contexts, their shared main purpose is to guard against evil interferences with one's life while seeking protection through the ownership of a tangible object. The crafting of amulets is often undertaken by ritual specialists that may act at the margins of orthodoxy, though operating in a ritualized context with a recognizable spatial and temporal framework. In outlining the characteristics of amulet-lore, Kotansky identifies three types of amulets: unlettered, semi-lettered, and lettered (Kotansky 2019: 508–9). The first type involves the exclusive use of natural substances of mineral, herbal, and animal origin, which are associated with magical properties or are deployed in specific ritual actions with the purpose to make them acquire special powers. The second and third types both include the more or less extensive use of text and iconographic symbols, which together are entrusted to make the amulet work. While this distinction is useful, "lettered" may be a misleading label, if taken with the implication that the amulet maker must possess a certain degree of literacy. As we shall see in the second ethnographic case presented below, this does not consistently apply to Tibetan-script amulet-lore, since the text that constitutes the amulet can be also reproduced by someone who is not literate in Tibetan. Therefore, to avoid an automatic implicit connection between literacy and lettered amulets, I prefer to define "textual amulets" as those amulets whose content and efficacy are primarily defined by the use of writing—broadly understood as the combination of graphic signs that may or may not retain their semantic significance—in possible combination with other material substances.

The simplest type of textual amulets can be realized by writing short texts on small pieces of paper. This is a widespread practice in the Mediterranean area in Jewish, Christian, and Islamic traditions as well as in East Asia in Daoist and Buddhist contexts, due to its characteristic of producing objects that are "relatively inexpensive, lightweight, portable and concealable and even disposable" (Skemer 2006: 1). Tibetan textual amulets are crafted on the basis of textual instructions that prescribe what material substances should be prepared and what text and drawings should be reproduced on paper, either by hand-drawing or using carved wooden printing blocks. While the latter is usually well preserved thanks to the durability of the material, the amulets themselves, made of paper and wrapped in cloth, tend to last much shorter. In addition, once amulets deteriorate materially, owners don't have a particular interest in keeping them. In the introduction to a recently published article about a collection of

Bonpo texts for the production of amulets, Charles Ramble recalls that since the first systematic study on the functions and material aspects of Tibetan amulets included in the *Tibetan Tantric Charms and Amulets* authored by Nik Douglas in 1978, the majority of publications focused on the block-printed reproductions of amulets (Ramble 2023). Conversely, Ramble presents the interesting case of the realization of a hand-copied amulet that he observed in a Bonpo community in Dolpo in 2018 and notices it to be an unusual practice compared to the more widespread use of block prints (ibid.).

In what follows, I present and discuss two ethnographic cases related to the crafting of Tibetan textual amulets that didn't involve the use of a wooden matrix. The first case study is based on my fieldwork in 2014 in eastern Qinghai Province (PRC), where I observed the making of an amulet based on the instructions contained in a Tibetan text printed in a book in a modern layout. The second case study is based on my fieldwork in 2018 in a Baima community in western Sichuan Province (PRC), where I witnessed the hand-copied preparation of a Tibetan-script amulet based on an older undated color-scanned copy. In both cases, the efficacy of the amulet was primarily tied to the ritual specialists' personal authority, who operated in their domestic space, unsanctioned by any religious establishment, and only partially based their actions on the textual instructions at their disposal. The material crafting of the amulet and its transformation into a magical device was shaped by the combined use of words and substances, which were not treated as belonging to segregated fields, but were rather put in communication with each other by the actions of the ritual specialists. While the two ethnographic contexts apparently bear little resemblance to each other, the comparison between the two ritual specialists' self-explanatory discourses of their choices and actions regarding the making of amulets sheds light on the nexus of authority–words–materiality that makes Tibetan amulets part of a transcultural phenomenon.

First ethnographic case: Aku Ta and a textual amulet for the protection of the livestock

Aku Ta (?–2017) spent most of his life as a monk in the Dge lugs pa monastery of Banshul, located in the border area between Mangra (Chinese: Guinan) and Rtsekhog (Chinese: Zeku) Tibetan autonomous counties in Qinghai Province (southeast Amdo). During the Cultural Revolution (1966–1976), he renounced his vows and got married, but returned to the Banshul monastery in the 1980s, where he stayed until the early 2010s. Between 2012 and 2014, I paid four visits to him at his home built at the feet of the Amye Drakar mountain, where his relatives took care of him as he had become too old to live in the monastery. Aku Ta was well-known in the area for his knowledge of local history as well as for his skills in crafting protection amulets and preparing offerings to different classes of beings.[5] He was also an expert collector of medical herbs and plants and an amateur painter of mountain deities. On one occasion, I brought with me a text containing instructions about the preparation of an amulet for protecting the livestock, with the hope that Aku Ta would agree to make an amulet based on it.

The text is titled "*Daki'i snyan brgyud zab mo las phyugs nas srung ba'i 'khor lo zab mo god kha gcod pa'i man ngag*" ("Instructions from the profound transmission of the *ḍākinī* for preventing the loss of livestock by means of the profound circle that protects from livestock diseases"). It is part of a group of five short texts that feature amulets as part of the tool kit of veterinary remedies to be prepared and utilized for the specific purpose of protecting the livestock.[6] These texts are published in a book titled "*Slob dpon pad 'byung gi sman yig gcen btus*" ("Collection of medical instructions from Guru Padmasambhava"), edited by the Qinghai Tibetan Medicine Research Center and republished in 2013 in modern layout after the first publication in 2006 by the Minzu Publishing House in Beijing (Mtsho sngon shing chen bod kyi gso rig zhib 'jug khang 2013). As the title indicates, the book is attributed to Guru Padmasambhava and includes textual instructions accompanied by mantra and drawings for the prevention, diagnosis, and treatment of different medical conditions.

After holding the text in its photocopied form, Aku Ta complained about his poor eyesight and handed it back to me to read it out loud. My attempt to read it in my hesitant Amdo Tibetan was however quite unsuccessful, prompting him to read it instead by himself wearing glasses.

The text opens with an invocation to the "*ḍākinī* that subdues the demons" (*bdud 'dul mkha' 'dro*). In the first lines it clearly states that "when seeking protection from respiratory diseases and all kinds of other diseases, there are two remedies: wheels (*'khor lo*)[7] and substances (*rdzas*)" (*phyugs nad glo gor tal ba sogs nad rigs mtha' dag srung ba'i skabs ni/ 'di la gnyis te 'khor lo dang rdzas*). It then provides detailed indications about the drawing of concentric wheels and the syllables to write within the respective inside and outside rims:

> At the center, make a round wheel and exactly in the middle of it write: GA BRA TSHWA GRA DRI. At the margins of it, bearing in mind OM SARBA SA TU RBAD HA RI NI SA HUM PHAGS, write: four lion-faced dakini protect cattle,

horses, and sheep from contagious and infectious diseases, rinderpest, smallpox, and all kinds of wolf injuries! RAKASHA. Beyond this wheel, write in the four spokes: OM DHAR SENG YE RBAD SAHA Protect! In the four intermediate spokes, write: OM NIR SENG YE RBAD BHYO Reverse! In the wheel beyond that, write: OM SA TU RBAD RBAD CHOD CHOD DZA DZI ZHI RBAD BHYO Reverse! Write it until the wheel is completely filled up. Beyond that, draw two circles. In the inner one, write: A LI KA LI YE DHA MA. In the outer one draw a *vajra* and fire mountains. In this way, there will be one male and one female wheels. For the male wheel, the letterheads should face the outside of a wheel with spokes; for the female wheel, the letterheads should face the inside of a four-petal lotus. At the center of these two, after smearing the back with the substance, apply it and place it on the altar in front.

The text then offers further instructions about the offerings to be made and the empowerment of the amulet:

Meditate in front of the dakini, offer white torma to the owners of the ground (*gzhi bdag*) and ask for clearing any sort of sickness that affects domestic animals. In front of the five groups of dakini represented in *yab-yum* union; underneath put the syllables OM SA RU RBAD CHOD DZA DZA ZHI RBAD BHYO ZLOG and attend for one week. After preparing the substances and the blessed water, it will sever the diseases. About extinguishing with a session of destructive actions: after a pure girl who looks like a deer at the water spring and prostrates three times, collect three little stones. Cover it with the wheel and put it on the cattle. Then, think about the empowerment and the blessing from the seven white deities that guard the wealth.

This first part concludes with the confident statement that "there is no doubt that this will work" (*des thub par the tshom med*). The second part of the text introduces the list of substances to be prepared. While the purpose is to restore the health of domestic animals, the elements required for preparing the amulet include a number of substances of wild animals' origin. The complete list includes: human flesh (*sha chen*), bear flesh (*sre mo'i sha*), steppe polecat flesh (*te lo'i sha*), deer flesh (*sha ba'i sha*), vulture flesh (*bya rgod sha*), tiger flesh (*stag gi sha*),[8] fennel (*shing kun*), musk (*gla rtsi*), white garlic (*sgog skya*), frankincense (*gu gul*), saussurea (*ru rta*), and wild aconite (*bong nga*).[9]

After having made these twelve substances into powder or pills (*phye ma'am ril bu byas*), utter the mantra above or alternatively the mantra: 'A GA SA MA RA TSA SHA DA RA SA MA RA YA PHATA/ OM NIR SING YE RBAD BHYO. Recite all the mantras for protection and meditation and place them into the various substances (*rdzas dud sna la bdug*). After preparing water blessed with mantras, it will accomplish (*sngags chu byas pas thab par 'gyur ro*) [the result].

The last part of the text is titled "instructions for interrupting the loss of any cattle and horse" (*rta phyugs gang yin god kha gcod pa'i gdams pa*). It starts with the instructions: "after separating the flesh from the bone of the head of a cow or a horse, draw a crossed vajra on the skull. Draw in the same way a sequence of them in the four intermediate directions." A long list of mantras to recite for different classes of beings follows. The text concludes with the statement: "there is no doubt that the loss of horses, cattle, and sheep will stop" (*rta phyugs gnag lug sogs god kha chod par the tshom med*).

Upon hearing the conclusive line, I expected that Aku Ta would have started drawing the wheels and placing small quantities of the listed substances in the cloth bag that he had arranged in front of him. However, not much of what Aku Ta had just read actually happened. To my surprise, he reached out for a sheet of paper from my notebook and cut it into small squared pieces of approximately the same size. Then he copied the name of each substance (*rdzas*) from the text onto a separate piece of paper, while skipping the part concerning the drawing of wheels (*'khor lo*) altogether. Blaming his elderly age, Aku Ta explained that drawing the wheels requires a firm hand that he no longer had. Meanwhile, he maintained that the act of copying the substances' names was sufficient to make the amulet equally effective. Acknowledging the unavailability of most of the required substances, Aku Ta took *sha chen* as an example of the necessity to seek substituting elements. Pointing at my arm, he gestured cutting it with an imaginary knife before bursting into laughter. My perplexed reaction triggered his explanation that the prescribed use of human flesh should not be taken literally, adding that the same was true for the other substances since he didn't have them.

As Aku Ta was inserting the papers into the cloth bag, our conversation further explored the topic of efficacy. How many amulets were needed to protect an entire herd of yaks? How long does it take to prepare and bless tens or even hundreds of amulets? My questions were to find an unexpected answer. The amulet in fact works like a metonymy: once one amulet is put around the neck of a single animal in the herd, it will be effective for the protection of all. To further explain, Aku Ta emphasized that this practice conveniently reduced the time and resources to be committed without compromising the amulet's efficacy. After the material preparation of the amulet was completed, I was told that its blessing and empowerment needed to take place at a different time and be carried out by him alone.

A last reflection should be made about the response of Aku Ta, a Dge lugs pa monk, to the text I had brought to him—a Rnying ma text directly attributed to Guru Padmasambhava. Although Aku Ta immediately recognized it as belonging to the Rnying ma tradition, he declared to be familiar with both its structure and content and didn't hesitate to follow the instructions for the amulet's preparation. This nonsectarian attitude testifies to the fact that the practice of amulet-making is both widespread and untethered to a specific monastery or lineage of transmission. Ritual specialists like Aku Ta might be comfortable with using texts different from their own tradition due to the high degree of similarities.

Second ethnographic case: Cidanji and an amulet for the protection of the household

Cidanji (1992–) is a ritual specialist who lives in a Baima village in northwest Sichuan Province (PRC). The Baima community numbers about ten thousand and is officially classified as part of the Chinese state-endorsed Tibetan nationality (Chinese: *zang zu*). Despite this official classification, the Baima people consider themselves to be an ethnic group of their own. From a linguistic point of view, no variant of oral Tibetan is intelligible to Baima, while written Tibetan does not have any currency in daily life. However, Baima ritual specialists (*bembo*) own a corpus of Tibetan scriptures that are read and chanted in the course of apotropaic, good fortune, healing, and other ritual ceremonies. While these texts are largely memorized during the apprenticeship and used as a trigger to remember the sequence of ritual actions that accompany the recitation, Baima ritual specialists' competence in written Tibetan is limited to the reading ability that excludes any semantic processing.

Like many young people who grew up in rural China during the 1990s without receiving high education, Cidanji left his village after middle school and ventured into the wage-paid job market in the fast-developing cities of Eastern China. After having stayed in Mianyang, Chengdu, and Beijing for several years working as a glass factory worker, a cook, a karaoke singer, and a hairdresser, he returned to his home village. Thanks to the financial support of his family, he undertook three years of apprenticeship under a master who is presently recognized as a bearer of intangible cultural heritage for Baima religion and customs. In Cidanji's words, this decision was motivated by his desire to follow the footsteps of his father and paternal grandfather, who were both well-known ritual specialists in the Baima community during their lifetime. At the time of our meeting, Cindanji had already completed his training and was himself mentoring two younger apprentices. While continuing to perform rituals for the community, he was also getting increasingly involved in the provincial government-led efforts to promote Baima culture to the tourism market. This double interest conflates into the self-perception of Cidanji, who sees his role as not only a "traditional" ritual specialist but also a "community representative" responsible for the preservation of Baima culture.

During my six months of fieldwork in 2018, I witnessed the preparation of an amulet for ensuring the protection of a household whose members repeatedly fell sick. According to Cidanji, the reason for the sickness was ascribed to two classes of beings. In the evening before visiting the family, Cidanji prepared two different amulets at his home. Although Tibetan texts are recited during ritual performances, to my knowledge no textual instruction is available for preparing amulets or other complex ritual objects commonly crafted by Baima ritual specialists with paper-cut and wood carving techniques. Therefore, to make the amulets Cidanji had to rely on his memory and previous experience, in addition to the visual aid of a color-scanned copy from an older original amulet that used to be part of his grandfather's manual (Figure 6.1). Using a compass and colored pens, he drew a structure of concentric circles within which he copied Tibetan syllables (Figure 6.2).

When asked about the meaning of the Tibetan text that he had just copied, Cidanji simply replied that he didn't know it and that, although he was curious about it, there was no Baima ritual specialist whom he could turn to. He had plans for a long stay in the neighboring Tibetan area in Songpan county to study Tibetan scriptures, but so far didn't have the opportunity to do so. He emphasized that the ability to read Tibetan was sufficient for the purpose of the rituals he performs, while deepening his knowledge of Tibetan was mostly his own initiative.

Once the amulets were ready, Cidanji placed them in the car boot together with the drum and the manual for recitation to be used the next day. The ritual for the empowerment of the amulet took place in the house of the client, who was the oldest female member of the family. After we parked the car in the courtyard in front of her house, she walked out and introduced herself as Liu, her family name. We followed her inside, where she had already prepared a pot of boiled water and some juniper branches. As Cindanji sat down near the stove, he placed the amulets in a flat open basket and sprinkled some seeds over them

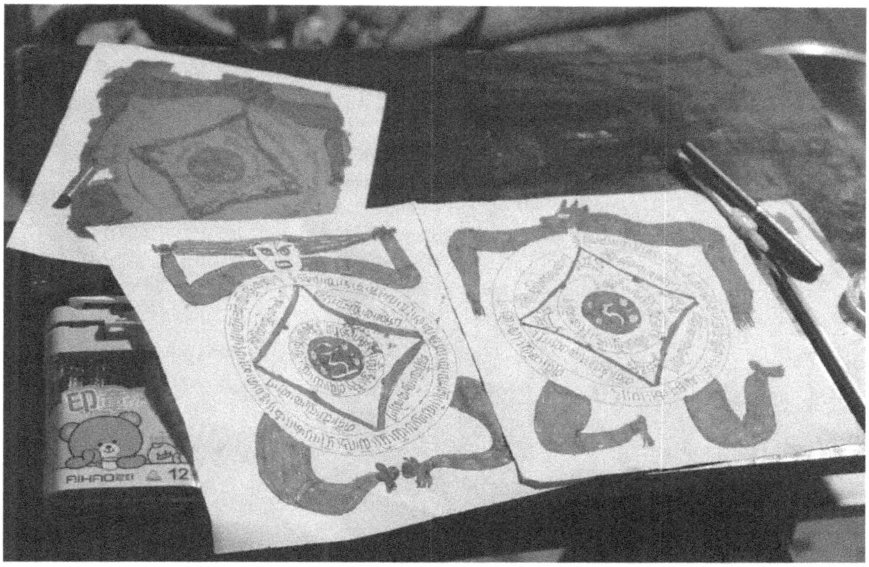

Figure 6.1 The color-scanned copy used by Cidanji to make the two amulets. Photo by the author.

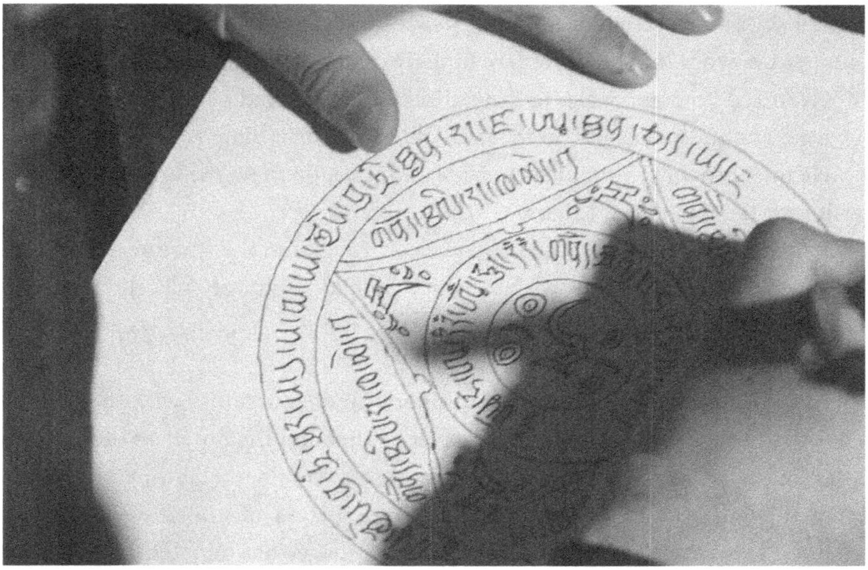

Figure 6.2 Cidanji drawing the wheels of the amulet. Photo by the author.

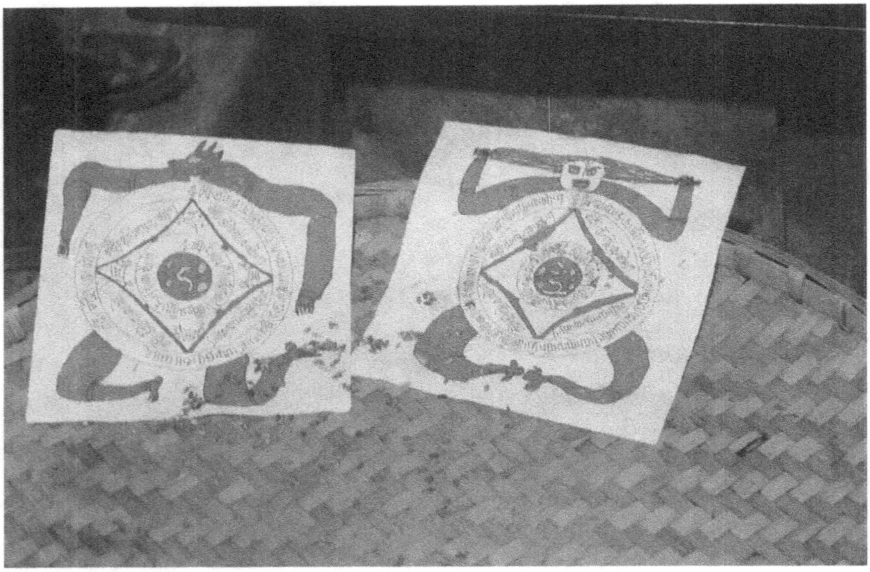

Figure 6.3 The two amulets placed in the basket. Photo by the author.

(Figure 6.3). He then prepared a bowl full of toasted grain, a bowl containing five boiled eggs, a bowl containing sunflower seeds, walnuts, and peanuts, and some juniper branches that he lighted up directly on the stove (Figure 6.4).

He mixed flour and water in a metal ladle and prepared a sticky dough, which he used as glue and spread on the back of the amulets (Figures 6.5 and 6.6).

He then brought the amulets outside and stuck them on the upper part of the wall near the main door (Figure 6.7).

Returning inside, he cracked and peeled the eggs on the stove and had them arranged into a separate bowl into which he had previously placed fermented barley (Figure 6.8). He then inserted small juniper branches on the top of each egg.

After bringing the still-burning juniper branches together with the bowl of eggs to the backyard of the house, he placed them on the top of an improvised altar made of a rusty tall tank (Figure 6.9). While the juniper branches were turning into ashes together with some pieces of boiled eggs, Cidanji chanted for about ten minutes in Baima language that he later explained to be "auspicious words" (Chinese: *jixiang ci*) to accompany the offerings for the beings that had caused sickness to the Liu family. During the entire time when Cidanji was performing these actions, Ms. Liu had silently observed and followed him.

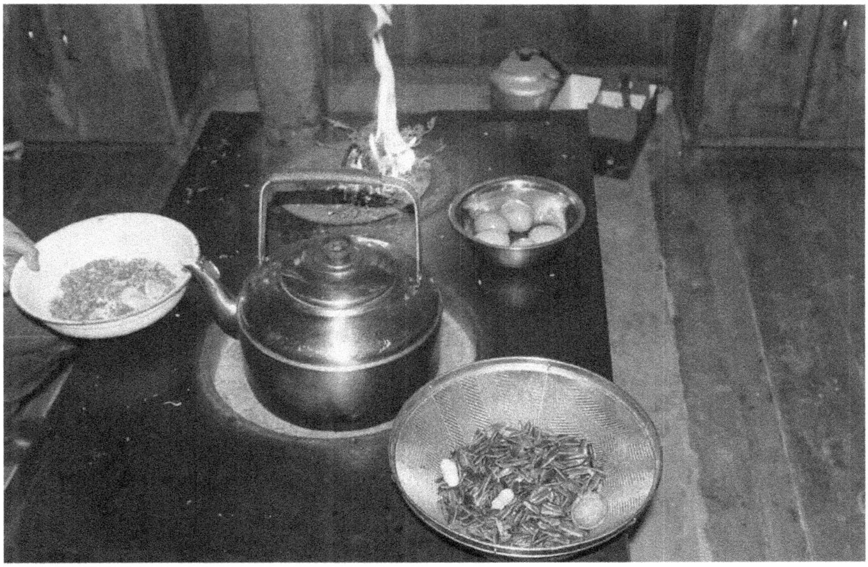

Figure 6.4 The materials prepared for the ritual. Photo by the author.

Figure 6.5 The glue made of flour and water. Photo by the author.

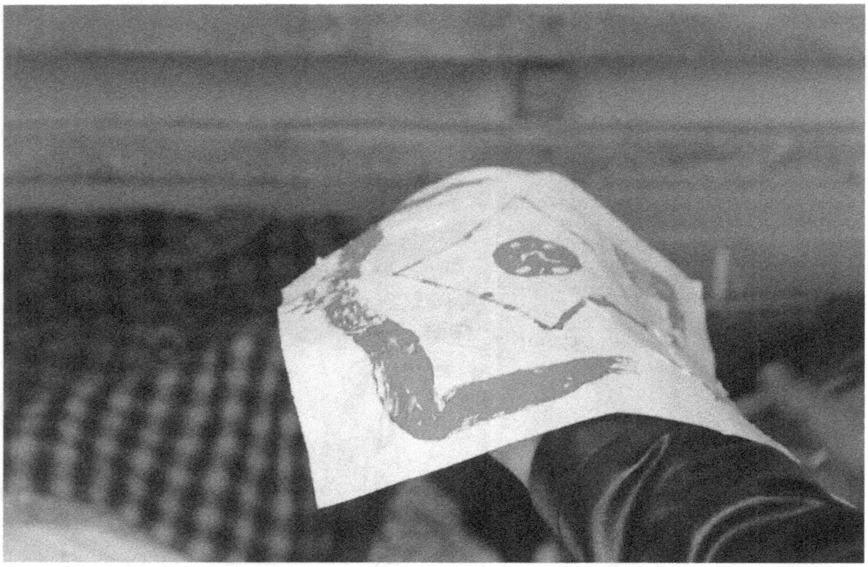

Figure 6.6 The amulet is spread with glue. Photo by the author.

Figure 6.7 The amulet stuck on the wall. Photo by the author.

Figure 6.8 The eggs prepared for burning. Photo by the author.

Figure 6.9 The eggs are burnt with the juniper branches in the backyard. Photo by the author.

When Cidanji went back inside and sat near the stove again, Ms. Liu finally spoke and offered him some tea and toasted sunflower seeds. With the general atmosphere relaxing, Ms. Liu asked Cidanji if the boiled eggs would be as good as a chicken for the purpose of the offering. She then apologized for not having been able to provide a chicken and explained that she couldn't afford it before selling her cabbages, something that would not have happened until a week later. However, since the divinatory calculation performed by Cindanji had indicated that very day was the most suitable one for preparing the amulets, she had given up the idea of the chicken and provided the eggs instead. Cidanji reassured Ms. Liu that he had made the eggs just as appropriate as the chicken by placing the juniper branch on top of each of them, thus making them resemble the mountains covered in forest that surround the Baima village.

After entering the car, I asked Cidanji why he had left the drum and the ritual manual in the car boot, two key objects in all the Baima rituals that I had observed until then. Cidanji replied that he learnt by heart the main "auspicious words" in Baima language to chant and that those were more important than the written text. Regarding the drum, he didn't set it up because it would have taken too long to prepare the poles' structure to hang it. After the ritual, he had to rush back to the county seat where he had some other business to attend to.

Magic as a semiotic domain with a design grammar to master

While the descriptions of my ethnographic encounters with Aku Ta and Cidanji might appear anecdotical, they provide a glimpse into the creative strategies implemented by the ritual specialists to cope with the contingent circumstances of their practice. With regard to my use of the appellative "ritual specialist," it is important to clarify that during our conversations neither Aku Ta nor Cidanji self-identified as such. Aku Ta simply introduced himself as a monk, whereas Cidanji introduced himself as a *bembo*, adding that he belonged to a family of *fashi*, a Chinese honorific title that is translatable as 'master' with reference to someone who is credited with great accomplishment in a religious, usually Buddhist, tradition. The term, however, is also commonly used in Chinese scholarship to describe the main actors of a broad range of ritual traditions that don't pertain to any specific orthodox religions, but go under the broad category of *minjian zongjiao* (folk religion). Nevertheless, I find ritual specialists an adequate appellative to value the expertise of Aku Ta and Cidanji in a field of knowledge. In these two cases, the choices and actions are in fact legitimized by a body of knowledge and a set of practical skills that together shape a semiotic domain. Gee (2008: 137) defines a semiotic domain as "any set of practices that recruits one or more modalities (e.g., oral or written language, images, equations, symbols, sounds, gestures, graphs, artifacts, etc.) to communicate distinctive types of meanings." To make a competent use of the semiotic domain of magic, a ritual specialist needs to master its design grammar, which in Gee's definition is "a set of principles or patterns in terms of which materials in the domain are combined to communicate complex meanings" (ibid.: 138). Such meanings, though not directly accessible, are intelligible to the community wherein the ritual specialist operates. To highlight that the cultural referents within a certain semiotic domain are shared by the specialist and the community, Gee calls the community an "affinity group" (ibid.: 138). In the context of ritualized magic, the affinity group is familiar with and recognizes certain activities as ritual magical actions, in spite of not mastering them in practice. In other words, while the affinity group owns the cultural framework to evaluate the aesthetics of the practice, its design grammar is only mastered by a few—the ritual specialists who use the resources and the knowledge at their disposal to accomplish the purpose of magic practice.

The content and the coherence of the semiotic domain of magic are not just maintained but actively (re)created by individuals through their personal entry point into an existing tradition. Once the ritual specialist masters the rules of the design grammar, he can manipulate and alter them according to his needs and external circumstances. However, within the domain, meanings and their possible combinations are limited by what is materially and culturally available. In addition, the ritual specialist cannot go completely free about his practice, but needs to confine himself within the shared sense of acceptability and familiarity with the lore of ritual actions. The exclusive access to magic by the ritual specialist depends on the recognition of his special qualification and status by the affinity group. The latter is expressed as "a way of acting, interacting, believing, valuing, and using signs, symbols, objects, and technologies so as to enact a particular socially recognizable identity as 'a certain type of person' doing 'a certain type of thing' (ibid.: 147). In this way, the efficacy of magic practice is generated through the relationship between the ritual specialist and the affinity group. This setup is the source of legitimacy for performing magic and making it effective. On the one hand, the affinity group recognizes the authority of the ritual specialist as long as he confirms the mastery of the domain through his practices. On the other hand, it is in the interest of the group to recognize the authority of the ritual specialist and the specialized knowledge associated with it because the efficacy of the practice is ultimately predicated on such acts of trust and recognition.

The reflections of Aku Ta and Cidanji highlight some aspects of their meta-level thinking that allow them to mobilize, discard, and play up a range of material and textual resources from the semiotic domain, while retaining the efficacy of the practice. In the context of making an amulet, the textual instructions are but one of the modalities used in the domain. While the text and the amulet are the two material items that are tangibly present and recognizable to the affinity group, the way to get from the text to the amulet is a journey of choices that the ritual specialist undertakes within the limits of the relevant cultural framework. By orienting himself in a multimodal design grammar, the ritual specialist needs to simultaneously master competence in reading textual instructions, manipulating material substances, writing and reciting texts.

By discussing magic as a semiotic domain, I do not intend to reduce the efficacy of magic to a matter of discursive practice, thus embracing a fully linguistic-semiotic approach that would contribute to the tendency of "pervasive logocentrism in anthropological theory" (Brown 1997: 126). I rather wish to propose a sympathetic approach that values ritual specialists' mastery of magic as a body of specialized knowledge and practical skills that effectively constitute a way to engage the world and its contingencies.

Words and substances: The process of transubstantiation

Nicolas Sihlé offered important reflections about the need for an "ethnography of the written word" (Sihlé 2010: 48), emphasizing the importance of situating the usages of ritual manuals in the ethnographic contexts where semiliterate ritual specialists operate. Ritual specialists build their legitimacy on texts, yet their practice in the specific ethnographic milieu exceeds them. These two case studies show that the use of text in the crafting process of amulets is situated at the juncture between informative and performative. Sam Gill qualified the use of texts in amulets that are crafted by semiliterate experts as performative in opposition to informative (Gill 1985). This is indeed evident in the approach taken by Cidanji to the copying of the Tibetan text, which can be considered a fully performative action. In the case of Aku Ta, however, such a distinction cannot be meaningfully applied, since the text maintained its semantic value, thus providing information that the ritual specialist took into account in the practice. At the same time, both Cidanji and Aku Ta are aware that their exclusive access to the texts and the very act of writing in Tibetan confer them a solid base of authority in performing the rituals. In both cases, amulets, in fact, gain efficacy not directly from the texts themselves but from the authoritative use of them, thus combining textual and personal authority.

In the practice of both Aku Ta and Cidanji, words synergically work with substances for achieving efficacy: incomprehensible words, that is, mantra syllables, and unusual material substances, that is, human flesh, signal a space–time framework, which is distinct from the course of ordinary life and is the precondition for magic actions to happen. Different specific functions appear associated with words in the two ethnographic contexts. In the case of Aku Ta, there are three distinct types of written words. First, the words of the text that Aku Ta read and followed as instructions. Second, the words designating the substances that Aku Ta copied from the text and transformed into the equivalents of the substances because the latter was not available. Copying the text itself was therefore sufficient to evoke the "power" of the items that were supposed to be present in their material form as components of the amulet. Third, the mantra syllables that the text prescribed to write into concentric wheels, which Aku Ta disregarded. In the case of Cidanji, Tibetan words were treated as powerful graphic signs that empowered the amulet without being semantically intelligible. Overall, in both cases, writing is imbued with a power that goes beyond the purpose of conveying immediate meaning.

In spite of the ephemeral character of textual amulets, as Frankfurter noted, "'magic' seems bound up with materiality in so many ways that it is worth querying the object, the thing, that so readily and vitally conveys ritual force" (2019: 661). Once gathered and empowered, different substances in fact become the material vehicles of messages for healing, protecting, and warding off (Frankfurter 2019: 664). However, the fact that textual amulets derived their efficacy from the text does not make their materiality any less relevant.

In the case studies presented, different material substances were missing in the preparation of the amulets. In the case of Aku Ta, none of the twelve substances listed in the textual instructions was used. In the case of Cidanji, the chicken that is usually slaughtered during Baima rituals for protection was not prepared. However, a substitution was employed in both cases. In the case of Aku Ta, even without any material substance being directly involved, once words were written down, they became themselves tangible materials and were treated as such. In the case of Cidanji, eggs were used as stand-in for the chicken. Both ritual specialists acted out of pragmatic considerations, yet to better understand their choices we need to take a step further.

Susan Greenwood pointedly argues that it is possible to counter the limits of Western analytical and causal logic by embracing participation as a cognitive approach that allows one to "entertain the possibilities of flexible, transient, and transformatory boundaries between things" (Greenwood 2009: 39). Such flexibility is also characteristic of how ritual specialists operationalize magic procedures. In the two ethnographic cases presented, the crafting of textual amulets sheds light on the flexibility of the practice, which ritual specialists acknowledged and coped in a way that didn't come at the expense of efficacy. Accordingly, rather than speaking of substitution, we may choose to participate in the transubstantiation process from substances into words-substances and from substances into other substances—which Aku Ta and Cidanji respectively operated—and recognize it as a meaning-generating process.

Substitution (*tshab*) is often practiced in Tibetan ritual and medical contexts wherein certain substances are substituted with others that are considered equally powerful and suitable for achieving the designated purpose (Czaja 2017). Such substitutions are rather standardized and based on textual prescriptions. However, in the two case studies presented, Aku Ta and Cidanji practiced something more radical than substitution, which can be defined as transubstantiation.

In the case of Aku Ta, the names of the substances written on paper were not standing for the substances listed in the *Daki'i snyan brgyud zab mo las phyugs nas srung ba'i 'khor lo zab mo god kha gcod pa'i man ngag*, but became the same as them, in spite of not exhibiting any quality that can be recognized when substitutive material substances are chosen. I am not aware whether this is a common practice undertaken by ritual specialists in Tibetan communities, but the explanation provided by Aku Ta that resorting to this choice was a matter of necessity would suggest that the act of writing the list was just one of the options to cope with the impossibility of following the textual instructions verbatim. In contrast to the standardized eucharistic transubstantiation that takes place in the institutionalized framework of the Catholic church, the transubstantiation operated by Aku Ta was one of the possibilities available to him in the semiotic domain. What suited Aku Ta well in this case might be different if another ritual specialist was acting. While the repertoire of options shares similar features, the individual choices can vary. In the case of Cidanji, Ms. Liu prepared eggs instead of a chicken for the purpose of the ritual out of financial considerations. This substitution, however, was not casually proposed, but acknowledged both by Ms. Liu and Cidanji as an acceptable solution to cope with material scarcity. Based on this shared recognition of the value of the offering, a process of transubstantiation took place. The ritual procedures carried out indoors and outdoors in fact involved the same actions that Cidanji would have performed with a chicken: fumigation, boiling, cutting, arranging into bowls, and burning.

By handling different materials and relying on different methods, in both cases the ritual specialists turned the amulet into an effective means of protection thanks to their authority. In spite of the apparent rigidity of the prescriptions that should have been closely followed in order to ensure efficacy, crafting the amulets was a process of adaptive open-ended semiosis in which the agency of the ritual specialist played a key role in determining what actions were legitimate and conducive to attain the desired outcome. Though starting from a recognizable framework, the process of signification, in fact, took place in the very moment and place where the transubstantiation occurred. While certain patterns make magic recognizable, its actual practice is a one-time event that is temporally and spatially situated and, therefore, unique. The availability of substances, the reading competence of the text, the time constraints, as well as the personal inclinations and interpretations play a fundamental role in the practice of magic. These contingent aspects become evident when engaging the ritual specialists' emic views on their practices and especially their meta-analytical reflections.

Conclusion

The avoidance of "magic" in scholarly works related to Tibetan culture can be overcome by focusing on specific phenomena, such as the crafting of objects, the undertaking of individual and collective actions of learned magic as well as small-scale rituals that are carried out by nonspecialists.

The two ethnographic cases disclose emic perspectives on the ways in which Tibetan words and texts are expected to activate the magic of amulets, which further shed light on how magic works in the context of the two different communities. While in the first case the ritual specialist closely read and interpreted the textual instructions for the purpose of preparing the amulet, in the second case the ritual specialist simply copied the drawings and the words that compose the textual amulet from an existing scanned color copy. The choices that Aku Ta and Cidanji made display self-scrutiny of one's practice in order to ensure efficacy.

Behind the choice of not embracing emic perspectives lays the fear of becoming too rooted in a specific historical and geographic context where a certain tradition of magic was formed, which—almost paradoxically—would reiterate an ethnocentric perspective that considers only Others' beliefs and practices as "magic" (Lehrich 2013). In addition, such a deep-rootedness would undermine the possibility to elaborate etic theorizing and further prevent the identification of patterns that are necessary to generate a cross-cultural definition of magic. Therefore, an emic-based theory, at least the way it is commonly reproduced in the academic venue, would lack the abstract quality that a theory is expected to display. However, it is only through the in-depth documentation and analysis of specific magical phenomena that we can obtain qualitatively and quantitatively significant data to be put in a comparative perspective and further concur to an advancement in theorizing magic. In order to do so, ritual specialists, the contexts wherein they acquire knowledge, their relations with the communities wherein they operate, the choices available to them, and their meta-level reflections need to be taken seriously.

A last note. Of course, my own position as a young female Western researcher has affected the answers of my interlocutors in ways and to an extent that I will never be fully aware of. One may wonder how the way I posed questions and reacted to the answers shaped the direction and the content of my conversations with Aku Ta and Cidanji. However, a skeptical approach that questions the sincerity of any verbal interaction in the fieldwork setting would enter a blind alley of doubts, thus undermining the basic trust and sympathy that seeking the emic understanding of magic requires. After all, if omitting information, lying, or making up stories occur with the aim of meeting or disattending the researcher's expectations, they are but the verbal manifestations of the ritual specialist's right to choose what message to convey and how, just like in any other act of human communication.

Notes

1 An updated survey of the literature from the classical works to the most recent approaches to magic is offered in Otto and Stausberg (2013).

2 The relationship between magic and religion has been much debated. The debate tends to be polarized between those arguing for extreme difference and those arguing for a continuum.

3 With the exception of Geoffrey Samuel's book *Civilized Shamans*, the general categories of "shamanism" and "shamans," admittedly already controversial in themselves, equally struggle to be applied in the context of Tibetan Studies. For an overview of the topic, see Kvaerne (2009: 19–24).

4 For an extensive discussion about the misfortune of magic in Tibetan and Buddhist Studies, see the introduction in van Schaik (2020).

5 In 2013 I witnessed the preparation of tens of palm-sized handsewn bags made of white cloth and later decorated with the eight auspicious symbols painted in red ink. Aku Ta put small quantities of resins, precious metals, and fragrant woods into each bag that he later brought to Tsho dmar "Red Lake" and let sink into the water as an offering to the resident *klu* beings.

6 The use of amulets is in fact not limited to the protection of humans, but extends to the protection of animals. Textual instructions concerning the preparation of amulets to ensure the protection of the livestock are widely available in different traditions of Tibetan Bon and Buddhism (Ramble 2023).

7 For the use of *'khor lo*, or yantra, see Brown's and Wenta's chapters in this volume. For a detailed study of *yantra*s in Buddhism, see Bühnemann (2003) and Kuranishi (2013: 265–81).

8 *Stag gi sha* could be also *stag sha* or *locoweed.* This plant belongs to the genus of *Oxytropis* in the family of Fabaceae or Leguminosae. According to Dga' ba rdo rje (1995: 211–12), there are two plants subsumed under this name: (1) *Oxytropis reniformis* and (2) *Oxytropis microphylla.* These plants are also known under the name *sha rgyal dar ya kan* or "theriac king of meat." I thank Carmen Simioli for providing me with the information reported in this and the following footnote and for her generous help with the identification of the substances.

9 *Bo nga* can refer to one of the four categories of aconite enumerated in Tibetan pharmacopoeia: white aconite (*bong nga dkar po*) or *Aconitum tanguticum*; black aconite (*bong nga nag po*) or *Aconitum richardsonianum*, identified also with *ra dug* or *Aconitum polyanthum*; yellow aconite (*bong nga ser po*) or *Aconitum kongboense*; and red aconite (*bong nga dmar po*) or *Pedicularis trichoglossa*. Black aconite is also called *btsan dug*. See Byams pa 'phrin las et al. (2006: 526).

References

Brown, M. F. (1997), "Thinking about Magic," in S. D. Glazier (ed.), *Anthropology of Religion. A Handbook*, 121–38, Westport, CT: Greenwood Press.

Bühnemann, G. (ed.) (2003), *Maṇḍalas and Yantras in the Hindu Traditions*, Delhi: D.K. Printworld.

Byams pa 'phrin las and Tshe brtan 'jigs med (2006), *Bod lugs gso rig tshig mdzo chen mo*, Beijing: Mi rigs dpe skrung khang.

Czaja, O. (2017), "The Substitution of *Materia Medica* in Tibetan Medicine: An Inquiry into Traditional Tibetan Treatises," *East Asian Science, Technology, and Medicine* 46: 119–212.

Dga' ba rdo rje (1995), *'Khrungs dpe dri med shel gyi me long*, Beijing: Mi rigs dpe skrung khang.

Douglas, N. (1978), *Tibetan Tantric Charms and Amulets*, New York: Dover.

Frankfurter, D. (2019), "Magic and the Forces of Materiality," in D. Frankfurter (ed.), *Guide to the Study of Ancient Magic*, 659–77, Leiden: Brill.

Gee, J. P. (2008), "Learning in Semiotic Domains: A Social and Situated Account," in M. Prinsloo and M. Baynham (eds.), *Literacies. Global and Local*, 137–50, Amsterdam: John Benjamins.

Greenwood, S. (2009), *The Anthropology of Magic*, Oxford: Berg.

Greenwood, S. (2013), "Magical Consciousness: A Legitimate Form of Knowledge," in B.-C. Otto and M. Stausberg (eds.), *Defining Magic: A Reader*, 197–210, London: Routledge.

Kotansky, R. D. (2019), "Textual Amulets and Writing Traditions in the Ancient World," in D. Frankfurter (ed.), *Guide to the Study of Ancient Magic*, 507–54, Leiden: Brill.

Kuranishi, K. (2013), "Yantras in the Buddhist Tantras—Yamāritantras and Related Literature," in N. Mirnig, P.-D. Szántó, and M. Williams (eds.), *Puṣpikā: Tracing Ancient India, through Texts and Traditions. Contributions to Current Research in Indology*, Volume 1: Proceedings of the First International Indology Graduate Research Symposium (September 2009, Oxford), 265–81, Oxford: Oxbow Books.

Kvaerne, P. (2009), "Bon and Shamanism," *East and West*, 59 (1–4) (2009): 19–24.

Lehrich, C. I. (2013), "Magic in Theoretical Practice," in B.-C. Otto and M. Stausberg (eds.), *Defining Magic: A Reader*, 211–28, London: Routledge.

Lopez, D. S. ([1998] 2018), *Prisoners of Shangri-la. Tibetan Buddhism and the West*, Chicago: University of Chicago Press.

Mtsho sngon shing chen bod kyi gso rig zhib 'jug khang, ed. (2013), *Slob dpon pad 'byung gi sman yig gces btus*, Beijing: Mi rigs dpe skrung khang.

Otto, B.C., and M. Stausberg (2013), "General Introduction," in B.-C. Otto and M. Stausberg (eds.), *Defining Magic: A Reader*, 1–13, London: Routledge.

Ramble, C. (2023), "Notes on a Bonpo Manual for the Production of Manuscript Amulets," in A. Helman-Ważny and C. Ramble (eds.), *Bon and Naxi Manuscripts: Essays on Form, Function and Preservation*, 61–85, Berlin: de Gruyter.

Sam, D. G. (1985), "Nonliterate Traditions and Holy Books: Toward a New Model," in F. M. Denny and R. L. Taylor (eds.), *The Holy Book in Comparative Perspective*, 224–39, Columbia: University of South Carolina Press.

Sihlé, N. (2010), "Written Texts at the Juncture of the Local and the Global. Some Anthropological Considerations on a Local Corpus of Tantric Ritual Manuals (Lower Mustang, Nepal)," in J. Ignacio Cabezón (ed.), *Tibetan Ritual*, 35–52, Oxford: Oxford University Press.

Skemer, D. C. (2006), *Binding Words. Textual Amulets in the Middle Ages*, University Park: Pennsylvania State University Press.

van Schaik, S. (2020), *Buddhist Magic. Divination, Healing, and Enchantment through the Ages*, Boulder, CO: Shambala.

7

The Magical Causality of Poison Casting and Cancer among Tibetan Communities of Gyalthang

Eric D. Mortensen

Things became increasingly complicated when Tserang began vomiting into a hedge of stinging nettles on the edge of the packed dirt yard next to the huge old house where we had just finished conversing with Lobsang Yeshe and members of his family.[1] My son Søren, age ten at the time, was agitated, squeezing my hand and whisper-yelling at me to pay attention to Tserang and scolding me for actually eating the food our hosts had generously provided for everyone around the wood-stove during the interview conversations. Søren had, as politely as possible, consumed nothing. Tserang, looking awful, was grinning at me with raised eyebrows, and I was thanking Lobsang Yeshe and exchanging WeChat contact information with him as Søren was crushing my hand. My wife Dáša was busy shielding Tserang from the dog in the yard. By the time we got into Tserang's jeep for the hour-long drive home to town, I was nearly doubled over with stomach pain, Tserang was laughing nervously, and Søren was chastising both of us with incredulity and anxiety.

The insidious and contagious, often fatal contraction of poison, known in Tibetan as *dug*, in Chinese as *dú* (poison) and as *gǔ* (蠱, a term often translated as a "legendary venomous insect"), in Naxi as *gu*, Mosuo as *gu* or *doo*, and in Lisu as *gu* or *ddor*, is a socially sublimated practice involving the volitional yet somewhat obligatory nurturing and casting of a serpentine force.[2] Most typically, *dug* is cast into female family members as well as into visitors to homes that "have" *dug*. In the region of Gyalthang in far southeastern Tibet (southern Khams) in what is today northwestern Yunnan Province in Southwest China, some Gyalthangpa (Tib. *rgyal thang pa*, literally, "the people of Gyalthang"—Tibetans and their Lisu, Bai, Yi, Naxi, and Mosuo neighbors) wrestle with the reputation of being "*dug* households." Legacies of mortal illness leave families feeling persecuted, cursed, and bitter with sorrow about the compulsion of inflicting one's own nightmare on loved ones.

While the ontology of *dug* is invisible, manifesting symbolically as *nāga*-esque venomous suggested creatures, its rationality, if rationality is particularly relevant in understanding *dug*, is caught between the worlds of diagnosable cancer and of nefarious, magical poisoning and ugly rumor. This project examines the religious and folkloric patterns of *dug* casting, ostracization, diagnoses of cancer, and its reputed antidotes. In what ways are accusations of *dug* perpetuated, resisted, rectifiable, or treated in relatively poor villages in southeastern Tibet? To what degree can *dug* be understood as rumor, as religious, or as cancer? What are the roles of gender, wealth, fertility, power, resentment, and silence in the construction of *dug* reputations? How, precisely, does *dug* manifest? How is it "cast"? In what sense are the causal mechanisms of *dug* magical? Why and to what degree is the agency of the caster inhibited?

In terms of positionality and methodology, this research stems from five distinct fieldwork periods in Gyalthang and neighboring regions between 2017 and 2020. Specifically, our fieldwork in the Dêqên Tibetan Autonomous Prefecture (Ch. *Díqìng Zàngzú Zìzhìzhōu*, 迪庆藏族自治州, Tib: *bde chen bod rigs rang skyong khul*) centered on interviews with families in the villages of Tangmei (Tib. *thang dma'*) in Nixi (Tib. *snyi shar*), Mulu and Nagara (Tib. *nags rked rag*) in Geza (Tib. *skad tshag*), Haba (in Sanba), Nizu (Tib. *rmig zur*), Dröngray in Dongwang (Tib. *terma rong*), Dongba (in Sanba), as well as several satellite villages of Benzilan (Tib. *tri rang kar*) and Nyushu in Dechen (Tib. *bde chen*, a.k.a. *mjol*), just west of Gyalthang. Our most fruitful fieldwork involved interviews with family members of Lobsang Yeshe in the village of Tangmei (Tib. *thang dma'*) in Nixi Township, famed for its black clay pottery, west of the city of Xianggelila (Tib. *rgyal thang*).

"Tsering Dundrup has been bitten three times," we were told by Lobsang Yeshe, learning of his father's battles with unspecified cancer (Chinese *áizhèng*). He told us this in the local dialect of Chinese so that his monoglot Tibetan-speaking father would not understand our conversation around the wood stove. Asked if people can control *dug*, we were told, in front of the father, that "half the time people can sort of control it ... he did through good luck."

Conducting fieldwork interviews on the topic of *dug* is remarkably challenging. Most people are hesitant to discuss *dug*, and people who have been accused of having *dug* typically will not speak about it, deflect or deny, or abruptly end the conversation when *dug* is first mentioned. We were also flying under the radar of official fieldwork and would frequently need to pivot conversations when unfamiliar or untrustworthy (typically government or Communist Party-connected) people joined a conversation or entered into earshot. Much of my fieldwork in the region over the previous decades had been about Raven (*Corvus corax*) languages (Raven augury), *nags myi rgod* (wild people) stories, Naxi rituals and pictographs, invisible villages, and traditions of storytelling. In previous research, we would often hike to or roll up to villages and ask around for reputed storytellers or wisdom holders in a particular village, and then we would cultivate these friendships and relationships through long-term and repeated, informal yet careful, slow, and sometimes inexact fieldwork.

Here I would like to emphasize the "we." This work is not mine alone. I conducted the preponderance of the research with several close local friends who have long been my partners in this research. I cannot name them here for reasons of sensitivity, but please know that I am in no way solely responsible for this work and the research would not have been possible without their partnership. There are several Tibetic languages spoken in the region, languages that are often unintelligible from valley to valley, and fieldwork translation is typically a team effort, as is, after all, most storytelling around a family stove. Recording of conversations is typically impossible due to the informal nature of most conversations and political sensitivities. In addition, even when I conducted this research alone, the information is owned by the many generous Gyalthangpa from whom I learned what I share with you now. My own presence as an outsider is often an obstacle to our research. We had endeavored for several years to identify—through personal contacts, past fieldwork connections, and friends—anyone knowledgeable who would speak with us about *dug*.

Due to an abundance of caution, many of our *dug* fieldwork conversations began or reverted to *nags myi rgod* conversations when the makeup of the conversation's participants shifted. Bringing up the subject of *dug* can gravely offend people. Many people so deeply fear the social ramifications of *dug* accusations that they find any mention of the subject threatening. Nevertheless, we did find that certain people were unexpectedly eager to discuss *dug*, either relating their own experiences or unloading with suspicion about a neighbor. The subject of *dug* is officially considered to be superstition (and superstitious belief is illegal in China), and the dynamic patterns of *dug* fall largely outside the scope of a Buddhist framework (despite Tibetan medical traditions' emphases on the diagnosis and treatment of poisons). Gyalthangpa Tibetans are mostly adherents of Dge lugs pa Vajrayāna Buddhism, and it is commonplace for people to respond to questions about any topic deemed religious or supramundane to dutifully provide doctrinal responses. In addition, the overall political context of conducting ethnographic, religious, or folklore fieldwork in Tibetan and even Naxi and Lisu regions in China has, in recent years, become increasingly fraught and sometimes impossible. Ultimately, though, the culturally encoded shame that surrounds *dug* and *dug* accusations is the deepest challenge to learning about *dug* and speaking with people who have or have experienced *dug*. It is a profoundly sensitive topic. We were both thrilled and cautious to be welcomed into Lobsang Yeshe's family house in the summer of 2018 and spent several hours talking about Lobsang Yeshe's family history before ever getting to the subject of *dug*.

I have written elsewhere about the occasion of tradition-bearers and around-the-stove storytelling in Gyalthang and about how it is a collective conversation more than a one-to-one transmission of a tale (Mortensen E. D. 2021). Lobsang Yeshe's parents, father Tsering Dundrup and 83-year-old mother Tsering Yangzom, sat closest to the stove. And in and out of the room came Lobsang Yeshe's sister-in-law, who was doing most of the cooking for the guests. All contributed to the conversation. We learned about family members featured in black-and-white photographs on the family altar alongside images of Mao and the Nechung Oracle (see Mortensen E. D. 2020; Mortensen D. P. 2020). And we learned about the history of slavery in the area (Tsering Yangzom's mother was a slave) and heard a few tales about *nags myi grod*. We ate steamed bread dipped in melted butter and cheese. Then, abruptly, Lobsang Yeshe told us about his family and *dug*.

"Talking about it can be harmful," he related. "And even if you cast it, you keep it." Most commonly, infected people cast *dug* into people. "They have to pass it on, and if there are no strangers available, it is passed to their children." Soon thereafter, Lobsang Yeshe's uncle entered the room and interrupted, firmly informing us that we needed to first gain permission from the village government if we wanted to continue our conversation. Lobsang Yeshe was apologetic and told us, "He carries communism on his back all the time." We changed the subject, then spent about another hour with the family before departing for home—a rather fraught departure detailed at the outset of this essay.

Later that same evening, however, Lobsang Yeshe drove to town to continue the conversation with us in Tibetan, away from his family. We learned of his personal life-quest to eradicate "black magic" *dug* casting from his community. It was a challenge, he admitted, to know who was responsible for casting *dug* into his family. Who was opposing them? If he suspected a culprit, he'd ask them, "is your food clean?" Or, knowing that they did not have a dog, he'd say, "do you have a dog? If so, keep it away from us." The assumption was that they'd understand "dog" was code for *dug* and respond with honesty.

Four people in Lobsang Yeshe's family had been afflicted with *dug*, two of whom died. People who have *dug* are dangerous. Their breath is poison. One can protect oneself from the poison breath by keeping a clove of garlic in one's mouth, but one still needs to be lucky to survive a visit and meal inside a house that has *dug*. Unlucky victims usually feel a false sense of safety and let down their guard.

The neighboring Lisu people are said to have a diagnosis and cure. Drolma, from Nagara, explained that the Lisu *dug* diagnostic test involves heating a small smooth river stone until it is white-hot. One then puts the stone in a small cup and urinates on it (one's first urination of the day). If the stone turns black, you have *dug*. Alternatively, one can urinate into a porcelain cup—the cup cannot be fabricated of wood or metal—then insert a bamboo stick wrapped tightly with a cloth into the urine. If the urine bubbles, it is a bad sign. One can, according to Lobsang Yeshe, "cut a stalk of a special grass and insert it down your throat like a tube, all the way to your stomach, and then vomit to be cured."

Dug is illusory and often invisible (Tib. *ma mthong*) and can change forms between snakes and frogs, and sometimes turtles or tortoises, or even scorpions.[3] Such creatures fall into a class of beings known as *klu* (Skt. *nāga*, Mosuo *ssù* or *lv* or *llû-mûn*, Naxi *ssù* or *llû'-mûn*, Lisu *fu*, and related to the Chinese *lóng*, which is commonly and somewhat problematically rendered in English as "dragon"). As Lobsang Yeshe put it, "normally, one cannot see *dug*; if you can see *dug* is it because its appearance has changed." People with whom we spoke in Gyalthang insisted that *dug* is not *klu*. It is worth noting that almost none of the species of snakes in Gyalthang are venomous, and that the frog, snake, and turtle as candidates for a *dug* more closely match the notion of Indic *nāga*, Tibetan *klu*, and Naxi *ssù* than they do a list of venomous creatures. Gyalthangpa are hesitant to associate the negative *dug* with *klu* given the complex yet largely positive valences associated with *klu* in Buddhist, Naxi, and Bön communities.[4]

That *dug* is serpentine is not disputed. The association of snakes with venom clearly connects the *dug* creature with poison. In a famed series of annotated medical paintings published as *Tibetan Medical Paintings: Illustrations to the* Blue Beryl *treatise of Sangye Gyamtso (1653–1705)*, we find extensive coverage of poison, its causes, and its cures.[5] On plate 51, we find a rendering of a woman, arms outstretched, seemingly sending forth a snake. The text by the image reads: "Hatred is a primary cause behind the giving of poison (*dug ster pa'i rgyu zhe sdang*)," followed by the notation "Inferiority complex is a primary cause behind the giving of poison (*ster rgyu mtho dogs*)."[6] On plate 40, an illustration of a *nāga/klu* is used to represent the statement, annotated next to the painted image, "harmful demons" (*gdon gdug can*) as a secondary cause of "tumors" (*skran*).[7] Above and beyond the clear sense that in late seventeenth-century Tibet it was understood by the medical community that poison was "given" or "bestowed" (the verb *ster ba* can carry the connotation of giving something to eat or drink) in serpentine form, by a woman, it was also understood that *nāga/klu* can inflict tumors (not just leprosy).

Homes with *dug* were required to prominently fly black prayer flags from their roof as a warning signal to would-be guests not to eat within those houses. Tashi Phuntsok in Nagara in 2019 explained the historical basis of this practice:

> The *bka' shag* [the governing council of Tibet in Lhasa, from 1751–1950s] needed to know who had *dug*, so they tried to identify them and then pressure them through the local headmen [Ch. *tǔsī*] to fly black prayer flags. As a Buddhist country, the *bka' shag* didn't want to hurt the *dug* families, but people needed a way to avoid staying in the homes of folks who would make them sick.

Every village in the Nixi valley, including those that had to relocate and rebuild following the 2013 earthquake, according to Lobsang Yeshe, has at least three houses that fly black prayer flags. Some people, though, hide the black flags: "these days there are only communist flags everywhere." To this I'd add the now widespread prevalence of orange prayer flags raised by adherents of the polarizing protector deity *rdo rje shugs ldan* in much of Gyalthang and southern Khams. Note that these black prayer flags and reputations of being poisoners are infamous stereotypes of the region Kongpo (Tib: *kong po*) in Central Tibet. En route to Kongpo in 1996, I was repeatedly and emphatically warned by friends in Lhasa to travel to Kongpo with my own food and not to eat in the houses of local villagers.[8] Black prayer flags can occasionally be seen in areas of Khams such as Sok (Tib. *sog*), Chamdo (Tib. *chab mdo*), Chatreng (Tib. *phyag phreng*), and elsewhere.

Whereas most families display images of protector deities on their family altars, according to Lobsang Yeshe, *dug* families have *dug lha*, depictions of *dug* deities, and the *dug lha* will follow someone with *dug* wherever they go. Images of *dug lha* are rumored to be kept hidden from the eyes of visitors to a house; the images are kept turned around on the altar, with Buddhist images on the reverse face. The *dug lha* are vital to the process of raising a *dug* at home.

It is primarily women who are afflicted with and transmit *dug*. They can do so with a simple gaze, in which case there is no cure. *Dug* will almost inevitably be passed from mothers to daughters. Passing it along does not cure one of the afflictions but can keep one alive. By far the most common method of transmission is through food. More nefariously, one can create *dug*. According to Ozer Wangdu in Nagara, "one can exhume at night, in secrecy, the bones of someone who died from *dug*, and put the bones in a jar and hide the jar." Growing a *dug* this way does make the incubator/nurturer sick. However, one is then compelled to cast it into someone close, someone intimate. This seems to always happen within the richest families in a community, who are less prone to dying of starvation. Families then have *dug* for generations.

The practice of *dug* casting and the social ramifications of having *dug*, whether understood as cancer or a demonic spirit, or both, remains at the center of social organization in numerous communities in the region. Yang Erche Namu, in her 2004 memoir *Leaving Mother Lake: A Girlhood at the Edge of the World*,[9] relates a story from her childhood of individuals in her Mosuo community of Lugu growing a "Gu." Her mother explained:

> The Gu is a very dangerous thing. … During the fifth lunar month, there are people who go into the mountains to collect snakes, centipedes, spiders, toads, sometimes bats—if they can catch them. They take all these dirty animals home and put them in a jar. Then they close the lid and all the poisonous things fight and eat each other until, at the end, only one is left. That one is the Gu, and it's the most poisonous thing in the world … it has to eat—just like everything else. Except that it eats only dirty things.[10]

Yang Erche Namu's sister Zhema then joined the conversation and explained: "If a man owns the Gu, he feeds it the sweat of his armpits, and if a woman owns it, she feeds it her monthly blood. … It has to give its poison to other people. If it doesn't make people sick, it will harm its own masters."[11] After Yang Erche Namu expressed her disgust and skepticism and defended the reputation of a friend who had the reputation of having *gu*, assuring her sister and mother that the girl, the beautiful Tsilidema, would assuredly not intentionally make someone sick, her mother continued:

> She can't do anything about it. The Gu cannot die and it is passed down the generations. Even if Tsilidema is the best person in the world. Even if she doesn't want the Gu anymore, she can't get rid of it. She's stuck with it forever and so are all her people and all their descendants. … The Gu can get anyone. That's why we don't have anything to do with Tsilidema and her family. And that's why nobody ever invites people who have the Gu into their house. That's why only Gu people can talk with Gu people. … You don't even have to touch someone

> who has the Gu to get sick from it. All you have to do is eat while you are near the, or even swallow your saliva when they look at you. All of a sudden you smell something very strange, like cigarette smoke or sweat or a wild animal, and then you lose your appetite. The next day your stomach swells up and you can't eat anything except the thing you were eating at the time the Gu poisoned you. Then you can't stop eating that thing, you crave it and eat and eat and eat. You can get very sick.[12]

The ostracization and scrupulous avoidance of those reputed to have *gu* mirror the Gyalthang dynamics of the social cost of *dug* accusations. In the case of the Mosuo ("Moso," in Yang Erche Namu's text), *gu* is not equated with cancer. Although potentially fatal, the affliction of *gu* can be treated by a Buddhist lama, who can administer medicine that will leave one with several days of diarrhea before a full recovery. It is notable that in this case, becoming sick with "the Gu" does not seem to mean that one is then a carrier of or "master" of a/the *gu*, but just that one has been victimized by the contagion.

Later in the memoir, Yang Erche Namu relates, with fear, the story of a different "beautiful girl" of their community by Lugu lake on the border of Yunnan and Sichuan provinces. The young woman, Zhecinamu, had rejected suitor after suitor, as men from as far away as Tibet learned of her beauty and sought her favor. In frustration, one of the resentful boys who had been betting on which suitor Zhecinamu would accept, decided to play a trick on her. He told his friends, "Last night I crept up to her window and I saw her, on her bed. She was naked and she was … oh, yes, so beautiful. But there was a huge snake with her. It was coiled around her waist with its head between her breasts. And she was asleep." As the rumor spread that Zhecinamu had "reared" a *gu*, according to Yang Erche Namu, the attention young men used to pay her evaporated. Soon thereafter Zhecinamu hanged herself in the forest.[13]

Erik Mueggler details similar odious *mə* spirits possessing women's wombs among the Lolopo/Lolomo (Yi), and relates the *mə* to contagious memories of starvation, suffering, and hauntings by ancestors.[14] Perhaps importantly, though, in the case of Lolopo/Lolomo *mə*, transference from household to household occurs through the magical dynamics of contiguity and adjacency, and less on notions of sympathy and mimesis. Drawing upon classical anthropological models of magical causality that developed in a trajectory largely instigated by Hubert and Mauss, Mueggler's description of *mə* is most notably comparable to Gyalthangpa *dug* in that in both communities women's wombs and notions of stomachs and starvation conspire in socially constructed patterns of vulnerability.

The Lolopo/Lolomo people about whom Mueggler writes are classified by the state as Yi nationality. There are several different groups of Yi in Southwest China. Communities of Nosuo Yi, who are in many ways quite distinct from the Lolopo/Lolomo, are neighbors to the Tibetans within Gyalthang. Lobsang Yeshe noted that whereas Naxi, Bai, and Tibetans have *dug*, the Nosuo Yi are "totally against it and don't have it." The Lisu, he claimed, are also "against" it, but the Lisu are said to have the best cures for *dug*.

E. Paul Durrenberger, in his 1993 essay "Witchcraft, Sorcery, Fortune, and Misfortune among Lisu Highlanders of Northern Thailand," details a dynamic of anxiety about and ostracization of witches whose "witch spirit" (*phyíphə*), similar to the Tibetan Gyalthangpas' *dug* phenomenon, is simultaneously an affliction for the witch and something the witch inflicts on others.

> People get the witchcraft spirit (*phwù swī*) ... by contamination, through close association with others who have it. The spirit is contagious, as communicable diseases are according to modern medical thought, except that the minimum exposure time is three years. The spirit and the person form one entity, and once infected, a witch "has" the spirit and cannot dispose of it ... the individual cannot control this evil power. ... Lisu hold that all members of the Gwa lineage are witch/were-animals. Since they are witches, no one from other lineages risks marrying them or allowing them to live in their villages. Gwa people live in Gwa villages and marry among themselves—incestuously by Lisu standards. Otherwise, they are like other Lisu. ... People of other lineages and villages attend feasts and events in Gwa villages. ... a witch spirit (*phyíphə*) may invade a victim's body with or without the volition of a witch ... accounts of witchcraft attacks usually attributed them to retribution for stinginess.[15]

Durrenberger glosses the Lisu term *khû* as "calamity spirit," postulating that the term is likely from the Shan *kho*. Addressing the symptoms and etiology of witchcraft, Durrenberger explains that "Victims who harbor the infectious witch/were-animal spirit are antireciprocal, harm others without provocation or reason, and are beyond the logic of social relations," concluding that "witches suffer as much as their victims."[16]

Perhaps the most pertinent study of Tibetan poisoning practices in the region is Giovanni Da Col's (2012a) work "The Poisoner and the Parasite: Cosmoeconomics, Fear, and Hospitality among Dechen Tibetans,"[17] wherein he emphasizes that fears about poisoning involve issues surrounding anxieties about the severing of "reproductive energies" in the context of hospitality. He identifies the dynamic of the fear of poison and poisoning as the character of a parasite. Da Col does not see *dug* as nefarious, writing: "Poisoning is not an act of sorcery or 'black magic' (*nak nkag*) [*sic*] since there is no malicious original intent coming from the poisoner."[18] Perhaps Da Col's informants in Dechen did not express to him that *dug* can be seen as wicked and intentionally employed, but it seems his formulation is relegated to the perspective of the poisoner only, and not the point of view of the victims.

Da Col's work in Dechen (Tib. *bde chen*, just to the northwest of Gyalthang), and Mueggler's work in Zhizuo (to the southeast of Gyalthang), when seen in the light of Mosuo and Lisu constructions of *gu* and poison and witchcraft spirits, illuminate a related set of practices and beliefs manifest within a multiethnic diverse geographic region. Adjacent cultural and distinct ethnic groups who have notably different religious traditions share the fear of poisoners, and dread becoming bound to the compulsion of inflicting one's own nightmare on loved ones.

Both Durrenberger and Da Col emphasize reciprocity and social relations in their analyses of Lisu witchcraft and Dechen Tibetan poison anxiety. While a direct causal transmission from Lisu to Tibetan, or for that matter from Naxi or Mosuo to Tibetan or to Lisu, or vice versa, remains a challenging dynamic to decipher, a possible explanation lies with the common linguistic and geographical ancestry of most of the peoples who today live in Northwest Yunnan Province, including the Na (Naxi and Mosuo), Yi, Lisu, Bai, and others. The prevalence of *dug*/*gu* traditions in Kongpo coupled with various parallel manifestations of the tradition among a broad swathe of Tibeto-Burman language speaking peoples along the periphery of southern Khams suggest an historical antecedence of *dug* casting and *dug* accusations further up the migratory river valleys of the eastern plateau.

Stories of poison and poisoners, while not ubiquitous, are widespread in Tibetan and its adjacent regions. Among the Lhopo of Sikkim, the fear of poisoning and of accusations of poisoning is rampant. Anna Balikci, in her 2008 book *Lamas, Shamans and Ancestors: Village Religion in Sikkim*, offers detailed anecdotes of cases of poison accusation, noting that the accusations are made of people, mostly women, of many different ethnic groups. "Poisoning or *duk* is considered a kind of cult wherein a woman enters into a ritual contract with a particular supernatural being … to accumulate wealth, power and knowledge, either for oneself or one's family."[19] According to Belikci, accusations of poisoning are inspired by feelings of jealousy for the success and wealth of another woman, often an outsider, although accusations are made of community members under an overarching sense that individuals should not profit off of one's own people. Belikci explains that the poisoner, often a restaurant owner, too, desires wealth:

> The woman poisoner is required to administer the poison by putting it in the food or drink of, preferably, a wealthy or knowledgeable person in order to magically inherit the victim's qualities after the victim's death ... she is obliged to find victims on a regular basis—otherwise the supernatural being may make her suffer, or worse, force her to administer the poison to her own child.[20]

The emphasis on the obligation to inflict the poison on a stranger or else have to lose it on one's own child is a pattern found across the Himalayas, and resonates with the nightmare of *dug* in Gyalthang. Balikci understands the accusation of poisoning as "a way of checking aggressively selfish behavior in others. Accusations of poisoning and *barmo* witchcraft are reserved for aggressive or covertly ambitious women."[21]

Importantly, many of the details of Yang Erche Namu's story of collecting venomous creatures in a jar to create a magically potent *gu* have explicit antecedents in medieval Chinese texts on sorcery and witchcraft. In the 2021 book *Healing with Poisons: Potent Medicines in Medieval China*, Yan Liu provides a thorough and insightful analysis of the history of the terms *du* and *gu* in China, addressing the ambivalence of the term *du* as both a poison and a medicine, the storage, worship, and use of cat demons and serpentine *gu* poison to inflict harm on others, the prominence of women in these practices, and the geographical marginalization of *gu* witchcraft practitioners to the south and southwest during the Sui and Tang Dynasties where they were increasingly associated with ethnic minority peoples. Christine Mollier's excellent 2008 study of Buddhist scriptures and Daoist rites and writings, *Buddhism and Taoism Face to Face: Scripture, Ritual, and Iconographic Exchange in Medieval China*, addresses *gǔ*. Mollier explains:

> The modus operandi of *gu* is derived from a singular, millennial recipe that involves filling a jar with insects, serpents, and other vermin and letting them devour one another. The last survivor, which presumably has concentrated within itself all the venom of the other pests, is called *gu*. This diabolical creature, subject to its master, enables him to apply its sorcery against enemies, notably by drugging their food. In all events, the *gu* places in high relief a semantic field that extends far beyond a rudimentary method of poisoning. As a nosological concept, rich with diverse connotations, it is synonymous with toxicology, demonic pathologies, and witchcraft. During the medieval period, medical treatises devoted whole chapters to the careful characterization of its etiology

> and to the prescription of remedies promising to cure the horrible illnesses occasioned by this scourge.[22]

Mollier addresses *sūtra*s and talismans from the tenth century that oppose the "way of gu." Thus, it is highly likely that the phenomenon of *gu/du/dug* is an exceptionally old and widespread concept, associated with magical affliction from the western Himalayas to eastern China and into Southeast Asia, and perhaps beyond.[23] Related to notions of purity and pollution and to the feminine, the fear of *gu/du/dug* and the efforts of established religion to oppose it have been active across an enormous region. In a certain sense *gu/du/dug* has become the stuff of folklore and popular religion, recognized but opposed by institutional religious traditions. In short, *gu/du/dug* is magic. Alongside the many ways in which magic in Tibet has been defined and discussed in this volume, it is important to note both that *gu/du/dug* is an affliction, a scourge, an anxiety, and a practice that supersedes the Tibetan geographical sphere, and that it rekindles one of the central aspects of the concept of magic: it involves mystery, confusion, and is *not* clearly understood.

In Gyalthang, it is dangerous to speak of *dug* (or to conduct fieldwork about *dug*). Additional interviews conducted in the Gyalthangpa villages of Geza, Nagara, as well as in neighboring Benzilan revealed similar understandings of *dug*. Stories abound of snakes dropping from rafters into bowls of food, and snakes seen among the vegetables for sale in a farmer's market stall, charges that can decimate a woman's reputation for generations. In Benzilan, in 2017, a photo of a snake among vegetables in a market stall circulated on WeChat, and within a day the farmer had been (unofficially) banned from the market. She told me that she believed the image was photoshopped, and that she "absolutely did not have *dug*." Lobsang Yeshe, in anger at the content, related to us the following story that he said took place in September of 1986:

> Some kids saw a woman wearing a snake around her waist. The children said, "Auntie! You have a snake!" She replied, "no … it's a belt." She turned around again to show them, and it was a belt. After one week, the same group of kids were going to school in the morning and encountered her as she was fetching water. When they passed each other, the kids turned to look and again saw the snake. They threw a stone, striking the snake, and the woman collapsed. She cried, "why did you hit my belt!?" It is one shared soul. Hurt the snake, hurt the woman.

Herein, understandings of cancer and of spiritual serpentine poison possession (or biting) are simultaneous. According to many in Gyalthang, *dug* is cancer. "It is not folklore. It *really* exists here … not just a story." *Dug* is also the maternally inflicted poison embodied by a snake. The *dug* is also like a *bla klu* (literally "spirit/soul serpent")—akin to a *bla mtsho* ("spirit/soul lake") or *bla shing* ("spirit/soul tree"), which functions in essence like a horcrux in J. K. Rowling's *Harry Potter* series. In effect, one cannot kill the person without killing the snake; the snake becomes the vital force of the woman, related to her stomach, to food, and to her womb and reproductive vitality. *Dug* people are understood to be greedy and takers—never givers—and thus wealthy and self-centered. Boys from *dug* families never become monks,[24] as a father with *dug* is obligated to pass *du* to his son. "It doesn't matter if a family is Buddhist, or even what kind of Buddhist. Ironheads [Tib. *lchags mgo*, practitioners/adherents of *rdo rje shugs ldan*] get *dug* too." By this point in my fieldwork, my initial theory that *dug* was basically the social memory of *nāga*-related leprosy had completely collapsed.[25]

According to Lobsang Yeshe, who, remember, is on a crusade against *dug*, people with *dug*: "do not want to get rid of it. *Dug* benefits them because they get rich and do not share. They can eat other people's things, but other people won't eat theirs. Sure, it is difficult to marry, but *dug* families bring in outsiders, like [Han] Chinese, to marry." When pressed and asked if there was any chance that village headmen merely identified rich folks of whom they were jealous, Lobsang Yeshi shook his head. "No, *dug* makes the entire community look bad. Other communities avoid yours. Inside the communities, *dug* people can take, but we don't take their things. I hate *dug*. My family members have died." When I explained that I felt rather sorry for people with *dug* he enjoined,

> No. Don't think like that. I know a lot because I ask, because I want to fight it. Everything has its natural place and has space to grow. For example, the food on the table—it might have viruses or give us cancer—or bugs on our bed might have viruses or give us cancer. *Dug* people are just survivors, and in order to survive they must harm others. They have chosen the wrong path toward survival. *Dug* people are *dug* … they are one and the same entity. It can't be explained scientifically.

Gerald Roche and Sa mtsho skyid discuss the notion of such related Tibetan terms as *rten 'brel*, *g.yang*, *bsod nams*, *bkra shis*, *las*, and *dge ba*, which they explain can be used to describe a range of things English speakers might render as "chance, fate, luck, fortune, Karma, destiny, happenstance, providence, and coincidence."[26] Important in their piece is the discussion of the terms *mi gtsang pa* ("unclean"), *sbags*, and *grib*, the latter two both meaning "defiled" or "polluted." "*Sbags* applies to things whereas *grib* applies to people's bodies."[27]

Being stricken with *dug* is *grib*, polluting, and unfortunate, but does not involve a valence of moral impurity. Raising *dug*, on the other hand, does. However, there is rarely a clear distinction between someone who has *dug* because of their own nefarious purposes and someone who has *dug* because they were victimized in the context of a situation of hospitality, for example, because they ate at the home of someone with *dug*. Nor, for that matter, is a distinction obvious between the grower of a *dug* and the original grower's daughter. In essence, once you have *dug*, you are contaminated, and the social ramifications depend on rumor, vitriol, fear, and severity of illness. Accusations can also be administered ex post facto, after someone dies of cancer.

Although I am not implying any causal connection between *dug* traditions and religio-folkloric traditions of Africa, I would like to draw on two theoretical contributions made in the context of witchcraft studies in Africa, as I find these ideas helpful in understanding the simultaneity of *dug* as cancer and as "black magic" poison-casting. In her piece "Witchcraft and Racecraft: Invisible Ontology in Its Sensible Manifestations," Karen Fields finds discontent in what she calls "granting the rationality" of witchcraft, while not granting rationality to what she terms "racecraft."[28] She writes:

> If we judge by the dependence of both on presuppositions that are demonstrably false according to modern science, then both sets of traditional beliefs should go down together as irrational. But if we discount their falsity by that standard, then they should rise together as rational. … We approach witchcraft and racecraft as if they belonged to two different orders of phenomena: the one is compelling belief and the other, a bad choice in matters of belief; the one, truth of a different order, and the other, false beliefs destructible through the propagation of truth; the one, an element of human diversity, and the other, an ugly reaction to that diversity.[29]

Following Appiah, Evans-Pritchard, and Durkheim, Fields locks on to the concept of "invisible ontology" and assesses the concept's applicability to both racecraft and witchcraft. She argues that indeed invisible ontology is what links the two concepts, and puzzles that employing the same critical lens that dismantles the rationality of racecraft should likewise allow us to dismantle the rationality of witchcraft and "condemn it accordingly." "Instead they give us racecraft as (objectively) false and witchcraft as true (in its own fashion), but not witchcraft as (objectively) false and racecraft as true (in its own fashion)."[30] Ultimately, she does not solve the dilemma, concluding that, following Appiah, if modernization (and thus, for Fields, rationality) is centered on the acceptance of science, we need to choose if the evidence is strong enough for us to give up our invisible ontologies. It is a most unsatisfying conclusion to an astutely identified ethical dilemma.

Dug in Gyalthang is most certainly an invisible ontology. There are strong parallels between *dug* accusations and witchcraft accusations; however distant the Azande are to Yunnan, what we learn, theoretically, about the importance of rumor and accusations in certain African witchcraft contexts can be illuminative of patterns of rumor and accusation of *dug* in Gyalthang. Setting aside the perhaps valuable purist polemic that witchcraft = rumor, it is, for instance, noteworthy that in much of the anthropological literature on African witchcraft, the term "witchcraft" itself has recently come more to mean the persecution of people accused of being witches than it means what it is that witches ontologically and invisibly (or even visibly) do. In other words, it might be helpful to look with more care at the social construction and ramifications of having or of casting *dug*, rather than focus attention on whether or not *dug* is either "real" or "cancer." Yet such a sociological or functionalist assessment need not discount the plausibility of *dug* as real, as cancer, or as a serpent being that can be cast into victims. *Dug* can certainly be both cancer and accusations of poison-casting, but we might be confusing ontological modalities and causal mechanisms in considering the secretive nurturing or raising of a *dug* in a jar as akin to raising cancer. For the *dug* is cast, but how is cancer cast? Is the issue one of cancer as the explanans and the *dug* as the mechanism for its contraction? I believe that the designation of cancer is rather recent in Gyalthang.

The Tibetan medical tradition's assertion that *klu* can inflict tumors might have influenced the people with whom I spoke in Gyalthang who believed, quite vociferously, that *dug* is cancer. There is, in *dug* casting, a *simultaneity* of intent and unavoidable necessity, and the transmission of *dug* is certainly blamed on individuals alongside an understanding, particularly within families, that it could not be helped. Mothers are compelled to cast cancer, as it were, into their daughters. Accusers demonize folks who "have" *dug*, and absolutely accuse them of maliciousness. It might seem that the apparent contradiction of volition and obligation is a matter of positionality—with the afflicted victim accusing the inflictor of intentional harm and the poisoner families emphasizing that transmission is involuntary. However, it is my assessment that the two understandings, regardless of whether or not the notions are contradictory, are indeed held simultaneously by each person involved. *Dug* poisoners see themselves as both victim and aggressor. Someone afflicted understands not only that the poisoner was both compelled *and* decided to "give" the *dug*, but that now they themself, the newly afflicted, will soon face the same tearing and impossible situation. Hereditary transmission, scalding assessments of the afflicted's greed, and the shame of illness and of community bullying (which is learned behavior, after all) conspire in the villages of Gyalthang.

There is a strange concurrence of Lobsang Yeshe castigating "*dug* people," yet seeing his own family primarily as victims. Instead of the notion of black magic sorcerers destroying themselves,[31] here we have a very long story (generations of pain) of slow illness and spite, of blame and accusation, of heredity and secrets. Whether or not *dug* is cancer seems largely irrelevant. That it can be fatal is relevant.

Dug is a pre- or non-Buddhist phenomenon in the Tibetan world. The manifestations of poison or demon creation/raising, casting, and inability to put the *dug*/*gu* back in the bottle, as it were, find parallels from Myanmar to Sichuan, from Kongpo to the Bai regions of central Yunnan. Lobsang Yeshe and others we interviewed are modern, scientifically minded Buddhists, and understandably wrestle with comprehending *dug* through these lenses of empirical or dharmic hermeneutical goggles. Yet, although the multivalent ways in which *dug* affects communities speak to invisible ontology and to rumor and accusation, it is vital to remember that people die from *dug*.

Tserang and I suffered several hours of acute pain and a few days of stomach discomfort as we recovered from our fieldwork interview visit with Lobsang Yeshe's family. We laugh about it now. A little. Dáša and Søren were fine. None of us have yet been afflicted with cancer.

Notes

1 Some names in this essay have been changed to protect the identity of our fieldwork partners and those we interviewed.

2 There are several senses in which variants of the Tibetan term *dug* are echoic of the phenomenon of poison casting in Gyalthangpa religious folklore. Etymologically, the term *dugs* can also mean "revenge" or "grudge." The verbal homonym *ldug pa* (or *ldugs*) can mean to sprinkle or cast, and *sdug pa* represents the notions of depression, ill luck, and affliction.

3 I refer the reader to the essay in this volume by Brown, pp. 13–33.

4 For more on the religious relationship between Bön, Naxi religion, and the Buddhism of southern Khams (including Gyalthang), see Mortensen (2019: 119–24).

5 Parfionovitch, Meyer, and Dorje (1992).
6 Parfionovitch, Meyer, and Dorje (1992: 273–4), plate 51.
7 Parfionovitch, Meyer, and Dorje (1992: 251–2), plate 40.
8 For more information on gossip and poisoning in Kongpo, see Schreiber (2011) and Ramble (1997). My thanks, also, to my colleague and dear friend Nicholas Sihlé for extensive comments on earlier drafts of this essay and for reminding me to return my scholarly gaze to the Himalaya.
9 Yang and Mathieu (2003), in particular, pp. 85–8 and pp. 129–31.
10 Namu and Mathieu (2003: 86).
11 Namu and Mathieu (2003: 86).
12 Namu and Mathieu (2003: 86–7).
13 Namu and Mathieu (2003: 130–1).
14 Mueggler (2001).
15 Durrenberger (1993: 50–2). For more ethnographic information about witchcraft (and poison) in Southeast Asian traditions, see Watson and Ellen (1993).
16 Durrenberger (1993: 48 and 63).
17 Da Col (2012a). Da Col also ascribes to the Tibetans of Dechen "innate conceptions of vitality and 'mystical' influence," which points to a theoretically valuable valence of "magic," and how it might best be conceptualized in the region. See Da Col (2012b and 2012c).
18 Da Col (2012a: 188).
19 Balikci (2008: 223). For information on poison, accusations, and possession in Ladakh, see Day (1989), and further afield on witchcraft accusations in Rajasthan, see Dwyer (2003).
20 Balikci (2008: 223–4).
21 Balikci (2008: 226).
22 Mollier (2008: 55–6). See, in particular, chapter 2 of the book: "In Pursuit of the Sorcerers" (pp. 55–99). I wish to thank the anonymous reviewer of an earlier version of this essay for bringing Mollier's work to my attention.
23 Mollier cites Obringer (1997) as postulating that *gu* was a southern Chinese practice.
24 This detail, which I heard in several interviews, suggests that Lobsang Yeshe's family first contracted *du* only after Geshe Lobsang Gyalwa became a monk and explains the family's consternation that Lobsang Gyalwa's reincarnation has never been identified or recognized.
25 *Nāga* (*klu*, *ssu*) are understood to be the cause of leprosy, and of hoar frost, and importantly among the Naxi and Tibetans of Gyalthang, of earthquakes.
26 Roche and Sa mtsho skyid (2011: 240).
27 Roche and Sa mtsho skyid (2011: 247). For an excellent contextual analysis of the term *grib* and the concept of pollution, see Gutschow (2009) and Chophel (1983).

For more in-depth discussion of the differences between terms relating to virtue and fortune, see Clarke (1990). For an intriguing discussion of causality in the Tibetan worldview, see Nielsen (2018).

28 Fields (2001: 308).

29 Fields (2001: 283–4).

30 Fields (2001: 308).

31 See, e.g., Devisch (2001).

References

Balikci, A. (2008), *Lamas, Shamans and Ancestors: Village Religion in Sikkim*, Leiden: Brill.

Chophel, N. (1983), *Folk Culture of Tibet*, Dharamsala: Library of Tibetan Works and Archives.

Clarke, G. (1990), "Ideas of Merit (bsod nams), Virtue (Dge-ba), Blessing (Byins rlabs), and Material Prosperity (Rten 'brel) in Highland Nepal," *Journal of the Oriental Society of Oxford* 21 (2): 65–84.

Da Col, G. (2012a), "The Poisoner and the Parasite: Cosmoeconomics, Fear, and Hospitality among Dechen Tibetans," *Journal of the Royal Anthropological Institute* 18: 175–95.

Da Col, G. (2012b), "Introduction: Natural Philosophies of Fortune—Luck, Vitality, and Uncontrolled Relatedness," *Social Analysis* 56 (1): 1–23.

Da Col, G. (2012c), "The Elementary Economies of Dechenwa Life: Fortune, Vitality, and the Mountain in Sino-Tibetan Borderlands," *Social Analysis* 56 (1): 74–98.

Day, S. (1989), "Embodying Spirits: Village Oracles and Possession Ritual in Ladakh, North India," Ph.D. diss., London School of Economics and Political Science.

Devisch, R. (2001), "Sorcery Forces of Life and Death among the Yaka of Congo," in G. C. Bond and D. M. Ciekawy (eds.), *Witchcraft Dialogues: Anthropological and Philosophical Exchanges*, 101–30, Athens: Ohio University Center for International Studies.

Durrenberger, E. P. (1993), "Witchcraft, Sorcery, Fortune, and Misfortune among Lisu Highlanders of Northern Thailand," in C. W. Watson and R. Ellen (eds.), *Understanding Witchcraft and Sorcery in Southeast Asia*, 47–66, Honolulu: University of Hawaii Press.

Dwyer, G. (2003), *The Divine and the Demonic: Supernatural Affliction and its Treatment in North India*, New York: Routledge.

Fields, K. (2001), "Witchcraft and Racecraft: Invisible Ontology in Its Sensible Manifestations," in G. C. Bond and D. M. Ciekawy (eds.), *Witchcraft Dialogues: Anthropological and Philosophical Exchanges*, 283–315, Athens: Ohio University Press.

Gutschow, K. (2009), *Being a Buddhist Nun: The Struggle for Enlightenment in the Himalayas*, Cambridge, MA: Harvard University Press.

Liu, Y. (2021), *Healing with Poisons: Potent Medicines in Medieval China*, Seattle: University of Washington Press.

Mollier, C. (2008), *Buddhism and Taoism Face to Face: Scripture, Ritual, and Iconographic Exchange in Medieval China*, Honolulu: University of Hawai'i Press.

Mortensen, D. P. (2020), "Historical Amnesia in Gyalthang: The Legacy of Tibetan Participation in the Cultural Revolution," in R. Barnett, B. Weiner, and F. Robin (eds.), *Conflicting Memories: Tibetan History under Mao Retold*, 274–310, Leiden: Brill.

Mortensen, E. D. (2019), "Boundaries of the Borderlands: Mapping Gyalthang," in S. Gros (ed.), *Frontier Tibet: Patterns of Change in the Sino-Tibetan Borderlands*, 115–39, Amsterdam: Amsterdam University Press.

Mortensen, E. D. (2021), "Of Monsters and Invisible Villages: Nags myi rgod Tales of the Tibetans of Gyalthang," in N. L. Mikles and J. P. Laycock (eds.), *Religion, Culture, and the Monstrous: Of Gods and Monsters*, 97–115, New York: Lexington Books.

Mueggler, E. (2001), *The Age of Wild Ghosts: Memory, Violence, and Place in Southwest China*, Berkeley: University of California Press.

Namu, Y. E., and C. Mathieu (2003), *Leaving Mother Lake: A Girlhood at the Edge of the World*, New York: Back Bay Books.

Nielsen, S. H. (2018), "Tibetan Buddhist Divination: The Genre and Its Concepts of Fortune and Causality," Master Thesis in Tibetology, University of Copenhagen (unpublished).

Obringer, F. (1997), *L'aconit et l'orpiment: Drogues et poisons en Chine ancienne et médiévale*, Paris: Fayard.

Parfionovitch, Y., F. Meyer, and G. Dorje (eds.) (1992), *Tibetan Medical Paintings: Illustrations to the* Blue Beryl *treatise of Sangye Gyamtso (1653–1705)*, vol. I: Plates, vol. II: Text. London: Serindia.

Ramble, C. (1997), "The Creation of the Bon Mountain of Kongpo," in A. W. Macdonald (ed.), *Mandala and Landscape*, 133–232, New Delhi: D. K. Printworld.

Roche, G. and Sa mtsho skyid (2011), "Purity and Fortune in Phug sde Tibetan Village Rituals," *Asian Highland Perspectives* 10: 231–84.

Schreiber, G. (2011), *Giftmorde in Nyingtri: Tratsch in einer osttibetischen Pilgerstadt*, Berlin: Weissensee.

Watson, C. W. and R. Ellen (eds.) (1993), *Understanding Witchcraft and Sorcery in Southeast Asia*, Honolulu: University of Hawaii Press.

8

Is There Magic in *Gcod*? An Expedition into (Some of) the Complexities of *Sādhana*-Text Enactments

Nike-Ann Schröder

To begin examining the question formulated in the title, I will describe a situation that occurred in Ladakh several years ago when, under the guidance of a Rnying ma Rinpoche, I wrote down a list of items needed for the inauguration and the eye-opening ceremony of a Guru Rinpoche statue. In the end, Rinpoche said: "And finally we need these things … in any case, a *kapāla* and if you manage, bring a real one [he displayed signs of slight discomfort], you know … this thing from the cremation ground. Go and ask your father, he is the kind of person who will have such things at home." He looked at me with a very controlled expression. However, some signs of disgust shone through, and he seemed to be a bit happy that he could delegate that task to me. My heart-father,[1] who is a lay *gcod* practitioner, contributed the "real" *kapāla*, an offering bowl made of a human skull. The question whether there is magic in *gcod* or not may, as I argue, also leads us to examine the relationship, interaction, or counterbalance existing between the monastic practitioners such as Rinpoche who holds a *khenpo* degree earned from a traditional monastic center (Tib. *bshad grwa*) and the lay tantrics, those, for example, who practice *gcod*.

Gcod is a tremendously complex Tibetan Buddhist and Bon tantric ritual and meditation practice. Various *sādhanas*, both Buddhist and Bon, provide the choreography for the practice, and there is a similar template to be found in all of them: the practitioner identifies and acts as a *ḍākinī*, offers her own body (of the ordinary self), and invites all sorts of beings to a tantric feast gathering (Skt. *gaṇacakra*), which serves to pacify suffering. *Gcod* is practiced both as a means to enlightenment and as a healing ritual. Accomplished *gcod* practitioners are assumed to have immunity against contagious diseases, and there are reports about the *gcod pa*s who served to treat affected people and the dead during epidemics (see Gyatso 1985: 222; Samuel 1993: 212).

Academic approaches to the representations of *gcod* practice seem to follow two different trajectories (see Schröder 2023: 244–7). On the one hand, most of the scholarly work on *gcod* is centered on its scriptural sources. It is generally assumed that the philosophical basis and theoretical premises of *gcod* can be found in the *Prajñāpāramitā* ("Perfection of Wisdom") *sūtra*s and literature (Gyatso 1985: 324, Edou 1996: 6; Orofino [2000] 2001: 399).[2] In this approach, the ritual action of *gcod* largely disappears from the scene. On the other hand, we have an approach focusing on the real-life *gcod pa*s, highlighting their ritual practice and lifestyle, which paints a very different picture of *gcod* as a whole. The often unconventional appearance of the practitioners, their affiliation with cremation grounds, together with such *gcod* procedures as ritual offering of one's body has been central in the early descriptions by the Western authors (Bleichsteiner 1937: 178; Eliade [1964] 1974: 436) and was since then being repeated in numerous publications. The source for the descriptions of *gcod* practitioners by the two Western scholars mentioned above seems to be a vivid account narrating meetings with *gcod pa*s provided by David-Néel ([1932] 2007: 120–34, in particular 121–2) in her book titled *Magic & Mystery in Tibet*.[3]

This title apparently refers to the exotic adventures of David-Néel herself and includes a promise of introducing the reader to the first-hand accounts of esoteric knowledge and practice of Tibet. The very term "magic," however, although seemingly straightforward, is nevertheless vague. The problem with the term "magic" perhaps lies in its various, wide-ranging applications, including miracles, ritual activities conducted to produce particular effects, a sense of wonder, ability to induce super-ordinary effects, and the power of transformation. In a certain period of the humanities, "magic" has been used as a pejorative term to interpret religio-cultural practices constructed from a colonial point of view. To deal with the present difficulty of finding a common definition of "magic," which encompasses a heterogeneity of practices, beliefs, and modes of thinking (Sørensen 2018: 1; Benussi 2019), I propose to sketch a "field of magic," rather than a single definition. This "field of magic" would stretch in between different landmarks or pathways following four different approaches toward the conceptualization of "magic." First, "magic" as a concept in Cultural Anthropology was established by evolutionists who separated "magic" from both "religion" and "science," and set these three categories into a trajectory of evolutionary development. I will critically examine this division and its presupposed hierarchy by discussing its relevance for the enactments of *gcod*.

The second landmark is a definition of magic proposed by Sørensen (2018: 1) who stated that: "Magic is about changing the state or essence of persons, objects, acts and events through certain special and non-trivial kinds of actions with opaque causal mediation." This definition speaks of a mode of operation and function of "magic," and I will follow this when examining the transformative techniques, effects, and powers of *gcod*. The third pathway follows the ideas of Chögyam Trungpa Rinpoche. When asked by his students about the meaning of "magic," "miraculous," and "miracle," he answered: "I think the fundamental idea … is … that your belief is challenged by its opposite. If you expect the world to be this way, downside up, and if you suddenly see it upside down, that's a miracle" (Trungpa 1999: 111). Here, "magic" is the experience of a miracle, an incident, or a practice, which cannot be explained by a conceptual framework a person holds, and thus it challenges them and potentially turns their worldview upside down. This framework will be prominent when investigating the question whether *gcod* induces miracles or not. The final landmark for analyzing the "field of magic" is a libertarian anarchistic slogan-poster, perpetuated probably in the year 1993 by David Lusmore, stating: "Life can be magic when we start to break free."[4] I take this as an inspiration to find more trajectories toward a (further) decolonization of anthropological views regarding practices and practitioners, and last, but not least, toward decolonization of "magic" itself.

In order to understand the colonial burden that has been put onto "magic" since this term's adoption into an evolutionary theory, it is crucial to consider the contributions of the two prominent cultural anthropologists, namely Edward B. Tylor and James Frazer. In his *Golden Bough*, Frazer introduced a three-stage model of cultural and intellectual development of human thought, which he claimed was universal, and allocated "magic" to the most backward stage of this development, prior to its advancement first to the stage of "religion" and finally to "science" (see Frazer 1920: 233–43; Sørensen 2018: 2). This evolutionary paradigm has to be understood in the context of colonialism and its proponents who sought to establish a "scientific" justification of the colonial oppression exploiting other countries, their resources, people, and cultures (Benussi 2019: 3). It is in this context that we have to understand first the connotation of magic as "primitive" or backward, and second, the division between "magic" and "religion" (and "science" as the supposed peak of civilization).

With this structure in mind, we can return to *gcod*, and its early descriptions and interpretations promoted by Western scholars, such as Bleichsteiner (1937: 178) who describes *gcod* as a "dreadful rite," a "rite, which, despite its Buddhist surface, is a gruesome mystery of a more primitive era" or Bell's description of a *gcod pa* whom he encountered in Lhasa. The photo, which his assistant Rabden took in the year 1920 (Bell [1931] 1968: 72), became iconic. It shows a man with a long, matted hair and naked upper body covered only with a meditation band over his shoulder and wearing earrings made of shell. He is sitting in front of a small tent, holding a *gcod* drum and a femur bone trumpet. Next to him is a long pole, most likely a skull-staff (Skt. *khaṭvāṅga*), a small table in front of him, with skull-cups, a bell, and a *vajra* on it. Bell (ibid: 72) introduces him in the description as follows: "I have met these Trup-thobs [Tib. *grub thob,* Skt. *siddha*] in Tibet, and can understand that there should be a measure of sympathy between them and the Pönists [Bon po], for certainly their actions and their equipment are far removed from those of the orthodox Buddhists." Bleichsteiner's description of *gcod* mentioned in the first example is both colonial and evolutionist, and also Bell's classification draws a line between the *gcod pa* and the "orthodox" Buddhism. By equating the *gcod pa*s with the *bon pos*, he perpetuates a division between a constructed "proper Buddhism" and "other practices." Here, the echo of a distinction between "religion" and "magic" is clearly heard. This classification has been repeated in numerous publications with the effect that the ritual elements of *gcod* are often conceptualized as "non-Buddhist," "shamanic," and/or "*Bon*," and, thus, as originating from other cultural layers.[5]

The historical roots of these divisions are manifold, and one root possibly stems from the evolutionary paradigm inherited from the colonial perspective as outlined above. The second root, however, derives from the history of the academic studies of Buddhism and its long-standing tradition of privileging texts over practice, partly due to a wider accessibility of texts, as well as a tendency to equate texts and philosophy with a "real Buddhism" (see Lopez 1995: 1–5; Gutschow 2001: 187–8). On the other hand, the ethnographic accounts of practitioners and ritual practices were often provided by missionaries, colonial officials, and travelers whose objectivity was tainted by an orientalist attitude. The split into the "proper Buddhism" and the "other," however, is not limited only to the Western academia but was already undertaken during the second dissemination of Buddhism in Tibet from the eleventh century onward. Major proponents such as King Ye shes 'od promoted a (re-)installation of a "pure Buddhism" in Tibet and eagerly supported monastic institutions, Indian scriptures, philosophy, and proper ethical discipline, while at the same time trying to counteract "foreign and heretic elements" and tantric ritual practices (see Snellgrove [1987] 2013: 170, relying on Karmay [1980] 1998: 9–16). We can conceptualize these historical roots as a three-dimensional colonization of (certain elements and practitioners of) Tibetan Buddhist tantric practice, which involved multifold divisions: between "magic" and "religion," "practice" and "doctrine," and "tantrics" and "monastics." These divisions resonate with each other, and there seems to exist a common stance of privileging religion, doctrine, and monastic institutions over ritual practice. However, I argue that we should not confuse the representations of *gcod* in the academic literature with the actual practice embedded in the contexts of the practitioners' lifeworlds.[6]

In order to decolonize the *gcod* practice in the academic discourse, first, we need to contextualize various authors' analysis and potential bias (and our own!) by understanding the respective worldview informing academic work in each case. This is important in order to understand the interaction between the authors' historical location in the world of ideas, their theoretical contexts, approaches, and interpretations. Second, I follow the working hypothesis that dichotomies that arise from theoretical frameworks such as the division between "magic" and "religion" do not actually match with the practitioners' realities. Although this statement is easy to make, it is nevertheless more difficult to reconcile this division when trying to come nearer to a practitioner's understanding.

On the following pages, I will discuss the opening sections[7] of a *gcod sādhana*, called "The Outspreading Laughter of the *Ḍākinīs* [*mkha' 'gro gad rgyangs*]," which serve as preparation to the ritual proper. I will, then, investigate and discuss various possible enactments and readings of these sections. Afterward, I will critically discuss a division between "religion" and "magic." "The Outspreading Laughter of the *Ḍākinīs*" is part of the *klong chen snying thig* text collection compiled by 'Jigs med gling pa (1729–1798). There are English translations of this *sādhana* available[8]; however, I rely on my own translation of a Tibetan version that I received from my heart-father in Ladakh. This text is handwritten with differently colored felt-tipped pen on pages taken from a school exercise book and cut into a palm-leaf format.

Sādhana enactments and alternative readings

Dancing to clear the ground

The choreography of the *gcod sādhana* "The Outspreading Laughter of the *Ḍākinīs*" starts with a dance. After the *gcod* practitioner has taken upon herself the identity of a wisdom-*ḍākinī*, she paces out the ritual place into the cardinal directions with dancing steps and by this action, she establishes a ritual space with the dancer and Mount Meru forming the center:

> When dancing in the East [on the continent of] Pūrvavideha, swirling around in the circular dancing ground of the *ḍākas* and *ḍākinīs* / … / when dancing in the South [on the continent of] Jambudvīpa / … / in the West [on the continent of] Aparagodānīya … / in the North [on the continent of] Uttarakuru … / in the center, on the peak of the Mount Meru…

This *sādhana* obviously follows the Buddhist geography of the earthly realms, as laid out in a text by Vasubandhu's exposition of the *Abhidharma*: the *gcod* dancer symbolically paces out the whole universe.

> Stamping upon the head of the evil king spirit [which is] hatred …, stamping upon the head of the Lord of Death, [which is] pride …, stamping upon the head of the demoness *rākṣasi* [which is] desire, …, stamping upon the head of the vowbreaker, [which is] envy …, stamping upon the head of evil spirit of the dead, [which is] ignorance.

The dance movement is intended to convey the act of *stamping upon somebody's head*. Each spatial direction has a twofold target, a combination of the outer and the inner hindrances. Each pair consists of a particular, personified and embodied, evil spirit, which is equated with one of the five disturbing emotions (Skt. *pañcakleśaviṣa,* Tib. *dug lnga*). The movements are choreographed in such a way that the dancer takes on a particular state of mind, namely one in which each of the disturbing emotions is subjugated. This trajectory unfolds a development from a changed mindset to an altered perception and, thus, reveals a distinct reality, as we can see in the initial statement at the beginning of the *gcod sādhana*:

> Phat! I, the *yogin*(ī) who practices, and who has absorbed and mastered fearlessness, will—with thought and deed which permeated the equality of *saṃsāra* and *nirvāṇa*—stomp and dance upon the gods and demons of ego-clinging [and] crush [all the] dualistic *saṃsāric* thoughts and experiences to dust.

The performing *yoginī* or *yogī* is prompted to hold a particular state of mind and perception, namely that *saṃsāra* and *nirvāṇa* are inextricably entwined. This mindset is a precondition for all the ritual activity that is to be carried out. Only with this understanding can the dualistic *saṃsāric* thoughts and experiences be crushed through the performance of the dance. In each stanza, the *gcod pa* is called upon to use the ritual instruments and sounds associated with different kinds of "pristine cognition" mentioned in the course of the *sādhana*. Here is an example:

> Make the trumpet-flute [of] a mirror-like pristine cognition echo eerily! ... Chime and clack the skullcup hand-drum [of] a pristine cognition of sameness! ... Let the hand-bell and small bells [of] the pristine cognition of discernment ring out!

There are five of the abovementioned "pristine cognitions," which together form a mental and perceptual "layout" of Buddhahood, each one representing an aspect of the cognitive quality of the *dharmadhātu* (Tib. *chos kyi dbyings*), sometimes referred to as the expanse of actual reality. Thus, the five aspects of wisdom, as evoked in the *sādhana* through the play of the ritual instruments, are the expression of *nirvāṇa*. The cosmos, which is paced out and subdued by the *yogī* or the *yoginī* during the dance, is the expression of *saṃsāra*. The *maṇḍala*, then, expresses the essential identity of both and that is the state, which the *gcod pa* seeks to establish during the course of this practice. The *gcod sādhana* concludes the procedure of the dance outlined above with the following instruction:

> [Reciting] this while stamping [the dance, you have] led the [ordinary] awareness [into a state of awareness,] which does not refer to objects or reference points [as being intrinsically existent].

We see here that the performative aspect of the dance and this specific mode of perception are intrinsically linked. The *gcod pa* subjugates the *saṃsāric* cosmos, the existence of which relies on the ordinary perception, and, thus, enters into a state of altered perception, which is being characterized as the recognition of the "ultimate truth" of emptiness of the self and the phenomena.

If we relate that back to Sørensen's approach to magic and ask: What kind of transformation and "special and non-trivial kinds of actions" take place during the dance? And furthermore: What effects arise and which powers are at play?, we find that the choreography of the opening part of the *sādhana*, as outlined above, is a skillful means for subduing and transforming destructive emotions, with the dance implementing a theoretical bedrock of Tibetan Buddhist philosophy in practice. Does this mean that we can read the *sādhana* (only) as a mere symbolic choreography drawing exclusively on the tenets of Buddhist philosophy and for the sake of inducing an altered attitude and perception? I argue that all this depends on the mode of enactment and the way the *sādhana* text is read. On the following pages, I will first look at different modi of how the dance outlined in the *sādhana* is enacted and then consider alternative (or parallel) readings.

Enactments and alternative readings

One enactment modus can be found within groups of (mostly) monastic practitioners performing *gcod* in the temple or the *dukhang* of a monastery. Sitting in rows, the practitioners perform the *gcod sādhana* through chanting (or reciting) the *sādhana* text, accompanied by playing the bell, the *gcod* drum (*da ru*), and possibly the bone trumpet (*rkang gling*). The enactment of the *sādhana*'s choreography, together with the dance, is (possibly) visualized while chanting. The second modus of enacting the dance choreography is its physical performance. The *mkha' 'gro gad rgyangs gcod*'s dances I have observed were performed by single practitioners and into the cardinal directions. This matches with the descriptions in literature (see David-Néel [1932] 2007: 121, 128; Crook and Low 1997: 325, for Low's reference to the *sādhana* see ibid.: 318). In Nepal, I observed the (physical) performance of a round-dance according to another Tibetan Buddhist *gcod sādhana*, requiring a group of practitioners. So we find the two different modi: first, through the visualization, when the dance is conducted with the faculty of imagination, and second, through the physical enactment of the dance choreography, when the *sādhana* is enacted in actual movement and physicality.

Next, I want to consider three alternative readings of the *sādhana*'s dance choreography. Rather than focusing on the symbolic interpretation of the *sādhana* explained through the cosmological framework of Tibetan Buddhist philosophy, these alternative readings are concerned with the relationship between dance and ritual place-making in Tibetan religious culture. For my conceptualization, I am relying on Schrempf's (1999) investigations on how the actual enactment of dance movements contributes to the creation of ritual space in *'cham* (dance in religious ritual) and *gar* (tantric initiation dance) in Tibetan Buddhist and Bon po contexts.

The first alternative reading is meant to set the *gcod* dance in continuum with a religio-historical event, namely the first ritual dance conducted by Padmasambhava to prepare a site for establishing the first Tibetan Buddhist monastery. A Tibetan dance manual compiled by the Fifth Dalai Lama Ngawang Lobsang Gyatso (1617–1682) refers to this enterprise as follows: "[He] subdued the ground (*sa 'dul*) of glorious Samye (*bsam yas*), by performing a ritual dance (*gar 'cham*), which relied on the same great *maṇḍala* of action ...."[9] The "great *maṇḍala* of action" refers to the Vajrakīla (*rdo rje phur ba*) *'cham* dance and its purpose: "The chief purpose [of this Vajrakīla *'cham*] is expressly the subjugation of Rudra by Badzra Heruka" (ibid.), namely the subjugation of evil forces by the embodiment of wrathful enlightened activity. The activity of Padmasambhava was credited with success: "With that [*maṇḍala* of action,] he created excellent conditions, such as pacifying the malice of the gods and the demons (ibid.)." Within the performative repetition and reenactment of this subjugation, the dancer is (potentially) empowered through a deep resonance with Padmasambhava and his activity[10] and is in action-based touch with a foundation stone of Tibet's traditional Buddhist history.

A second alternative reading I propose focuses on understanding the *gcod* dance as a condensed form of a *'cham* dance. The physical setting of a *'cham* consists of monk-dancers, and the succession of dances involves different protectors and deities. Even if the dancers take on multiple roles, there are still a number of participants required. A drawing of a *'cham*-dance by Filchner (1933: 296–7, plate 154; documented in Schrempf 1999: 203) shows five participants in the center, surrounded by an inner circle of about twenty-five dancers and a similar number in an outer circle, plus six musicians and a row of monks, who seem to be holding incense. By contrast, in the *gcod* practice although the dance *may* be performed by a group of *gcod pa*s, it is often performed by a single retreatant or practitioner. In that case, a *yoginī* or a *yogī* dances on her/his own, yet according to the *sādhana*'s choreography, she/he addresses the *guru*s, the deities, the *ḍākinī*s, the *ḍāka*s, and the protectors, to join in:

> [You] root-*guru*s and *guru*s of the lineage come to dance! [You] hosts of personal meditation deities and *ḍāka*s come to dance! [You] [great] assemblies of *ḍākinī*s and guardians of the holy places come to dance!

While dancing, the *gcod pa* plays the drum, and occasionally blows the bone trumpet. Moreover, the *gcod pa* assumes several roles herself, and the physical setting of a ritual *gcod* dance is much simpler than the elaborate *'cham* dance, which has many performers and musicians. However, I argue that the *gcod* dance reflects the *'cham* performance in dance and music and by evoking the *guru*s, the deities, and other participants, the dance not only mirrors the evocation of agents inhabiting a tantric *maṇḍala* but also points to a bigger assembly of a collective ritual when a *yoginī* or a *yogī* dances with the lineage holders, the deities, the *ḍāka*s, and the *ḍākinī*s called, as it were, into presence.

A third alternative reading of the dance is its recognition as a *maṇḍala* of action. This can be interpreted in a twofold way. The first is ontological, when the ritual dance does not necessarily only serve to prepare the site, but the dancers *and* their performance can, in combination with various mental acts carried out simultaneously, also *be* the *maṇḍala* itself. This state induces transformation:

> The performance of a publicly staged ritual dance (*'cham*) becomes itself a "great *maṇḍala* of action," where dancers act as … masked wrathful protectors of religion (*chos skyong*), empowered by their *being*, [carry out the further ritual activities]. (Schrempf 1999: 199)

The dance acts as a ritual strategy of place-making, and the dancer performs the evocation and the self-initiation into the *maṇḍala*, so that the dancer's body, identity, action, and perception all become part of the *maṇḍala*. Then, and this is the second dimension of action here, according to Schrempf, the *'cham* dancers, empowered by their being a part of the *maṇḍala*, conduct two acts of subjugation. The first is a *sa 'dul* (lit. "taming the earth") and it is performed by the dancers as they are taking the roles of "Black-Hat figures" or masked wrathful *dharma* protectors. As Schrempf remarks, the usual translations of this Tibetan term meaning "cleansing the ground" or "preparing the site" appear rather neutral, more precise rendition is "subjugating the earth," which Schrempf conceptualizes as a "means of taking control of and transforming space," an action that goes beyond symbolic reading:

> The actions [… performed in ritual to take control over space] are not mere symbolic representations of the religious order but powerful and physical means of transformation through subjugation. Dance movements not only create and inscribe ritual space, they simultaneously subjugate the ground physically. (Schrempf 1999: 212)

The second act is performed by the dancers taking the roles of higher tantric deities to subjugate obstacles preventing enlightenment, such as different classes of evil spirits, and outer and inner hindrances including enemies of religion

(Schrempf 1999: 199). I suggest that in the choreography of the *gcod sādhana*, these two acts of subjugation of the earth and of the evil influences are conducted simultaneously and in a condensed form.

If we now recall Sørensen's definition of "magic" and evaluate the enactments and four readings of the dance accordingly, we find various potential transformations at play: of conflicting emotions, *saṃsāric* views and perceptions, and of the mode of being in the world; potential identification with Guru Rinpoche's powerful act of subduing opposing forces, calling a tantric community of lineage holders, deities, and protectors into presence; and last, but not least, the transformation of one's own identity, and the whole environment into tantric ones. If we look at the transformative techniques, we find considerable variations between the different readings and possible enactments of the same text containing the *sādhana*'s choreography. The technique may consist of reciting the text and following it through visualization, while playing the bell, the drum, and the bone trumpet; or of performing dance and thereby reenacting the clearing of the ground for Tibet's first monastery. It can also consist of performing a condensed version of a *'cham*-dance and/or enacting a *maṇḍala* of action. And ideally, these potential horizons of practice and encounter all happen at the same time.

Location and exposure

The location where the *gcod* practice including the dance should be performed is, according to advice at the beginning of the *sādhana*, a *gnyan sa*—a place of rugged terrain populated by malicious spirits. A cremation ground matches well with these requirements and serves as a distinguished place of practice. The charnel ground has had a long symbolic history in Buddhism and is considered a critical locus for the performance of many different practices, such as meditating on impermanence and the selflessness of the self, cultivating mindfulness of the certainty of death in order to turn our attention to *dharma* practice, or contemplating one's own death in order to practice techniques of liberation from *saṃsāra* during the process of dying and so forth.

Of the many locations of actual *gcod* practices encountered during my fieldwork in Ladakh, Uttarakhand, and Nepal, in the majority of the cases, a literal cremation ground is substituted by a practice place at home, in the temple, in a retreat place, in a nomad tent, at a pilgrimage site, or in the monastery, where the practitioner visualizes the cremation ground and thus goes there virtually.

However, *gcod pa*s do practice in physical cremation grounds, which will be discussed in more detail below. The preliminary practice of meditating on one's own death, and the practice of *'pho ba* where one ejects their own or another's consciousness into a pure land at death, is meant to be enhanced by the outer conditions and the ambience of a cremation ground where dead bodies are treated. In the *gcod sādhana*, there are some alterations of the common *'pho ba* procedure. First, the consciousness is not projected into a pure land with its specific environment and perception, but it transforms into a female deity, who then dismembers the corpse of one's own conventional life and identity:

> That [wrathful female deity into which my awareness has transformed] [then cuts with her knife into the head of my] own body [which is now the corpse], cutting off the skull cap. [I/She] place/s it [turned upside-down] upon three hearth stones which are human heads [so big that they] pervade [the whole universe consisting of] 1000^3 [a billion worlds].

When the outer and the visualized ritual sites are congruent, they potentially enhance each other's power of transformation, since what the practitioner sees and experiences in the outer world may color the reality of the visualization of one's own death and dismemberment. And the more clearly the death of one's own conventional identity and body is imagined, the more powerful a new identity as a tantric deity with a new body of different quality and outlook may arise. The human heads, which make up the hearth, are described as being giant in size, so that they fill the whole universe, which means that, in this meditated ritual environment, the whole universe is turned into a charnel ground.

A second alternative reading of both, namely the enactment advice to practice at a *gnyan sa* and the choreography, is to set both in relation to other cremation ground practitioners and conceptualize *gcod pa* in continuity with other cremation ground specialists, known throughout the centuries. Historically speaking, we can trace back the selection of the cremation ground as a site for practice to Hindu tantric Śaiva practitioners such as the Pāśupatas, the Lākulas, and, in particular, the Kāpālika ascetics (see Sanderson 1988: 665–71). Tantric practice related to cremation grounds has been performed in order to attain salvation, yet also to attain supernatural powers (ibid.: 664) by gaining access to the power of the worshipped deities. The lifestyle of such ascetics interestingly seems to have followed the pattern of the living conditions of the criminals. According to Lorenzen (1972: 13), Sanderson (1988: 666), and Samuel ([2008] 2009: 243–5), a potential "role model" for the cremation ground practitioners' lifestyle was murderers who had killed a Brahmin. However, contrary to the murderers, who were expelled from the community as a punishment and were forced to live outside the human settlements, sometimes in cremation grounds, the tantric practitioners actually chose these places. With that choice, they moved closer to the "criminal" and the "dark," and their tantric practices became associated with transgression, night, death, danger, and horror. This culminated in various transgressive ritual practices, possibly including human sacrifice, which were ascribed to the Kāpālikas by their contemporaries (Lorenzen 1972: 85). This may have influenced *gcod* practice, and the contemplated sacrifice of—most likely in a version adjusted to Buddhist paradigms—one's own body. However, such a lifestyle and practice are not necessarily indicative of actual "dark" deeds, but possibly point to an alternative interpretation, namely their dedication to handle the "dark side" of life, from which people normally turn away: illness, misfortune, and death, which are the working fields of *gcod* healers.

A third alternative reading that goes beyond a symbolic reading of the cremation ground is the importance of mastering the challenge of physical exposure and practice at the site. David Neel ([1932] 2007: 126–31) vividly describes the exposure of a monastic *gcod pa* who practiced at night next to a corpse that had been cut into pieces to feed the vultures. In her report, the physical exposure includes the presence of a wild animal and a host of evil spirits to whom the *gcod pa* offers his body. I have documented elsewhere a *gcod pa*'s report about the beginnings of his cremation ground practice, when he reported to have met spirits, skeletons, wolves, and other wild animals and experienced strong winds, which was in accord with what he had been told by his teacher and other *gcod pa*s beforehand. He also told stories about other *gcod pa*s who had died because their meditation skills had not been sufficiently trained to deal with a number of wolves at a sky burial ground (see Schröder 2023). In any case, the *gcod pa*s who seek the physical exposure will encounter the cremation ground and its challenges more directly and without an "easy exit," in contrast to those who practice in a safe environment and merely visualize the scenery. In this regard, the *gcod pa*s literally frequenting cremation grounds are more near to the enterprise of "seeking out adversity to directly work with fear and terror" (Sheehy 2005: 41).

There are other alternative readings possible, such as practicing at the *gnyan sa* as a potential gathering place of local gods and spirits, to subdue them and simultaneously gather empowerments and spiritual realizations (see Nicoletti 2013: 24). Still another alternative reading of the cremation ground as practice site for *gcod* is to come into contact with deceased family members and members of the armed resistance who died in the battlefield, as well as to practice *gcod* to purify their (and one's own) karma accumulated during their fights against the invasion of Tibet (see Schröder 2023).

If we return to Sørensen's definition of "magic" and evaluate the possible interpretations of the significance of the cremation ground as a site of practice accordingly, we find various potential transformations at play: first of all, the great transformation of death itself; the meditated death of the practitioner's conventional identity and body; the transformation of perception and attitude when realizing the selflessness of the self; the practitioner's transformation into a tantric deity; and the transformation of her ordinary body into the offerings for the *gaṇacakra*; the history of transforming cremation grounds into the sites of tantric practice; and other transformations, such as the accumulation of power and the purification of karma. If we look at the transformative techniques, we find Buddhist contemplations about death and meditations to stabilize the insight into the ultimate reality of emptiness of the self and the phenomena; the *'pho ba* technique to project the consciousness into another realm (or here: identity); and the practice of *gcod* in the physical exposure of the cremation ground. In short, the transformative power of the *gcod* practice partly relies on its stable connection with various Buddhist practices, and the practitioner's readiness to leave the comfort zone to conduct the said practice.

The *gcod pa*'s tent

The *sādhana* text lists seven items required for the *gcod* ritual: a beast of prey's intact skin with all its claws, a small tent, a skull-staff (*khaṭvāṅga*), a bone trumpet, a *gcod pa*'s drum, a bell (with its counterpart, the *vajra*), and a crown or head dress with a veil. The tent is introduced as follows:

> For that [performing the *gcod* ritual] the required utensils [are]: / … [Secondly, he/she needs] a small square tent that is pitched [by throwing it] from above [down onto the ground] [like] the view /.

The tent is mentioned as being "small" and "square," and its pitching is set up in the analogy to "the view." Here, the "view" refers to the realization of "emptiness of the self and the phenomena" as conceptualized in the Buddhist philosophical notion of the ultimate truth or reality. There are two possible enactments: first, pitching the tent may serve as an analogy of the view of ultimate truth. This can be meditated on in the assembly hall of a monastery or in a shrine room at home.

In that case, the practice is entirely visualized and conducted in an imagined cremation ground. In the second case, the practitioner pitches a material tent in the physical cremation ground and *thereby* practices "the view" so that an action (with a resulting pitched tent) is performed simultaneously with the cultivation of a particular way of perceiving the world, and becomes its tangible analogy.

The materiality of a *gcod pa*'s tent is described by David-Néel ([1932, 1965] 2007: 128) and Evans-Wentz ([1935] 1958: 277, note 2). Bell's photo ([1931] 1968: 72) mentioned before shows the *gcod pa* sitting in front of a square tent made from cloth. David-Néel and Low describe how such a tent was used in an active ritual practice: at night near a corpse (David-Néel [1932] 2007: 128–9) and during several months lasting *gcod* practice—pilgrimage to 120 cremation grounds in Ladakh (Crook and Low 1997: 323, 325–30). From these reports describing its physical use, we can derive a second interpretative reading of the tent, which goes beyond a symbolic one, namely in the actual cremation ground, the tent becomes a place to practice, live, and sleep in. It becomes a physical shelter—though due to its material—possibly weak. Since it is located in the physical environment, it may contribute to keeping away the cold, wind, wild animals, gods of the place, and spirits (when they are not called in for the *gaṇacakra*). The use of the actual tent for the *gcod* practice possibly enhances also the second alternative interpretation: the tent itself represents a *maṇḍala* and becomes one when it is set up during the *gcod* dance (Crook and Low 1997: 323; conversation with James Low). It becomes a particular realm, populated by various tantric beings, including the practitioner who changes her identity into that of a wrathful *ḍākinī*. The most profound transformation, however, is that of the conventional perception that changes into the enlightened one.

Discussion

The enactment modi of the opening parts of the *gcod sādhana* differ, firstly, in the degree of physical involvement needed to enact the choreography of the dance; secondly, in the choice of the place of practice; and thirdly, in the presence or absence of material ritual items mentioned in the *sādhana*.

If we now apply the magic/religion division current in Cultural Anthropology, which is partly based on Tylor's and Frazer's evolutionary trajectory, to the findings of these different enactments of *gcod*, we come to several conclusions. First, if we consider "magic," we find a physically conducted dance in an actual cremation ground, and a ritual tent pitched there, at night, where the practitioner practices, dwells, and meditates, using various ritual items such as a skull-staff, a trumpet made of a human femur, and potentially the skin of a wild animal with all its claws. Then, if we consider "religion," we find the visualization of a dance, a cremation ground, which is visited by a practitioner merely in imagination, pointing to the typically Buddhist doctrines such as mindfulness of death, and a virtual tent referring to the famous doctrine of the emptiness of the self and the phenomena. All of these are merely symbolic acts, referring to the view of ultimate truth outlined in the *Prajñāpāramitāsūtra* and applied for soteriological goals. The actual site of religious practice would be a monastery or a shrine room at home, the ritual items would be music instruments, and the main performative activity is chanting or recitation of the text.

This classification apparently grants a rather clear picture of a distinction between "magic" and "religion." However, *gcod* is *not* two different practices: we look at *one gcod sādhana*. I suggest two other perspectives that cross-cut this division. The first is the consideration of the historical development of Tibetan tantric Buddhist practices, which in parts accords with the development of Śaiva-Śākta tantric practices in India. White (1998) formulated a three-stage model for Śaiva-Śākta practices, relying on Sanderson's more detailed descriptions (1988: 660–704). During the first of these phases from about the sixth century CE, practices were carried out in actual cremation grounds and were centered on "terrifying" worship of Śiva-Bhairava, his consort, and the *yoginīs*, as well as the worship of Kālī. Among these practitioners were the Kāpālika ascetics whose practice and lifestyle were closely related to the cremation grounds. In the second phase of this development, from about the ninth century CE onward, the cremation ground practices became interiorized and greater emphasis was put on the erotic elements of the *yoginī* cults and sexual initiations. Finally, in the third phase, which took place in the eleventh century CE, the practices were "sanitized" for the public, and the original practices were carried out in secret only. This phase involved the progressive internalization of the tantric ritual scenario (see Samuel 2008: 327). This transformation of practice was accompanied by the development of a sophisticated philosophical basis for the practices, and by converting transgressive practices into a gnoseological system that made use of the (meditated) aesthetics of the divine encountered through vision, light, and sound (see White 1998: 172–3; Samuel 2008: 326–30). If we now consider the first and the third historical phase as relevant for the development of *gcod*, we find the importance of the actual cremation ground characteristic of the first phase, and then, the internalization of the tantric ritual scenario as well as development of an elaborate philosophical basis as characterizing the third phase. If we assume that not only the practices but also the practice sites have been internalized, then in *gcod*, we find an internalized cremation ground. Applying the three-phase model, just described, to the *gcod* practice itself, we notice a progressive shift from the material to the imaginative, from the physicality and (supposedly) transgressive ritual practices to visualization, and "symbolifications" of those transgressive practices. However, contemporary practitioners seemingly work across the phases of that model, and so I suggest that, rather than applying a model divided into historical phases that are terminated in terms of their respective modes of practices, we can conceptualize them as a historical field of practice that provides different possibilities of *gcod* enactment available to practitioners of the current era.

The picture of clear-cut differentiation also changes when we leave the synchronical perspective and look diachronically at the practices in the biographies of individual practitioners. For example, among the practitioners I worked with during my fieldwork, there is the Bonpo Geshe who practices *gcod* in his monastery and in patients' homes for healing, but has the experience of having practiced *gcod* at the cremation ground of Pāśupatināth during his early years of education. There are the nuns who regularly practice *gcod* in the temple, but occasionally at the cremation ground, when a dead body is cremated. There is the *gcod* healer who practices *gcod* for patients in his home, but also goes to the mountains to conduct sky burials with a simultaneous *gcod* practice. We find a lay tantric practitioner, who, in the past, conducted the *gcod* dance physically in his backyard, and *gcod* without a physical dance at the cremation ground, yet presently practices at home only through visualization since his age and arthritic degeneration of his knee joints prevent him from going to distant places and performing dances. We find *gcod* practitioners who employ different sets of ritual items at different occasions, and we find numerous lay practitioners who join monastic *gcod* practices at particular practice dates. There are monastic *gcod* practitioners who practice *gcod* together in the temple, but have completed short-term or long-term solitary mountain retreats to practice *gcod* and other practices—and some have spent nights alone in "dangerous places." This diachronic perspective reveals that the different enactments—instead of being distinct—are rather entwined in the experience of many practitioners. I argue that against the background of the historical and the diachronic perspectives, we can formulate an antithesis to a clear dichotomy between magic- and religion-related practice elements, and rather than as fundamentally different ways of practice, we can conceptualize them as a field with different enactment modes that inform one another.

If we now conceptualize this field of practice as a spectrum, apply the classifications and add our alternative interpretative readings, we find two ends of enactment modes. On the one end there are the physical enactments, a potential reenactment of Guru Rinpoche's dance to subdue the opposing forces, a *'cham* dance with the lineage holders, the deities, the *ḍāka*s and the *ḍākinī*s, and the echo of the tantric Kāpālikas and their lifestyle at the edge of society. We find practice at gathering places of local gods and spirits, the generation of power, and the experience of staying in a little tent alone at night at the cremation ground, where the practitioner dwells, dances, and evokes various tantric beings. Here, the practitioners transform their mindset, attitudes, and perception *in action*, with the physical investment into movements, activities, and into exposure.

On the other end of the spectrum, we find visualized activities reduced to the imagined sites of practice. The actual (visible) practice is performed at home, in a monastery, or another practice place. For the observer, the *gcod* practice may look like a majority of other Tibetan Buddhist practices: the practitioner sits, chants or recites a text, and plays ritual instruments, which provide a unique soundscape to the ritual during which the ritual becomes a "*pūjā*." The practitioner is required to follow the visualized choreography to transform the mindset, attitude, and perception. Thereby, the aims and accompanying settings outlined in the Tibetan Buddhist philosophy are being actualized and the *sādhana* forms a skillful means for this realization. Here, the core practice is the *gcod meditation*. The *gcod sādhana* presents a choreography that provides a symbolic window to conduct Buddhist trainings, such as cultivating renunciation and practicing the doctrine of emptiness of the self and the phenomena.

I argue that if we however think about the spectrum of *gcod* practice with all its enactment modes *together*, and their potentials entwined, then, this combination bears the potential of bringing the *sādhana* text to dynamic life. If we stay for a moment with the classical dichotomy but are ready to reconcile both ends, the religio-philosophical end provides an array of meanings, elaborate techniques of transformation, and a means of embodying all this within a fine-grained Tibetan Buddhist cosmology. The "magic" end with its physicality, materiality, performance, and tangibility, on the other hand, provides the life-blood, energy, and power to accomplish a deep and profound transformation. The unification of the two ends guarantees that the practitioners understand the meaning, but are not necessarily conducting a merely intellectual or a recitatory exercise. They seek the real experience, they work with "real" material items and physicality, and, in that way, engage with their whole being-in-the-world. In this way, the *gcod* practice may become a powerful means with the potential to radically transform places, actions, beings, material items, and ultimately: the practitioner's mode of being-in-the-world, that changes her attitude and perception during the path to (and of) enlightenment.

Conclusion

Returning to the question whether there is magic in *gcod*, I will seek the answers in relation to different "magic" definitions and landmarks, outlined in the introduction. To begin, let's start with the first question, namely: Is there such a type of magic in *gcod* as depicted in the evolutionary theory, where the separation of magic from both religion and science is highlighted and where magic is associated with a backward position in terms of (proper) development of a society? One may notice that the division between transgressive rituals seen as "magic" and the institutionalized proper religious practice had its historical predecessor with the person of the King Ye shes 'od and others, who differentiated the two. The former was associated with lay tantrics, while the later with official monastic religion. However, the development of Tibetan Buddhism was more entwined and complex than this simple division suggests, and it still is. In this chapter, I have presented different interpretations of the opening parts of the *gcod sādhana*, and applied a division between "religious" and "magical" practices to its contents. The result is that this division is artificial and does not exist in opposition to one another, but, instead, forms a unit that informs one another. Seen from this perspective, "magical" and "religious" elements enhance each other's power of transformation when applied together during the *gcod* practice.

The second approach to "magic" mentioned by Sørensen defined it in terms of transformations that take place through certain special and non-trivial actions with opaque causal mediation. In *gcod*, many transformations are induced and potentially take place; one may recall a few of the many that were mentioned: a *gcod pa* changes the mode of being from a conventional personality and perception into that of a *ḍākinī*; while dances, tents, people, and other beings are transformed into a *maṇḍala*. We have seen that the transformative techniques can be read symbolically, recited and meditated as visions, and some of them can be performed physically. All these acts are non-trivial actions, and most likely seem opaque for audiences of laypeople, even more so when the techniques are kept in secrecy for non-initiates. In that sense, we find a lot of Sørensen's magic in *gcod*. For the initiate practitioner however, none of these activities are opaque: rather, they are logical, acquired through rigorous training and explained through a detailed system of empowerments, reading transmissions, and oral explanations, so that the way they work is perfectly understandable. For the initiate, *gcod* is not magic but rather: skill.

With that explanation in mind, we should now look at the third definition of "magic" by Chögyam Trungpa Rinpoche who defined magic and miracle as a belief instigated by a sudden incident or a practice, which cannot be explained by the theoretical framework a person holds. Whether the effects of a *gcod* ritual are seen as magic, or not, depends on the level of skill as well as cosmology in which a person lives and operates: for someone it might be a miracle, and for somebody else, it is an enactment of logical processes outlined in scripts and illuminated through the teacher's oral instructions that leads to success. The Tibetan Buddhist tantric and Rdzogs chen paths, as such, and their effects, however, can be conceptualized as "magic" in terms of their efficacy in transforming the mindset and, with that, they result in a transformed mode of encountering the world. Chögyam Trungpa (1991: 132) states:

> The Vajrayana, the tantric teaching of the Buddha, contains tremendous magic and power. Its magic lies in its ability to transform confusion and neurosis into the awakened mind and to reveal the everyday world as a sacred realm.

And James Low (Crook and Low 1997: 330) describes such a state of magic for *gcod*:

> Cutting a way through cultural limitation, cutting off the demands of others, cutting into the innate clarity of presence—this is the task of Chod (*gcod*). And it is a task that calls us, the soft reverberating drum of Machig Labdron, echoing down through every moment of experience, transforming the corpse of reification into the living dancing beauty of the ceaseless play of becoming.

So, yes: there is magic in *gcod*, definitely, if the practitioner is ready (and skilled) for a radical transformation of her attitudes, perception, and mode of being-in-the-world.

Notes

1 My Tibetan heart-father and I adopted each other as father and daughter more than a decade ago. We shared close family ties, took care of each other, and undertook many activities together—among these several pilgrimages (for an account of a shared pilgrimage see Schröder 2019).

2 Several authors added that this was not a new conclusion, but already explicit in Tibetan historical works; see, for example, Stott (1989: 222).

3 For a detailed discussion of David-Néel's "culture of magic," see Thévoz's article in this volume.

4 For the poster documentation, see the entry "Lusmore, David" on the website of the Fédération Internationale des centres d'"études et de documentation libertaires (FICEDL), poster reference Aff1285—305336 (ciraL): placard.ficedl.info/article3730.html.

5 Especially Mircea Eliade's classification of *gcod* as being "clearly shamanic in structure" ([1964] 1974: 436) has been repeated many times.

6 For a fieldwork and text-based ethnography of (mostly Tibetan) *gcod* practitioners in Ladakh, their worlds, and their practices, see Schröder (2018).

7 For a contextual description and more detailed discussion of the entire practice and a second *gcod sādhana*, see Schröder (2018).

8 See Evans-Wentz ([1935] 1958: 301–19) and Duff ([2008] 2010).

9 See Schrempf (1999: 198), translation by Toni Huber, transcription and transliterations adjusted.

10 The concluding sentence of the Fifth Dalai Lama's dance manual states that the ritual dance was especially powerful because of its historical association with Padmasambhava and its usage in the establishment of the first monastery in Tibet: "[This *'cham*] is associated with the source of Tantra and has a great deal of empowerment (*byin rlabs*)" (see Schrempf 1999: 198).

References

Bell, Sir C. ([1931] 1968), *The Religion of Tibet*, Oxford: Oxford University Press.

Benussi, M. (2019), "Magic," in F. Stein (ed.), *The Cambridge Encyclopedia of Anthropology*. http://doi.org/10.29164/19magic.

Bleichsteiner, R. (1937), *Die Gelbe Kirche: Mysterien der Buddhistischen Klöster in Indien, Tibet, Mongolei und China*, Wien: Josef Belf.

Crook, J. H., and J. Low (1997), *The Yogins of Ladakh. A Pilgrimage among the Hermits of the Buddhist Himalayas*, Delhi: Motilal Banarsidass.

David-Néel, A. ([1932, 1965] 2007), *Magic & Mystery in Tibet: The Classic Account of a Woman's Extraordinary Journey to Tibet*, London: Souvenir Press.

Duff, T. (ed.) ([2008] 2010), *The Longchen Nyingthig Chod Practice "Sound of Dakini Laughter,"* Kathmandu: Padma Karpo Translation Committee.

Edou, J. (1996), *Machig Labdrön and the Foundations of Chöd*, Ithaca, NY: Snow Lion.

Eliade, M. ([1964] 1974), *Shamanism: Archaic Techniques of Ecstasy*, Princeton: Princeton University Press; Bollingen Series LXXVI.

Evans-Wentz, W. Y. ([1935] 1958), *Tibetan Yoga and Secret Doctrines*, London: Oxford University Press.

Filchner, W. (1933), *Kumbum Dschamba Ling*, Leipzig: Brockhaus.

Frazer, S. J. G. (1920), *The Golden Bough. A Study in Magic and Religion, 3rd Ed., Part I., The Magic Art and the Evolution of Kings, Vol. 1*, London: Macmillan.

Gutschow, K. (2001), "What Makes a Nun? Apprenticeship and Ritual Passage in Zangskar, North India," *Journal of the International Association of Buddhist Studies* 24 (2): 187–215.

Gyatso, J. (1985), "The Development of the gCod Tradition," in B. Azis and M. Kapstein (eds.), *Soundings in Tibetan Civilization*, 74–98, Delhi: Manohar.

Karmay, S. G. ([1987] 1998), *The Arrow and the Spindle: Studies in History, Myths, Rituals and Beliefs in Tibet*, Kathmandu: Mandala Book Point.

Lopez, D. S., Jr. (ed.) (1995), *Curators of the Buddha. The Study of Buddhism under Colonialism*, Chicago: University of Chicago Press.

Lorenzen, D. N. (1972), *The Kāpālikas and Kālāmukhas: Two lost Śaivite Sects*, New Delhi: Thomson.

Nicoletti, M. (2013), *The Nomadic Sacrifice: The Chöd Pilgrimage Among the Bönpo of Dolpo*, Kathmandu: Vajra Publications.

Orofino, G. ([2000] 2001), "The Great Wisdom Mother and the Gcod Tradition," in D. G. White (ed.), *Tantra in Practice*, 396–416, Delhi: Motilal Banarsidass.

Samuel, G. (1993), *Civilized Shamans: Buddhism in Tibetan Societies*, Washington, DC: Smithsonian Institution Press.

Samuel, G. ([2008] 2009), *The Origins of Yoga and Tantra: Indic Religions to the Thirteenth Century*, Cambridge: Cambridge University Press.

Sanderson, A. (1988), "Śaivism and the Tantric Traditions," in S. Sutherland, L. Houlden et al. (eds.), *The World's Religions*, 660–704, London: Routledge.

Schrempf, M. (1999), "Taming the Earth, Controlling the Cosmos: Transformation of Space in Tibetan Buddhist and Bon-po Ritual Dances," in T. Huber (ed.), *Sacred Spaces and Powerful Places in Tibetan Culture: A Collection of Essays*, 198–224, Dharamsala: Library of Tibetan Works and Archives.

Schröder, N.-A. (2023), "The Cremation Ground, the Battlefield and the Path of Compassion. Or: What Makes the Fabric of an Individual's Tantric Encounter?," in C. Lorea and R. Singh (eds.), *The Ethnography of Tantra. Textures and Contexts of Living Tantric Traditions*, 243–68, New York: SUNY Press.

Schröder, N.-A. (2019), "Places, Rituals, and Past Worlds: Encounters on a Tibetan Pilgrimage in North India," in C. Bergmann and J. Schaflechner (eds.), *Ritual Journeys in South Asia: Constellations and Contestations of Mobility and Space*, 85–118, London: Routledge.

Schröder, N.-A. (2018), *Belonging, Encountering and Transformation: An Ethnography of Suffering and Its Negotiation through Ritual Gcod Healing in and around Tibetan Refugee Settlements in Ladakh*, Ph.D. thesis, Heidelberg University.

Sheehy, M. R. (2005), "Severing the Source of Fear: Contemplative Dynamics of the Tibetan Buddhist Gcod Tradition," *Contemporary Buddhism* 6 (1): 37–52.

Snellgrove, D. (2013), "The Rulers of Western Tibet," in G. Tuttle and K. R. Schaeffer (eds.), *The Tibetan History Reader*, 166–82, New York: Columbia University Press.

Sørensen, J. (2018), "Magic," in H. Callan (ed.), *The International Encyclopedia of Anthropology*, Hoboken, NJ: John Wiley. doi: 10.1002/9781118924396.wbiea1756.

Stott, D. (1989), "Offering the Body: The Practice of Gcod in Tibetan Buddhism," *Religion* 19: 221–226.

Trungpa, C. (1991), *The Heart of the Buddha*, Boston, MA: Shambala.

Trungpa, C. (1999), *Transcending Madness. The Experience of the Six Bardos*, Boston, MA: Shambala.

White, D. G. (1998), "Transformations in the Art of Love: Kāmakalā Practices in Hindu Tantric and Kaula Traditions," *History of Religions* 38 (2): 172–98.

9

"Trainings for Sorcery, Magic, Mystic, Philosophy—for That Which Is Called 'the Great Accomplishment' ": Alexandra David-Neel's Written and Unwritten Tibetan Grimoires

Samuel Thévoz

Alexandra David-Neel's name is closely tied to Tibetan magic both in the—often critical—academic and the—usually more encomiastic—public opinion. This is testified not only by a large number of her published and unpublished writings and talks but also by a profuse collection of letters sent by readers and listeners who reached out to her with sometimes bewildering questions about Tibetan magic.[1] Interestingly enough, neither Tibet nor magic were explicit topics of David-Neel's official fieldwork mission to Asia in 1911. They stood out as chance encounters on the field. Furthermore, in her first press reports and serial narratives of her journey to Lhasa in 1924, a widely acclaimed tour de force, David-Neel immediately opted for the genre of adventure literature but hardly touched upon the topic of magic. Only in her second book, *Mystiques et Magiciens du Tibet* (David-Neel 1929b), published in 1929 and quickly translated into many European languages, did magic become the author's signature topic. In highlighting a selection of David-Neel's written and unwritten Tibetan grimoires,[2] I will argue that her exposition of what she herself designated as Tibetan magic, its practitioners and practices, needs to be understood both in her own trajectory and in a larger literary and epistemological context, since it has several literary models (e.g., Oman 1905) and many copycats (e.g., Mahuzier n.d.) as well. Using print, manuscript, and photographic archive material, I will aim at understanding the inception and, to a large extent, invention of Tibetan magic by David-Neel as a cultural translation.[3]

Considering the difficult question of defining magic without either reifying and limiting the concept to one aspect in space and time or dissolving the notion into a polythetic perspective, an issue with which the editors of the present volume had to struggle in their introduction, I opt here for a historical and contextual approach of the use of "magic" as a translation of Tibetan cultural features with reference to David-Neel's enduring focus and legacy on the topic. I will first ask what Tibetan magic *is*—and even more importantly who Tibetan magicians *are*—in David-Neel's presentation. I will then analyze how her use of the word "magic" correlates with coeval studies, theories, and even performances developed in scientific, occultist, and artistic milieus at the time of her return to Europe. In doing so, I will highlight simultaneously the main historical features that account for and David-Neel's own agency in her fashioning of Tibet as a "land of marvels" (Thévoz 2016), a fashioning of which readers and scholars are certainly still—for better or for worse—in the grip today.

Magic and mystery beneath and beyond a book title

David-Neel's second book title itself is a telling editorial maneuver. The first intended title was *Le Thibet mystique* (*Mystical Tibet*). Here only the rather loose religious category of mysticism prevailed. It implied that Tibet itself was metonymically pervaded by the special quality of its inhabitants, characterized by their personal spiritual experience and practice, as opposed to religious institutions and doxology. Magic was not an explicit topic at first and only became one in the editorial process when David-Neel suggested *Parmi les mystiques et magiciens du Tibet* (*Among Mystics and Magicians of Tibet*) as an alternative title. The couple "mystics" and "magicians" either fused the idea of spirituality and special practices and powers in a general category or denoted an opposition inside the combined terms. Ultimately, the publisher preferred the title that would become definitive (David-Neel 1929b), probably because it was shorter and simpler. This last title also distanced itself from the genre of the subjective and partly autobiographical account already used by David-Neel in her first book in 1927, *Voyage d'une Parisienne à Lhassa* (*My Journey to Lhasa*). This subjective dimension was still strongly suggested by the word "among" in David-Neel's title proposition; instead, the publisher's choice promised an objective portrait of a specific category of actors in Tibet or, one could more exactly say, of a category of actors (deemed as) specific to Tibet. In English, two titles prevailed.[4] In Britain, the book was published as *With Mystics and*

Magicians in Tibet in 1931 (David-Neel 1931b). This title was a straightforward translation of the French title David-Neel had first proposed and enacted the semantic effects suggested above, much in line, one must immediately say, with the content and setup of the narrative, which the definitive French title tended to betray. Interestingly, the American edition and translation in 1932 featured still another combo: *Magic and Mystery in Tibet* (David-Neel 1932). Unlike the previous titles, it gave a significant prominence to magic as an umbrella category rather than to human actors. Moreover, it weaved the term, reminiscent not only of occultist practices but also of theatrical conjuring, together with a term especially familiar to readers as a specific literary subgenre rather than as a religious connotation as was the term "mystics." It also resonated with many previous publications on "mysterious" Tibet, as in McGovern (1924)'s *To Lhasa in Disguise: A Secret Expedition through Mysterious Tibet*, a couple of years earlier. As an outcome of these editorial maneuvers, magic became the defining feature of David-Neel's presentation of Tibet in her second book. The multiple titles tell a lot about the interest the topic of Tibetan magic and magical Tibet was expected by the publishers to capture in the 1920s–1930s readership while they sketch slightly varying national contexts of reception.

As a consequence, David-Neel's books, talks, articles, and public interviews prompted a long-lasting imaginaire of Tibet. They also have often been used as main sources of reference on certain phenomena characteristic of Tibetan magic according to David-Neel's classification (especially *gcod, rlung sgom, 'pho ba, sprul pa, ro langs,* and *gtum mo*) in Western literature from all genres and even in art and music pieces. As far as academia is concerned, when Rolf Stein (1954) welcomed George Roerich's edition of the *Blue Annals*, which provided more details on *gcod*, for example, as those which were so far only available in David-Neel's writings, already fifteen years had passed since the publication of *Mystiques et Magiciens du Tibet.*

How magic became a topic in David-Neel's literary career

David-Neel's first book after her sojourn in Tibet, her travelogue *My Travel to Lhasa*, almost did not mention magic at all. Remarkably, the word and idea of magic here was merely limited to the landscape of Tibet ("a land of marvels") and to David-Neel and her son lama Aphur Yongden's inventive tricks and feats inspired from Tibetan magic that famously enabled them to succeed in reaching Lhasa in 1924 disguised as pilgrim-beggars.[5] The book itself, published simultaneously in English under the title *My Journey to Lhasa* (David-Neel 1927a, 1927b) and in French under the title *Voyage d'une Parisienne à Lhassa* (David-Neel 1927c), was a rewritten version of a series in twenty-nine episodes initially published in the French daily newspaper *Le Matin* from June to July 1925 under the title, with some variations, *Souvenirs d'une Parisienne au Thibet*. There, magic already characterized the two heroes of the adventure narrative and only pertained to Tibetan agents and actions in episodes 25 to 28, as if the topic had only belatedly emerged in the process of writing. As we will see there is some evidence to substantiate this hypothesis.

David-Neel's first two books after fourteen years spent in Asia had a determining function for her literary career and each, in its own way, testifies to the author's tactics of self-positioning in the growing literature on Tibet. First, David-Neel decided to publish her travel account in order to ascertain her feat in regard of other recent and obvious publications such as that of William Montgomery McGovern's (1924) *To Lhasa in Disguise* or Ferdinand Ossendowski's (1922) *Beasts, Men, and Gods*. Tentative titles jotted down in David-Neel's 1924–5 notebook provide us with evidence that she was very much aware of these publications and tactically challenged the literary rivalry that they involved: her own travelogue promoting a daring French, and even mischievous Parisian, woman can thus be read as the response to a reputedly male domain both of activities and writings. Her second book, in contrast, explicitly elaborated on the topic of magic that the author had only touched upon in her 1925 travel account in the press and was excluded from her volume published in 1927. Obviously this was done for the purpose of forthcoming publications, since, as part of her publishing agreement, she was liable for a series of three books.[6] As a matter of fact, David-Neel's first intended book-project since 1912 in Sikkim had been quite different and was supposed to present for the first time in Europe the life of the Tibetan magician and saint Milarepa. When David-Neel came back to France, she found to her own dismay that Milarepa had already become an icon of Tibet on European book-shelves. Berthold Laufer (1922) had recently published a selection of texts in his *Milaraspa* and Jacques Bacot (1925)'s *Le Poète tibétain Milarépa* was just hot off the press. Moreover, David-Neel was probably aware that Walter Evans-Wentz, the champion of esoteric Tibetan studies (Schlieter 2021), was planning to publish his *Tibet's Great Yogi: Milarepa* (Evans-Wentz 1928) when she came back from Tibet to Sikkim in 1924 and gathered material belonging to her first Tibetan language instructor Kazi Dawa Samdup (1868–1922). Milarepa and his "initiate's occult power" (David-Neel 2021: 204) were David-Neel's first encounter with the world of Tibetan magic under the guidance of Dawa Samdup. The latter handed to her his own translations from Tibetan into English and then, barely three years after she had left, to Evans-Wentz. Not without opportunism, they both successively appropriated the figure of Milarepa as a literary valuable, which they elected to promote their own authority as writers and scholars of Tibetan Buddhism.[7] Yet David-Neel now had to leave her first literary project on Tibet behind.

What is Tibetan magic?

With the figure of Milarepa, Tibetan magic entered the stage of scholarly and public debates. Surprisingly perhaps, this yogi and magician is hardly present in David-Neel's second book, as though the author felt that she needed to take a step to the side of existing publications on Tibet. In fact, *Magic and Mystery in Tibet* can be viewed as a creative response to this situation, since it featured under the label of Tibetan magic a wide array of magicians and magic practices. David-Neel wrote:

> A broad classification of Tibetan magicians and students of the magic arts divides them into two categories. The first includes sorcerers, soothsayers, necromancers, occultists who seek the power of coercing certain gods and demons to secure their help. They believe in the real existence of the beings of the other worlds.
>
> The second category only includes a small number of adepts who employ the very same means as their less enlightened colleagues, but they hold the view that the various phenomena are produced by an energy arising in the magician himself and depend on his knowledge of the true inner essence of things. (David-Neel 1932: 245–6)

In the narrative, these figures were randomly displayed. Comparing the French original to the English translation even shows how much the material has been rearranged and reordered in these two distinct narrativized grimoires of Tibetan magic. Yet here David-Neel made clear that the Tibetan proponents of magic belong to two distinct categories, mirroring the binomial distribution of the title of the book in the French and British editions, even though the notion of magic pervades from end to end the spectrum of practices and practitioners at stake here. Of course, these categories are not natural and only superficially mirror an emic dimension: the grid is for the most part the author's own schematic classification. David-Neel herself inscribed and ordered her characters in a layered architecture (and an elitist social scheme) within a skillful narrative. Earlier in the book, David-Neel summed up this framework in her own words:

> As for Tibetan mystics, they patronize a certain kind of commerce with demons that is connected with psychic training. This consists in meetings deliberately sought by the disciple, either to challenge demoniac beings or to give them alms. These rites are very different from those which have been described at the beginning of this chapter. Though they, too, may sometimes appear ridiculous or even repugnant, according to our ideas, their purpose is useful or lofty, such as liberating from fear, awakening feelings of boundless practical compassion leading to complete detachment and, finally, to spiritual illumination. (David-Neel 1932: 142)

Remarkably enough, this passage, taken from the fourth chapter, is inserted in a different context in the French and the American editions. In the former, it is part of a concise introduction to magical practices and serves as a justification of sorts to the presentation of the rite of *gcod*. In the latter, it is embedded in a much longer (ten pages), more detailed, and possibly complacent presentation of "lugubrious" practices (David-Neel 1932: 131). The passage provides us with a series of keywords that will guide our inquiry: the notion of "psychic training," the existence of private and public rites, the axiological opposition between the means (such as *materia magica*) and the purposes of magic, the range of the goals of the magical action and its effects, either instrumental or spiritual. What prevails here is the idea that the same practices, envisioned from the (Western) reader's perception ("ridiculous or repugnant according to our ideas") can be used for different purposes: the highest purpose of the practice of magic being spiritual illumination. As we will see, not only this conception has a long and complex history but also it implicitly legitimates, in David-Neel's view, the choice of magic as a defining feature of Tibetan Buddhism as a whole.

Who are Tibetan magicians?

As suggested above, David-Neel's work stands out as unique in its specific focus on magic among a wide corpus of publications on mysterious and esoteric Tibetan beliefs and practices. David-Neel herself stated:

> There is hardly any country which can vie with Tibet as to the riches, variety and picturesqueness of its folklore regarding ghosts and demons. If we were to rely

on popular beliefs, we should conclude that evil spirits greatly outnumber the human population of the "Land of Snow." (David-Neel 1932: 141)

David-Neel deliberately fashioned Tibet as the elective—and elected—location for magical feats. Yet it would be wrong, and to some extent unfair toward her, to consider the author as the *inventor* (like an ex nihilo demiurgic magician) of Tibetan magic. Here I do not intend to address the question of whether David-Neel did or did not actually witness and experience the actors and practices she writes about, sometimes eloquently and with a distinguishable sense of staging. I rather aim at debunking what her *culture of magic* was and how she came to apply the notion to the wide—and bewildering—variety of characters and phenomena, ranging from gruesome black sorcery to pristine high magic, brought back from the fieldwork, in her writings.

It is interesting to note that David-Neel did not seem to be directly familiar with academic studies on magic, popular in her time, like the works by Edward B. Tylor, James Frazer, Émile Durkheim, Marcel Mauss, or Lucien Lévy-Bruhl. In one of her notebooks, David-Neel critically quoted from and commented on Frazer's *The Golden Bough* in regard of Tibetan magic practices[8] and of sympathetic magic,[9] but these notes were written down rather late, after 1933. Yet she relied—like the aforementioned scholars—on an esotericist conception of magic, or what Wouter Hanegraaff (2012 and 2016) has called the "Enlightenment's wastebasket of rejected knowledge," namely the "occult philosophy" of the Renaissance, which had synthesized and reordered a wide array of scattered practices under the generic label of "magic," or more precisely *magia naturalis*. Like them, and we will see, alongside many occultists and scholars alike at the beginning of the twentieth century, David-Neel supported the idea that magical feats like those she witnessed in Tibet, far from reversing the laws of nature, testify on the contrary to a deep understanding of natural phenomena.

In *Mystiques et Magiciens du Tibet*, the variety of practitioners, whom David-Neel calls magicians, are not only distributed in the narrative in the form of lively descriptions and arresting episodes but also feed most of the rich illustration of the book, contributing to give the reader a concrete, palpable picture of the Tibetan magicians and arguably ascertaining the reality and admissibility of the feats the author describes. In addition, the photographic archive collection housed in David-Neel's estate helps us document them in more detail than they are in David-Neel's, often deliberately loose, narratives. They range from the figures of the sorcerer and the soothsayer to several figures of *ngags pa* (tantric practitioners, a figure David-Neel especially helped promote in the West) and *rnal 'byor pa* (yogis), the Tibetan tantric practitioners. One also finds in David-Neel's collection pictures of *gsang yum* (tantric consorts) and *rnal 'byor ma* (yoginis), important female figures, which David-Neel herself embodied in her travel and narratives, and with whom she herself has been photographed on several pictures, as if to imply a complicity of their personae.

One also finds more intimate figures and informants such as the key "cultural broker" Kazi Dawa Samdup to whom she owed so much, even though she downplayed him in her letters and narratives. In the book, David-Neel turned his character into a magician:

> Dawasandup was an occulist [*sic*] and even, in a certain way, a mystic. He sought for secret intercourse with the Dâkinîs[10] and the dreadful gods hoping to gain supernormal powers. Everything that concerned the mysterious world of beings generally invisible strongly attracted him, but the necessity of earning his living made it impossible for him to devote much time to his favourite study. (David-Neel 1932: 15)

The tone of this portrait of the "good interpreter" and "schoolmaster" (David-Neel 1932: 19) as an occultist is rather ambiguous and very much in David-Neel's witty, ironic style. One should be aware of the author's idiosyncratic sense of portrayal since such a passage can even be read as a eulogy, considering that Dawa Samdup is the very first character mentioned in the narrative and that an important part of the first chapter, featuring photographs, is then devoted to him. Nevertheless, despite his key role as an informant and as a Mephistophelian character, Dawa Samdup is at odds with the highest representatives, to David-Neel's eyes, of Tibetan spiritual practices: the *bsgom chen*,[11] and especially the most central of them in her trajectory, the gomchen of Lachen, Kunzang Ngawang Rinchen, who acquainted her with *rdzogs chen pa* teachings.

A modern magician in Tibet

Ultimately, photographs depicting David-Neel and Aphur Yongden show them attired as various instances of what David-Neel held as Tibetan magicians. Some were minutely staged in studios in India and Europe after the trip in order to be sent to correspondents, the press, and the publishers who reproduced them in newspapers and her books, some others were taken during the journey itself. For example, on the front page of both the French and British editions, one finds a mesmerizing portrait of "the author wearing the dress of Tibetan anchorites" and several tantric tools; further in the book one finds that of lama Aphur Yongden. These were taken in a studio either in Calcutta or in Toulon. In the book, the two protagonists were themselves staged as the main magicians of the narrative, both visually and textually, reinforcing the "With" ("Parmi") of the initial book title with not only the idea of observation but also of participation. As a matter of fact, *Magic and Mystery in Tibet* was itself staged as a magic show of sorts. The narrator opened the narrative with a dialogue with the lama-prince Sidkyong Tulku portrayed as a "genie." She adds: "I doubt his reality. Probably he will vanish like a mirage. … He is part of the enchantment in which I have lived these last fifteen days. This new episode is of the stuff that dreams are made of" (David-Neel 1932: 1). The storyteller functions thus as a kind of magician capable of giving flesh to her characters and writing a "real" and "true" narrative in the tone of a mystery tale. Furthermore, in the vein of *My Journey to Lhasa*, the two protagonists were themselves staged as performers of magic tricks. Unpublished photographs taken during the journey such as PHDN93 that shows David-Neel as a *rdzogs chen ngags pa* and PHDN633 that shows lama Aphur Yongden practicing *gcod* provide a quite different, if authentic, flair of their personae on the field than the ones featured in the books. The archive material nonetheless documents this bluffing dimension of the narrative. Even when not fully dressed as a *rnal 'byor ma,* once in Europe, David-Neel would go on wearing in public two rings given to her by gomchens that still roused the curiosity twenty years after her first journey to Tibet: "nowadays the famous explorer is dressed in the European fashion. Only her high red-golden-hued hairdress and a strange ring carried in the annular of the left ring give her an air of adventure" (Carrière 1946). In terms of the history of magic, David-Neel, a former opera singer "conjuring Asia" both in her writings and in her public talks (reputedly spectacular with Aphur Yongden performing Tibetan dances and rituals), turned out to instantiate a radically *modern* magician committed to Oriental magic, to follow Chris Goto-Jones's book title and argument on the rise of modern magic:

> Oriental magic opened up new possibilities … enabled and encouraged new ways for magicians to exhibit a form of commitment to magic that resembled a process of becoming a magical being. In other words, while Oriental magic arose as a core component of modern magic, it also proved to be a radical force within it, undermining and creatively transforming some of the foundational assumptions of magic in the modern West (such as that a magician is only an actor). (Goto-Jones 2016: 306)

In the narrative, magic thus works beyond the antagonism of a rational(ist) narrator-observer set against the phenomena witnessed and episodes told. Magic is fully integrated within the literary setup in a similar way as a magician performing on stage or even "on the ground" so to speak (see Goto-Jones 2016: 197–204 on "magical American yogis"). I will later discuss how this conception of the writer as a magician and the narrative as a magical feat fitted in David-Neel's vision of her own literary agenda as a Buddhist inspired by her contact with Tibetan tantric Buddhism. *Magic and Mystery in Tibet*, as well as her (published and unpublished) works and performances in general turned out to instantiate her own written and unwritten grimoires of Tibetan magic.

A scientific magical culture?

Designed with the support of publishers and literary agents for a wide readership, *Magic and Mystery in Tibet* was the result of a series of talks and articles published in literary periodicals (David-Neel 1928 and 1929a) and scientific reviews (David-Neel 1927d). This largely explains why David-Neel equated Tibetan magic with psychic training, a topic that attracted attention from the Institut général psychologique in Paris, the French response to the famous Society for Psychical Research. The Institut's president, Jacques Arsène d'Arsonval, was a pioneer in the medical application of electricity. He had invented the first telephones commercialized in France, and was especially interested in electromagnetic and psychic phenomena such as thought transference, or telepathy, and animal and human thermogenesis (Blondel 2002). D'Arsonval strongly supported David-Neel's work, and, despite her statement that she wrote *Mystiques et Magiciens au Tibet* in response to many readers' and listeners' requests, he himself alleged to be the one who prompted her to write the book to which he wrote the preface. In a talk at the Society of Biology, D'Arsonval eloquently legitimated David-Neel's work in regard of scientific investigations:

> I found her interesting enough to engage my learned friend to write a book dealing especially with psychic training in Tibet. This book, of which I have read the most interesting passages, will be published very soon. It will be of interest to the physiologists and the psychologists. Even though we do partly know the influence of mind on the physical, we are far from having experimented this study as fully as the masters of the Land of Snow. (D'Arsonval 1929: 25, my translation)

He ended with quoting David-Neel (1927d: 27–8) herself:

> As far as the spirit with which Mrs Neel wrote her book, suffice it to quote the conclusion of one of her talks held at my request at the Collège de France: "Everything that more or less closely pertains to psychic phenomena and to the effect of psychic forces in general must be studied like any other science. There is here no miracles, nothing supernatural, nothing liable to superstition. The reasoned and scientifically driven psychic training can bring useful results. Therefore data collected on such a training—even though it is empirically practiced and based on theories to which we can not always adhere—constitute useful and worthy documents. Based on the imperfect attempts of our forerunners we can reach a larger amount of knowledge." (D'Arsonval 1929: 25–26, my translation)

This tie with the scientific study of magical feats clearly highlights David-Neel's focus on magic. Such a study, championed by the Institut général psychologique in 1900, was a defining feature of the first two decades of the century in French scientific milieus. Contrary to the spiritualist approach and convictions of the Society for Psychical Research in London, the French scholars endeavored to develop an experimental method based on the achievements of the physical sciences (such as D'Arsonval's). In this perspective, they especially focused on what was called material psychic phenomena instantiated in spiritist séances (Bensaude-Vincent and Blondel 2002). This was a notable turning point in the history of science, since even inventions and discoveries as D'Arsonval's medical electricity or telephone, were deemed mere quackery by political representatives and mainstream scientists (Blondel 2002: 165–7). In 1910 Gustave Le Bon (1910) viewed the collaboration of spiritists and scientists as the "renaissance of magic," a view that triggered much debate (Dubuisson 1910; Blondel 2002: 161–3). In this context the notion of psychical training was especially developed in the course of experiments (Blondel 2002: 166–7). David-Neel was actually not a newcomer to this scene. She may have met D'Arsonval before her departure for Asia in 1911, as testified by her personal library that contains previous issues of the *Bulletin de l'Institut général psychologique* and by her address books.[12] More explicitly, her 1927 talk on Tibetan psychic training eloquently mirrored her own 1903 study on "physical training in yoga" at the Society of Anthropology of Paris, which was known for its physicalist approach to human phenomena, and whose members were, like scholars at the Institut général psychologique, mostly physicians. While this explains the scientific roots and epistemological conceptions of David-Neel's discourse on Tibetan magic, one must bear in mind that when David-Neel came back to France such an interest was fading. Psychic phenomena, as they had been understood, were now out of the scope of official psychology in the process of the institutionalization of the discipline and were more and more labeled as "parapsychological" and "parascientific."[13] In a way, as David-Neel transferred her own epistemological background to the general readership together with her widely acclaimed narrative on Tibetan mystics and magicians, she made a move comparable to the "renaissance of magic" now transposed in Tibet, and as some journalists remarked, Tibet could well be the dreamed-of laboratory for what was called in France metapsychic studies. Such an imaginaire has had a lasting effect in pop culture that probably the mere title *Magic and Mystery in Tibet* without reference to the content of the book or to the author herself still prompts today. The connection of the scientific context of the Belle Epoque in France and this rather unscientific imaginaire is not haphazard: not only is the interaction of scientific and occultist milieus a specificity of this period, but it also accounts for David-Neel's own relationship and understanding to magic.

Magic in the writer's literary laboratory

One aspect I would like to briefly deal with here is the question of the literary feats achieved by David-Neel who addressed herself to quite different audiences. Was magic envisioned in the same way in a talk to a learned audience as it was in a book for a larger readership? How did storytelling interact with factuality (whether the facts are "true" or not is not the question here)? One of her personal notebooks offers further insights into her vision of magic in relation to the ritual of *gcod*, a feature of *Magic and Mystery in Tibet*, which has been widely commented upon and is still a canonical reference point today, as evidenced by Nike-Ann Schröder's chapter in this volume. Suffice it to say that in the rather long presentation of the ritual, the "dreadful mystic banquet" (David-Neel 1931b: 148–66), illustrated by a famous photograph of a *gcod pa*,[14] David-Neel assimilated the ritual to an inner drama developing on a private stage (Thévoz 2019). One striking feature is the distant and slightly ironic tone of the narrator toward the practitioners and practices described, induced by the observer's own position as a hidden observer in the episode. The "inner drama," in contrast, was accounted for in a thrilling skillful art. A last notable feature is how David-Neel portrayed herself as sitting in a peaceful meditation surrounded by nature, in clear opposition to the nightmarish experience of the initiate practicing *gcod* not far from her (David-Neel 1931b: 157). David-Neel here mentioned that her meditation took place in the presence of a corpse. She does not say that this was her own initiation to *gcod* but rather implies that her meditation could have been, in a more orthodox Buddhist conception, with the corpse simply as a support of meditation.

Essentially, the relationship between the narrator and the characters delineated in this rhapsodic passage opposed two types of magicians: the "subject" and the conjurer, the master of illusion, implying both the possibility of a demystification and the idea of a (psychic) training. This setup very much recalled the framework of the "theater of proof" that had been developed in the observation of material psychic phenomena at the beginning of the twentieth century. In fact, these experiments often staged not only a "subject" (the term came to replace that of the "medium" in this context) and scientists (physicians with their apparatus of technical devices, psychologists, and, most notably, stenographers!); they also appealed to stage magicians and prestidigitators, who were held as the most skilled and trained individuals capable of perceiving a fraud, whereas scientists were considered easy to fool (Blondel 2002: 160–1). This setup took place in a period that needs to be understood in its own terms:

> We consider today that mediumistic materialization, trances, hysterical simulations, performances of prestidigitation, and psychological experiments constitute quite distinct and identifiable categories. It was absolutely not the case at the end of the nineteenth century. (Blondel 2002: 169, my translation)

Acutely aware of this state of the art, David-Neel certainly had a clear preference as to which position she would rather choose for herself.

This specific "scientific" staging of psychic phenomena, familiar to the reader at the time, is best highlighted when compared to David-Neel's archive material. For example, in a notebook (CADN-13: 38), she wrote down the beginning of a first-person narrative of her (supposedly) own initiation to *gcod*, which reversed completely her self-portrait in *Magic and Mystery in Tibet*. In turn, this unpublished narrative echoed a narrativized description of the ritual in Tibetan written in *dbu med* script probably by Aphur Yongden (E2-TB-43). One delves here into the writer's alchemy laboratory.

An occult culture of magic

If one can explain the conception of *Magic and Mystery in Tibet* by David-Neel's former publications and talks, as well as by the author's reworking of manuscript material, the book was not the endpoint of the concept of magic in the author's literary projects. Indeed, there is significant further archive material available. For example, David-Neel sketched a book proposal for Harper (CADN-42), probably soon after *Magic and Mystery in Tibet* had been published, as a third (contractual) book project. In this project titled *The Tibetan Secret Lore*, David-Neel methodically—in contrast to the narrative economy of *Magic and Mystery in Tibet*—detailed the "trainings for sorcery, magic, mystic, philosophy—for that which is called 'the Great Accomplishment,'" describing in her own (English) words her vision of magic in Tibet, as we have examined it above. Yet here David-Neel brought more clearly to light than in *Magic and Mystery in Tibet* the Tibetan source for her own conception of magic in Tibet, the doctrines and practices she was acquainted with (first and foremost by the Gomchen of Lachen) and which she privileged in her presentation of Tibetan Buddhism: oral and textual teachings of *rdzogs chen* emerged here as seminal to her own written and unwritten grimoires.

Before turning to the question of David-Neel's (potential) Tibetan sources, one needs to grasp more firmly the translation process of magic with regard to European terminology. Later, in her 1947 diary, David-Neel came back to the topic as she mentioned several title proposals regarding a talk at the Theosophical Society on *lhag mthong*, "the life intense,[15] and its relation to Tibetan High Magic." Interestingly, the word "high" was crossed afterward, as though David-Neel was both reluctant to limit Tibetan magic to "high magic" and willing to inscribe Tibetan magic under this honorable subcategory. Magic explicitly reappeared later as the main topic of a popular horror novel (David-Neel 1938) in which travel adventures and spiritual adventures here again were the basic ingredients of the plot and in which romanticized "high magic" and terrifying "black magic" opposed.

The very notion of "high magic" needs scrutiny. One needs first to remember that David-Neel had been an active albeit critical Theosophical member from 1892 onward and had been close to many esotericist milieus in fin de siècle Paris. In that regard, it is worth mentioning that one of David-Neel's most precocious object of interest, yoga, was precisely considered—and looked up to—as an instance of "theurgy" or "High magic" in the 1890s by eminent occultists in Paris, such as Paul Sédir and Ernest Bosc in many publications starting from the 1890s. In his introduction to his *Yoghisme et Fakirisme hindous* (1913), Bosc explained:

> The teachings given in the present book are part of yoga, Royal Yoga (Radja-Yoga), which is the true Magic, which is that revealed by Iamblichus in his *De*

> *Mysteriis* when he explains *Theurgy* as the divine Science. … Theurgy is no other thing than *Yoga Radja* and is attained by the *Manteia*, or the highest state of ecstasy (*Samadhi*). By this Theurgy, man reaches:
>
> 1 Prophetic discernment thanks to the superior *Ego*;
> 2 Ecstasy and Illumination;
> 3 Action by the Spirit [or Mind], i.e. the astral body, or by Will;
> 4 Lastly, domination over elementals (inferior demons).
>
> Radja Yoga must be preceded by the training of our senses and by the knowledge of *human Self* in relation to the *divine Self*.
>
> This is why the earnest, righteous and honest man can study Yoga without danger, for he is protected by his invisible guides.—Therefore, go onwards, Students! Do not be scared. (Bosc 1913: 9–11, my translation)

Bosc's passage is but one instance of the translation of Oriental religious trends into the occultist and theosophical language of the time. Bosc, like many French esotericists, was heir to the father of occultism, Éliphas Lévi, whom his famous successor (who had not known him in person), Gérard Encausse aka Papus, credited with the invention of occultism itself. In fact, Lévi mostly used the word "magic" to speak about the large scope of teachings and practices that would be stored under the label of "occultism" after him (D'Andrea and Lagrange 2002). We have already observed that David-Neel inherited such a hotchpotch conception of magic. Here we can more precisely trace back this conception to the context in which David-Neel actually became familiar with the idea of magic. David-Neel took over not only the occultist repertoire of magic practices but also a set of concepts and values such as "method," "training" linked to psychic experiences, and spiritual practices common at the time to both occultist and scientist milieus in that regard. These were all associated with a specific conception of magic and many publications in the 1890s (Lermina 1890; Papus 1893), in the aftermath of Éliphas Lévi (1854 and 1861)'s foundational *Dogme et Rituel de la Haute Magie*, that promoted the notion of practical magic, with its insistence on private or secret, elitist rituals. At the time David-Neel left for Asia, Tibetan magic was already a topic for occultists (Pouvourville 1912; Carnoules 1913). Bosc himself assimilated some Tibetan practices to his study of "Yoghisme," but most authors envisioned Tibetan magic under the guise of black magic and sorcery: "Thibet is prey to a strange, fanatical religion, which is both tied to Buddhism by its arts and philosophy and to inferior magism by its mysterious practices" (Carnoules 1913: 121). In particular, these inferior magic practices are characterized by the use of power objects, the "magical weapons made by the Tibetan sorcerers" such as ritual daggers, drums, and horns, as well as by the uttering of magic sounds, incantations, and spells, in the art of which these "fearsome characters" are "past masters."

Remarkably, this perception of magic constituted the background against which David-Neel's books were read by French esotericists and (reductively, one must admit) criticized, as shown by a series of reviews of her books in esotericist periodicals such as *Le Voile d'Isis* or *L'Initiation*. In fact, David-Neel's publications on magic following *Mystiques et Magiciens du Tibet* can be regarded as a response against accusations that Tibetan magic merely amounted to left-hand path magic, or that there simply was nothing of interest in that regard in Tibet. On the contrary, she insisted that "there is everything." Yet "magic and magicians are awkward words to describe the way Tibetans perceive extra-normal phenomena. For them, there is no reversing of natural laws, but only skillful means of using little known forces" (David-Neel 1931a: 47). In saying so, David-Neel both referred to her understanding of Buddhism, Tibetan Tantrism included, and to a problem articulated at the time in regard of psychic phenomena: are subjects the source of phenomena or merely reflecting exterior forces undetected by technical devices (Blondel 2002: 169)? Here David-Neel gave her own answer to both scientists and occultists.

Translating magic: Sources in Tibetan studies and in Tibetan texts

Of course, David-Neel was not the first to identify the characters and practices she gathered under the label of Tibetan magic. From the 1900s, she herself made reference to and made extensive use of Jäschke's *Dictionary*, and, among a few others, of Waddell's (1895) *Lamaism*, who depicted the *'grub (thob) chen* (siddhas) as "degraded Indian Buddhist priests most popular with the Lamas, credited with supernatural powers, by being in league with the demons; … their chief is St. Padma-sambhava."[16] One sees here that Tibetan magic was discredited by Waddell in using the concept of supernatural. Not only did David-Neel depict mostly real and not legendary magicians, but she also never used the term "supernatural" (nor superhuman or suprasensible or even metapsychic). She replaced it instead with the term "supernormal," much to the credit of Tibetan magic.[17] As Egil Asprem (2014) has shown, the term was first coined by Frederic Myers in 1903 to account for phenomena "above the norm of man rather than outside his nature" (Myers 1903, xxii). The concept was taken over by many authors such as Joseph Maxwell in France whose books (Maxwell 1903, 1927, 1929) belonged to David-Neel's shelf on "magic" in her library. She also personally met him in Paris after her journey to Asia, as testified by a dedication in one of these books. Except for Maury (1860), all her books on magic and psychic phenomena belonged to the post-Myers era instantiated in France by the Institut général psychologique.

With these historical interpretations of magic in mind, one can grasp more tightly David-Neel's translation of magic. Did she actually translate anything Tibetan by the word "magic"? Her presentation of the magic rites named *sgrub thabs*, "methods of success," is a revealing feature, especially as regards the question of *materia magica*. The word "*doubthabs*" appears only once in the French original of *Mystiques et Magiciens du Tibet*, as an instance of a "magical rite" (David-Neel 1929a: 137), whereas it occurs four to seven times in English, depending on the edition. In the editions in English, the word "*dubthabs*" stands for either the French [magical] "rite" or "invocation." In displaying agents and practices of Tibetan magic in *Magic and Mystery*, David-Neel provided the reader with many colorful portrayals and awe-inspiring magical feats of the Tibetan "psychic sportsmen." Yet she did not go into detail about the practical rites nor explicitly referenced her oral or textual sources. In her next book published in French one year later (David-Neel 1930) and translated into English the very same year, *Initiations and Initiates in Tibet*, she dedicated a whole chapter to this subject (David-Neel 1931c: 91–9). This third book, an explicit supplement to *Magic and Mystery*, was not published by the contractual publisher. As such, it was not the third book agreed upon in the initial convention. In French, it was published this time for a smaller readership by the French Theosophical Press Adyar, hinting at the fact that David-Neel was engaged in an ongoing dialogue with occultist milieus. Likewise, in Britain, it was published by yet another publisher, Rider & Co, and translated by Fred Rothwell, who had specialized in the translation of French works on philosophy and occultism. No American edition seems to have been published.

After stating the goals of *sgrub thabs* and detailing the practical aspects and process of the ritual, David-Neel described the "method consisting in projecting, like images on a screen, deities mentally conceived and in imagining a series of changes through which they pass, in the course of very prolonged and complicated rites" (David-Neel 1931c: 92). Not only the focus on this particular type of ritual deserves attention here, but also the rather positive treatment of it and the means of translation. In particular the use of comparisons and metaphors is quite telling: here a cinematographic screen, later the notion of electromagnetism, as a discrete allusion to her friend D'Arsonval. These references were not merely David-Neel's own stylistic effects, for they were used and overused since the end of the nineteenth century to describe psychic phenomena. David-Neel simply incorporated the same scientific imaginaire into the Tibetan context.

In David-Neel's collection of more than four hundred Tibetan manuscripts bequeathed at the author's death to the library of the Guimet museum in Paris, Samten Karmay (1980?) has inventoried in the 1980s four *sgrub thabs* texts (BG5862, BG54739, BG54832, BG54756) and one text on divination (BG54552).[18] This notwithstanding, in *Initiations and Initiates in Tibet*, David-Neel only mentioned a couple of oral and written sources. In particular, she alluded to a treatise by Longchenpa (Klong chen rab 'byams dri med 'od zer, 1308–1364)—she did not say which treatise—and other unidentified *sgrub thabs*. She felt that these were worth summarizing on the grounds that these rites were "so different from any practiced in the West" (David-Neel 1931c: 94). She obviously hinted at the theatrical setups and social decorum of "ceremonial magic," which she herself was familiar with and recalled in her 1954–5 series *Le Sortilège du Mystère* (David-Neel 1972: 7–65). The only text she mentioned with its full title (David-Neel 1931c: 94) is *dPal rdo rje 'jig byed kyi sgrubs thabs* (Konchok between 1497 and 1557) without identifying its author, the tenth Konchok Lhundrup (Ngor mkhen chen dKon mchog lHun grub, 1497–1557).

What matters in David-Neel's translation of *sgrub thabs* is her heavy insistence that: "Be it said at once that all the ingredients enumerated are imagined" (David-Neel 1931c: 97). The meditation material support (here a thangka of either rDo rje 'jig byed [Vajrabhairava] or 'Khor-lo bde-mchog [Cakrasaṃvara]), the basic set of ritual instruments (*gtor ma*, butter lamps, *dril bu*, *damaru*, human skulls were mentioned),[19] the *materia magica* (here the *pañcatattva*s) are to be successively perceived by the *sgrub pa po* in their "exoteric, esoteric, and mystical significations" ("mystical" being her translation for *gsang:* "secret"). In terms of translating magic at the time, David-Neel's presentation of such a Tantric ritual accounted for a deliberately distinct interpretation of *pañcatattva* from John Woodroffe's version of Śaivite Tantric *cakrapūjā*s (Woodroffe 1929: 593), with which he himself had acquainted her when they met in Calcutta in 1912. Likewise, there was a clear rivalry with Walter Evans-Wentz—one only needs to read some disparaging comments by David-Neel in the margins of her copies of his books—on the question of translating Tibetan secret teachings for a Euro-American readership, as denoted by several remarks by Evens-Wentz. This author simultaneously relied on David-Neel when describing *gtu mo* and *gcod* in his *Tibetan Yoga* (Evans-Wentz 1935: 158–9, 320) and boasted of providing the reader with more complete textual translations than her colleague (Evans-Wentz 1935: 57, 101).

David-Neel's approach of *sgrub thabs* reflected her positive yet psychologized—or more exactly imaginational—exposition of Tibetan magic rites, in contrast with former understandings of such texts and practices, as rituals of coercion taken at face value or rites designed to ensure the efficacy of material ingredients (Jäschke 1881: 121; Waddell 1895: 151–3), such as in curative drugs (Schlagintweit 1863: 266). In doing so, she aligned herself with the principles of modern magic, which held the magician as the source of magic (Sofer 2020).[20]

Conclusion: A modern Buddhist vision of Tibetan magic

In a book review of *Mystiques et Magiciens*, a French critique wondered: "Isn't Tibetan magic like any other magic?" (Bellessort 1929). Things, I have argued, are more complicated than that. David-Neel has been instrumental in making Tibetan magic a worthy topic in its own right in the scope of the psychic sciences of her time, on the edges of science, esotericism, Asian studies, and literature. More precisely, as some readers of the time suggested, David-Neel did not so much as *invent* Tibetan magic, as *relocate* the "renaissance of magic" *to* Tibet. But that was not all. As a committed Buddhist, David-Neel nurtured a more personal reflection and assessed her discovery of the "Tibetan Secret Lore," as she calls it, by her own understanding of "true" Buddhism as a "mental training" (David-Neel 1936: 117, 134). In 1936, in her *Le Bouddhisme du Bouddha* (translated in 1939 as *Buddhism, Its Doctrines and Its Methods*), David-Neel wrote that "although peculiar in form, the [Tibetan] methods [of spiritual training] often tend toward a goal entirely in conformity with the Buddhist ideal" (David-Neel 1939: 98). The other way round, Tibetan magic gave an unexpected turn to her work as a Buddhist author. In this sense, her book *The Secret Oral Teachings in Tibetan Buddhist Sects* (David-Neel 1967) published in French in 1951 completed the "magic" trilogy begun with *Magic and Mystery in Tibet* and *Initiates and Initiations in Tibet* and reflected in David-Neel's career her own conception of Tibetan magic.

As such, David-Neel's exposition of Tibetan magic complied with and fulfilled her literary agenda, designed as early as 1914 in Sikkim during her two-year retreat under the guidance of the Gomchen of Lachen. At that time, she had written to her husband:

> The *Buddha* saw something. … My *lama-yogi* "saw" too. … In study and meditation, I seek to see what the Buddhas have seen. If I can transcribe this vision in a lived and lively way as the [Buddhas and the *lama-yogi*] have, then maybe is it worthwhile for me to write and speak. (David-Neel 2000: 394, my translation)

A few weeks earlier, David-Neel had already formulated such a vision in words that both referred to the magical culture of her time and to her understanding of Buddhism: "The one who knows the great secret can only smile at the phantasmagoria that the world is, and the great peace will surround them" (David-Neel 2000: 342, my translation).[21] This "creative process"—as David-Neel used to translate the Tibetan *bskyed rim* (David-Neel 1931c: 96)—would be materialized in her forthcoming work that launched Tibetan magic on the global stage. In revisiting Tibetan magic, the present volume certainly addresses the complex historical encounter of European and Tibetan cultures David-Neel has conjured in her written and unwritten grimoires.

Notes

1 Many such letters, and sometimes David-Neel's first-draft replies, are held in the Maison Alexandra David-Neel archive collections (hereafter MADN). Unless specified, all manuscript material referred to in this chapter is held by the MADN.

2 I somewhat unilaterally refer to David-Neel's work on magic as grimoires, not only because the author partly relied on Tibetan spells heard in Tibet or possibly read in spell-books, but mostly because David-Neel displays a wide collection of Tibetan practices and practitioners in such a way that her oeuvre—comprising her magnum opus *Magic and Mystery in Tibet*, her numerous other publications as well as her unwritten talks and potentially her unpublished literary projects on the topic—ended up casting a spell on her audience and turned Alexandra David-Neel into an unprecedented kind of Tibetan magician in the public sphere. Hence her own books gained a special authoritative quality which she herself held as a specificity of Tibetans' relationship to books: "reading sacred texts, according to Tibetans, is less intended to instruct than to [produce] magical effects" (David-Neel 2021: 166).

3 As the data pertaining to the topic in the author's personal papers and collections is under research at this stage, my intention here is not to provide a full survey of David-Neel's writings on magic or even an in-depth analysis of her literary treatment of the topic. Similarly, the question of—especially Tibetan—sources, either oral or textual, still needs further inquiry.

4 The book titles usually chosen with the complicity of the author in the many languages into which her books were translated deserve attention. In this chapter,

I will limit myself to the French and English versions and refer either to the French or American titles according to the specific context.

5 Aphur Yongden (1899–1955) played an important role both during David-Neel's journeys in Asia and in the course of her literary career, since he would live alongside her until his death. He contributed to many of her writings, even when he was not credited as an author or a coauthor.

6 When David-Neel came back from Asia, she decided to become a writer. Literary contracts and written exchanges with her French, British, and American publishers and literary agents testify to her thorough understanding of book marketing. In particular here, she obtained an agreement that three books would be written, translated, and published right after *My Journey to Lhasa*.

7 David-Neel's partial and sometimes loose French rendition of Dawa Samdup's English translation gave way to some creative license and free personal comments. See David-Neel (2021). It is clear from her narrative that David-Neel was exposed to Tibetan magical practices early on through Milarepa's biography, since she reports phenomena such as *'pho ba* (David-Neel 2021: 199, 208) and *sprul pa* (158–9), for example, although these terms are not explicitly identified.

8 She comments: "Frazer p. 492 of The Golden Bough in one vol. is completely wrong when telling about Tibet and a 'Old Mother Khönma (khon ma?) who has all the demons under her authority. Never heard about it!'" (David-Neel, CADN-33: 6).

9 She copied a large passage taken from page 49 where Frazer compared sympathetic magic to modern science as "it assumes that in nature one event follows another necessarily and invariably without the intervention of any spiritual or personal agency."

10 Here David-Neel adds a footnote: "Feminine deities. Dâkinî is their Sanskrit name used also in Tibetan mystic literature. Their Tibetan name is *mkah hgroma*, pronounced Kandoma. They are often styled 'mothers' and are said to impart esoteric profound doctrines to their devotees." The reader was already familiar with this figure, since in *My Journey to Lhasa* David-Neel told how she was acknowledged as such a *kandoma* accompanied by her son, the lama Aphur Yongden.

11 Coupled with the narrative and several manuscript archive files, these photographs, often identified and labeled by David-Neel herself, help document the learned contacts she had established during her journey. The teachings she was given by them still need further scrutiny.

12 As early as March 1925 did David-Neel mention appointments with D'Arsonvsal and attend the Institut général psychologique's lectures, such as René Sudre's "Metapsychics and Science," as testified by her 1925 diary. This obviously triggered her late mentions of such a topic in the series of her travel account in the press and her own first talk at the Institut on December 7 (David-Neel 1925). On November

23, she wrote to her literary agent that she was "preparing a series of articles under the title 'Mystics, magians [*sic*] and philosophers of the Land of Snow' for the *Revue de Paris*" (William A. Bradley Literary Agency collection, Harry Ransom Center, University of Texas, folder 16.9). The topic still required time for reflection, since such papers would only be published in 1928 and 1929 (David-Neel 1928 and 1929a) and developed into her 1929 book-length Tibetan grimoire, which reused this very first title idea.

13 This shift that turned esotericism from a niche phenomenon into a wide cultural stream has been well documented by several studies. See Lagrange (2005). David-Neel's personal library and some of her later publications testify to her connections with this new field, famously represented by Louis Pauwels (1920–1997) and Jacques Bergier (1912–1978) in their 1960 book *Le Matin des Magiciens [The Morning of the Magicians]*. The book published by Jean Paulhan (1884–1968) in the prestigious Gallimard's "white collection" was followed by the creation of the periodical *Planète*. David-Neel held copies of these publications, in which her name was sometimes mentioned, as well as Kurt Seligman's *Histoire des magies* published in 1964 in Pauwels's collection "Encyclopédie Planète." Seligman (1900–1962) was André Breton's (1896–1966) main informant on esotericism and magic. David-Neel's (1931) article explicitly titled "Tibetan magic" (mentioned later on in my chapter) was published in a special issue dedicated to "exoticism" of the periodical *Jazz*, a venue closely connected to the Surrealist scene at a time when the movement developed an interest in both "exotic" cultures and esotericism, and especially magic. Remarkably, such an interest from artists and writers was backed up by contemporary anthropologists, an obvious case in point being poet and essayist Michel Leiris (1901–1990) taking part in Marcel Griaule (1898–1956)'s ethnographic expedition to "phantom Africa" in 1930. Even though David-Neel was a lively and inquiring mind throughout her life who moreover benefited from a long-standing network in literary and artistic circles, she appears to have been only incidentally in touch with such avant-garde milieus. As she later did address such new issues as UFOs and paranormal phenomena, her presentation of Tibetan magic was firmly rooted in the "psychic phenomena" paradigm as delineated in this chapter.

14 The picture has a caption, but David-Neel does not name the *rnal 'byor pa*: from several pictures held in her archive collection, and contrary to many former erroneous identifications, one can affirm that the performer here is "Sakyong Gomchen" (*sa skyong sgom chen*), whom David-Neel mentions for other matters only in the book.

15 This interesting typo—"vie" (life) for "vue" (view, vision)—is her own.

16 Padmasambhava was a key figure of the imaginaire of Tibet at the time (Thévoz 2023). Remarkably, before becoming familiar with Milarepa, Jacques Bacot had

planned on writing a life of Padmasambhava. In her first publication on Tibet (David-Neel 1904), David-Neel herself focused on Padmasambhava and never mentioned Milarepa. From the standpoint of literary sensibility (Thévoz 2017), the latter's dramatic course of existence (a conversion of a black magician into a Buddhist saint) and its humane features largely account for the European authors shifting away from the legendary and epic lifestory of Guru Rinpoche and his magical achievements in Tibet.

17 In her earlier publications, notably in the *Bulletins et Mémoires de la Société d'anthropologie de Paris* (see, for example, David-Neel 1903) and in her manuscript of Milarepa's biography, David-Neel discarded the idea of "supernatural" without using a substitutive category: "[An Oriental] does not believe in supernatural, everything is possible, one merely needs to know the means of action" (David-Neel 2021: 175).

18 It is hard to estimate how much David-Neel relied on this set of texts when she wrote about Tibetan magic and such a study still needs to be done.

19 An interesting case in David-Neel's understanding of Tibetan magic is precisely instantiated by her presentation of magical objects. In *Magic and Mystery*, David-Neel provided two distinct narratives, in line with her storytelling trademark. The first narrative staged the author herself using for her own purposes (the acquisition of a magic dagger) the "popular belief" of the "credulous Tibetans" in a deceased "lama magician's "enchanted dagger" (*phur ba*), a "ritualistic implement" used in "coercion rites" (David-Neel 1931b: 137–141). The story is telling of the way David-Neel relied on the "[willing] suspension of disbelief" famously inherent to fiction and reports events on the edges of undecidability (between trickery and actual supernormal phenomena) in her written work. When accounting for the Tibetan conception of power objects, David-Neel explained that in the view of "a true initiate in the Tibetan secret lore" "the power of the magic weapon does not depend on the substance of which it is made but is communicated to it by the magician himself. … Yet, as time goes on, a certain portion of this energy remains attached to the *phurba*" (David-Neel 1931b: 138). As such, power objects were aligned with other magical phenomena such as *'phrul pa*, creatures endowed with the energy of their maker and progressively leading a life of their own. In the last chapter of the book, dedicated to the Tibetans' explanation of "psychic phenomena," David-Neel insisted that all these phenomena are produced by individuals, either consciously or unconsciously, and provide instances of strict determinism (David-Neel 1931b: 291). She here came back to the question of power objects as exemplifying "mystic masters" "concentration of mind": "An object can be charged by waves. It then becomes something resembling our electric accumulators and may give back, in one way or another, the energy stored in it" (David-Neel 1931b: 293–4). The author then went on to enumerate several instances and practices. What

matters here is the process described as a technique that ties the object to a subject (the transference of power) and the explanatory model given in terms referring especially to Arsène d'Arsonval's own technoscientific concepts: "waves of energy are produced which can be used in different ways. The term 'wave' is mine. I use it for clearness sake and also because, as the reader will see, Tibetan mystics really *mean* some 'currents' or 'waves' of force. However, they merely say *shugs* or *tsal*; that is to say, 'energy.'" David-Neel did not hide the translation process at stake; simultaneously she delineated her own field of inquiry—this mysterious "energy" being the main purpose of her next "mission" to Tibet and Central Asia. See Thévoz (2022).

20 In this regard, she may have been influenced by the conception of magic developed in a milieu like Max Théon's *Cosmic Movement* through her close connection with Paul and Mirra (Alfassa) Richard from 1901 onward.

21 Of course, this is only one aspect of Tibetan and Mahāyāna Buddhism upon which David-Neel builds her understanding of Buddhism per se. It goes without saying that it also echoes both her long-standing interest in Advaita Vedānta and her European literary and philosophical background (the world as a dream). See Thévoz (2016) and (2019).

References

Asprem, E. (2014), *The Problem of Disenchantment: Scientific Naturalism and Esoteric Discourse 1900–1939*, Leiden: Brill.

Bacot, J. (1925), *Le Poète Milarépa, ses crimes, ses épreuves, son nirvana*, Paris: Bossard.

Bellessort, A. (1929), "Voyageuses," *Journal des débats politiques et littéraires* 141 (357), December 29: 1.

Bensaude-Vincent, B. and C. Blondel (eds.) (2002), *Des savants face à l'occulte, 1870–1940*, Paris: La Découverte.

Bergier, J., and L. Pauwels (1960), *Le Matin des Magiciens*, Paris: Gallimard.

Blondel, C. (2002), "Eusapia Palladino: la méthode expérimentale et la 'diva des savants,'" in B. Bensaude-Vincent and C. Blondel (eds.), *Des savants face à l'occulte, 1870–1940*, 143–72, Paris: La Découverte.

Bosc, E. (1913), *Yoghisme et Fakirisme hindous (Introduction à la Yoga)*, Paris: G.A. Mann.

Carnoules, J. (1913), "Le magisme thibétain," *La Vie mystérieuse*, April 25: 121–2.

Carrière, P. (1946). "Alexandra David-Neel revient du Thibet," *Les Nouvelles littéraires, artistiques et scientifiques* 992, August 8: 1.

D'Andrea, P., and P. Lagrange (2002), "Définitions occultes," in B. Bensaude-Vincent and C. Blondel (eds), *Des savants face à l'occulte, 1870–1940*, 19–40, Paris: La Découverte.

D'Arsonval, J. A. (1929), "Remarques à propos du rapport de M. J[ean] Giaja [au sujet du facteur psychique de la thermogenèse animale]," *Comptes rendus de la Société de biologie et de ses filiales*, 2 (101), May 29: 23–26.

David-Neel, A. [Myrial, A.] (1903), "L'entraînement physique dans les sectes yoguistes," *Bulletins et Mémoires de la Société d'anthropologie de Paris* 5 (4): 201–14.

David-Neel, A. [Myrial, A.] (1904), "Le pouvoir religieux au Thibet: ses origines," *Mercure de France* 12, December: 599–618.

David-Neel, A. (1925), "Les Thibétains: leur mentalité et leurs mœurs," *Bulletin de l'Institut général psychologique* 25 (4–6): 111–31.

David-Neel, A. (1927a), *My Journey to Lhasa*, London: Heinemann.

David-Neel, A. (1927b), *My Journey to Lhasa*, New York: Harper and Brothers.

David-Neel, A. (1927c), *Voyage d'une Parisienne à Lhassa*, Paris: Plon.

David-Neel, A. (1927d), "L'entraînement psychique chez les Thibétains," *Bulletin de l'Institut général psychologique* 27 (4–6): 1–28.

David-Neel, A. (1928), "Le Thibet mystique," *La Revue de Paris*, 1: 855–99.

David-Neel, A. (1929a), "Les phénomènes psychiques au Thibet: théories et pratiques," *La Revue de Paris* 1: 566–95.

David-Neel, A. (1929b), *Mystiques et Magiciens du Tibet*, Paris: Plon.

David-Neel, A. (1930), *Initiations lamaïques: des théories, des pratiques, des hommes*, Paris: Adyar.

David-Neel, A. (1931a), "Magie thibétaine," *Jazz*, Special issue "Exotique," 42–7.

David-Neel, A. (1931b), *With Mystics and Magicians in Tibet*, London: John Lane The Bodley Head.

David-Neel, A. (1931c), *Initiates and Initiations in Tibet*, London: Rider.

David-Neel, A. (1932), *Magic and Mystery in Tibet*, New York: Claude Kendall.

David-Neel, A. (1936), *Le Bouddhisme du Bouddha*, Paris: Plon.

David-Neel, A. (1938), *Magie d'amour et Magie noire: scènes du Tibet inconnu*, Paris: Plon.

David-Neel, A. (1939), *Buddhism, Its Doctrines and Its Methods*, London: John Lane The Bodley Head.

David-Neel, A. (1967), *The Secret Oral Teachings in Tibetan Buddhist Sects*, New York: City Light Books.

David-Neel, A. (1972), *Le Sortilège du Mystère: faits étranges et gens bizarres rencontrés au long de mes routes d'Orient et d'Occident*, Paris: Plon.

David-Neel, A. (2000), *Correspondance avec son mari, 1904–1941*, Paris: Plon.

David-Neel, A. (2021), *Milarépa, le yogi-poète tibétain*, Paris: Plon.

Dubuisson, E. (1910), *À propos de la Renaissance de la magie*, Paris: Librairie des sciences psychiques.

Evans-Wentz, W. (1928), *Tibet's Great Yogi Milarepa*, Oxford: Oxford University Press.

Evans-Wentz, W. (1935), *Tibetan Yoga and Secret Doctrines*, Oxford: Oxford University Press.

Goto-Jones, C. (2016), *Conjuring Asia: Magic, Orientalism and the Making of the Modern World*, Cambridge: Cambridge University Press.

Hanegraaff, W. (2012), *Esotericism and the Academy: Rejected Knowledge in Western Culture*, Cambridge: Cambridge University Press.

Hanegraaff, W. (2016), "Magic," in G. Magee (ed.), *The Cambridge Handbook of Western Mysticism and Esotericism*, 393–404, Cambridge: Cambridge University Press.

Jäschke, H. (1881), *A Tibetan-English Dictionary*, London: Secretary of State for India in Council.

Karmay, S. (1980?), *Inventaire des livres tibétains de la collection d'Alexandra David-Neel donnée au musée Guimet* [index cards], Paris: library of the Guimet museum.

Konchok, Lhundrub (between 1497 and 1557), *dPal rdo rje 'jigs byed rwa lugs kyi sgrub thabs bdud 'joms snang ba*, https://library.bdrc.io/show/bdr:MW00KG01587

Lagrange, P. (2005), "Renaissance d'un ésotérisme occidental (1945–1960)," in P. Lagrange and C. Voisenat (eds.), *L'Ésotérisme contemporain et ses lecteurs: entre savoirs, croyances et fictions*, 45–96, Paris: Éditions de la Bibliothèque publique d'information.

Laufer, B. (1922), *Milaraspa, tibetische Texte*, Hagen: Folkwang-Verl.

Le Bon, G. (1910), "La renaissance de la magie," *Revue scientifique*, 1: 391–7, 426–35.

Lermina, J. (1890), *Magie pratique*, Paris: Ernest Kolb.

Lévi, É. (1854 and 1861), *Dogme et Rituel de la Haute Magie*, 2 vols, Paris: Germer Baillière.

Mahuzier, L. (n.d.), *Chez les magiciens et les sorciers de l'Himalaya*, n.e.

Maury, A. (1860), *La Magie et l'Astrologie*, Paris: Didier.

Maxwell, J. (1903), *Les Phénomènes psychiques*, Paris: Félix Alcan.

Maxwell, J. (1927), *La Divination*, Paris: Ernest Flammarion.

Maxwell, J. (1929), *La Magie*, Paris: Ernest Flammarion.

McGovern, W. (1924), *To Lhasa in Disguise: A Secret Expedition through Mysterious Tibet*, London: Kegan Paul.

Myers, F. (1903), *Human Personality and Its Survival of Bodily Death*, London: Longmann.

Oman, J. (1905), *The Mystics, Ascetics and Saints of India*, London: T. Fisher Unwin.

Ossendowski, F. (1922), *Beasts, Men, and Gods*, New York: Dutton.

Papus (1893), *Traité élémentaire de la magie pratique: adaptation, réalisation, théorie de la magie*, Paris: Chamuel.

Pouvourville, A. (1912), "L'Énigme tibétaine," *Le Journal*, August 23, 1.

Schlagintweit, E. (1863), *Buddhism in Tibet*, Leipzig: Brockhaus, Trübner.

Schlieter, J. (2021), "A Common Core of Theosophy in Celtic Myth, Yoga, and Tibetan Buddhism: Walter Y. Evans-Wentz and the Comparative Study of Religion," in Y. Mühlematter and H. Zander (eds.), *Occult Roots of Religious Studies: On the Influence of Non-Hegemonic Currents on Academia around 1900*, 161–86, Berlin: De Gruyter Oldenbourg.

Seligman, K. (1964), *Histoire des magies*, Paris: Planète, "Encyclopédie Planète."

Sofer, G. (2020), "The Reception of Ritual Magic in Max Théon's Circles," in J. Chajes and B. Huss (eds.), *The Cosmic Movement: Sources, Contexts, Impact*, 169–98, Beer Sheva: Ben-Gurion University of the Negev Press.

Stein, R. (1954), "George Roerich, *Blue Annals*," *Journal asiatique* 243: 285–6.

Thévoz, S. (2016), "On the Threshold of the 'Land of Marvels': Alexandra David-Neel in Sikkim and the Making of Global Buddhism," *Journal of Transcultural Studies* 7 (1), 149–86. https://doi.org/10.17885/heiup.ts.23541

Thévoz, S. (2017), "The Yogi, the Prince, and the Courtesan: *Izéÿl* in Europe and America," in P. Hackett (ed.), *The Assimilation of Yogic Religions through Pop Culture*, 7–34, Lanham, MD: Lexington Books/Rowman & Littlefield Press.

Thévoz, S. (2018), "En voix de libération," in A. David-Neel, *Le Grand Art*, 305–80, Paris: Le Tripode.

Thévoz, S. (2019), "Au bord d'un mystère: de Ceylan au Tibet, David-Neel, Segalen et le bouddhisme," in G. Louÿs (ed.), *Voyages extrêmes*, 139–92, Paris: Classiques Garnier/Lettres modernes Minard.

Thévoz, S. (2022), "Alexandra David-Neel," *Collectionneurs, collecteurs et marchands d'art asiatique en France 1700–1939*, Paris: Institut national de l'histoire de l'art, 2022. https://agorha.inha.fr/detail/761.

Thévoz, S. (2023), "'Ce vagabond érémitique, Sorcier des hauts pics embéguinés:' *Thibet*, autoportrait du poëte en Padmasambhava," in C. Doumet, A. Cavallaro, A. Schellino, and Z. Zhao (eds.), *Victor Segalen: la connaissance de l'Est*, Paris: Hermann.

Waddell, L. (1895), *The Buddhism of Tibet, or Lamaism: With Its Mystic Cults, Symbolism, and Mythology, and in Its Relation to Indian Buddhism*, London: Allen.

Woodroffe, J. (1929), *Shakti and Shâkta: Essays and Addresses on the Shâkta Tantrashâstra*, 3rd edition revised and enlarged, Madras/London: Ganesh/Luzac.

Afterword: Conceptualizing the "Magical" in Tibet and Beyond

Nicolas Sihlé (CESAH, CNRS/EHESS)

> *A monk who practises black magic is doctrinally on a par with a man who drinks; a bad Buddhist, if you like, but bad in the sense of wicked, not of inconsistent. A monk who says* pirit *[Pali verses] to cure sickness, whatever may be his theory to explain its efficacy, is a good Buddhist in every sense.*
>
> Gombrich (1971: 209), quoted by Gellner (1990: 105)

In part, it was the lure of "magic," one could say, that got me into the business of the anthropology of Tibet. Or, widening somewhat the notion, an "enchanted" quality to the religious side of Tibetan lives that struck a chord—something which, I suspect, may have worked its magic on many others too. One of the first academic studies of Tibetan religion that came into my hands, Stephen Beyer's complex but seminal *The Cult of Tārā: Magic and Ritual in Tibet* (1973), arguably deserves more than any other work to be mentioned at the outset, in these closing remarks for a collection of essays on Tibetan magic. At that time, the field of religious studies was still marked, to quite some extent, by the Durkheimian conceptual duality of "religion" vs. "magic," understood as opposed domains. In that context, the book's title signaled a bold and important claim: in Tibetan (and, for that matter, in tantric) Buddhism, something we can call "magic" constitutes a key component at the very heart of this religious tradition.

The book's foreword by K. Bolle promoted the study's seminal character in no uncertain terms: "Certainly, no study of magic can be undertaken from now on that does not take the present study into full account" (ibid.: viii). In retrospect, it comes therefore somewhat as a surprise to realize that the 2022 IATS panel that led to the present volume, as well as the contributions now assembled herein (including one that deals with a Tārā tantra), have hardly mentioned *The Cult of Tārā*. This relative neglect (by the author of the present lines included) may have been, in part, an indirect reflection of the book's weaknesses. It has organizational flaws, in particular, such as the lack of a proper table of contents (the one that is provided lists only the titles of the three long, dense chapters) or the absence of technical Tibetan terms in the main text itself (they are to be found in the index but under their English translations); we should note also that some of Beyer's uses of the term "magic" failed to convince some of his readers (e.g., Denwood 1975; Kalff 1976). However, another, major factor was certainly at play. The announcement of this panel followed closely in the wake of the publication of another key study on this topic, Sam van Schaik's *Buddhist Magic* (2020), which focuses even more centrally on the concept of magic itself. Convening the panel and bringing through the publication process this stimulatingly diverse collection of perspectives on a complex topic—from commonalities in magical recipes of early Buddhist and Śaiva tantras (A. Wenta) to present-day suspicions of poison-casting on the southeastern rim of the Tibetan cultural area (E. Mortensen)—was thus a very timely initiative, for which we have to thank Aleksandra Wenta and Cameron Bailey. In keeping with the spirit of the panel and the present volume, I will focus more on van Schaik's work than on Beyer's, but it will be important to note that they have conceptualized "magic" in significantly different ways.

A last word of preliminary disclosure: I am not convinced of the usefulness of "magic" as an analytical category. The noun seems somewhat blunt and may lead all too easily to reification; I will argue that the adjective "magical," used with due caution, may be more serviceable. The scare quotes in this text thus express a referential character and skeptical distance.

Defining "magic": Textualist paradigms and beyond

It is well known that the dominant approach in the academic study of Tibetan religion has been textual—that of the history of religions, in its different emphases: doctrinal/philosophical, philological, history of lineages and institutions, and so on. The present volume is pleasingly diverse in its disciplinary composition, with a mix of textual, ethnographic (or ethnographically informed), and literary studies. This diversity extends to the approaches to, and definitions of, "magic" that are deployed throughout the book—something which, in itself, is quite representative of the polyphonic state of recent studies of Tibetan (or even Buddhist, more broadly) "magical" practices. Some of the definitional discussions are substantial, and together they provide stimulating food for thought. A. Wenta and C. Bailey's introduction, the most extensive of these contributions, draws together a number of threads of thinking on "magic" in the West, from the original use of the term in ancient Greece, through the Western esoteric tradition (one of the more useful conceptual resources when considering Tibetan tantric magic, in their argument), to the major early figures of anthropological theorizing on this topic.

A small number of recent texts have provided the most inspiration for the contributors' definitional discussions. Bernd-Christian Otto and Michael Stausberg's "General Introduction" to their reader on magic (2013), to which I will turn further below, is one of the most quoted, along with van Schaik's (2020) aforementioned work, which is particularly relevant in its focus on *Buddhist* magic, and more precisely on a Tibetan book of spells. It is worthwhile to quote, in summarized form, van Schaik's "threefold definition of Buddhist magic" (ibid.: 40–1):

> 1. First, I will use the term in a Buddhist context to point to rituals entirely performed for "this-worldly" ends, in which the ultimate aim of Buddhism is only very indirectly linked to the practice. When buddhas and bodhisattvas appear in these practices, … their purpose is to guarantee the effects of the spell. The accumulation and transfer of merit is also of little importance in Buddhist spells. It is true that meritorious Buddhist activities such as recitation of scriptures and offerings … are also considered effective for … achieving … worldly aims, but this is different from the application of specific rituals by specialists, based on a book of spells. I am reserving the word *magic* for the latter.
>
> 2. Second, the rituals I am calling magic in Buddhism are characterized by a swift and clear relationship between ritual and result. In these rituals the result follows quickly after the accomplishment of the spell. … in many cases the spells address pressing concerns, including illness, the need for urgent answers …. Thus the expectation is that the result of the spell will be evident. … Thus, for the purpose of this book, I am not dealing with magical powers that arise as a side effect of meditation, as these are usually to manifest only after a long period of practice.
>
> 3. The third way I want to define what we mean by magic comes from the structure of Buddhist books of spells. These are collections of practices …. Each spell is usually quite brief, and the instructions are clear even to a nonspecialist. These books of spells are usually manuscripts compiled by practitioners, though some Buddhist scriptures … are also compendiums of spells.

One may note that the very project of defining "Buddhist magic" is straddling the line somewhat uncomfortably between defining cross-culturally applicable analytical concepts and examining particular sociocultural, historical traditions: it is neither nor. In a nutshell, for van Schaik, "magic" (in a Buddhist context) refers to rituals that are basically spells (or based on spells), aim at swift worldly results, and are gathered, with instructions, in books of spells (or similar scriptures). As definitions of "magic" go (even in Buddhist contexts), this is very specific. The key constitutive feature is the spell, which is found in "books of spells." We have here a logocentric, very selective text-centered vision of "magic"—actually, this is just a characterization of *magical spells* and the instructions for short rituals based on them that one finds in spell books. Larger tantric rituals with a magical character, such as large community exorcisms (like *torgyak* [gtor rgyag] rituals) or "war magic" (*makdok* [dmag bzlog] rituals), do not fit the definition well, and neither do small, domestic "magical" acts such as casting out a dough effigy on the evening of the twenty-ninth day of the last lunar month, or keeping a thread from a cloth that is given in a dowry, in order to keep the essence of prosperity (*yang* [g.yang]) that may be attached to it. Van Schaik's focus on the particular modality of spell books is not unreasonable in itself: collections of spells, with ritual instructions, are a prominent example of clearly magical elements. Some contributions in this volume (by Amanda Brown and Aleksandra Wenta, who refer, respectively, to "magical rites" and "magical recipes") analyze precisely this kind of texts; others (Susan Landesman's chapter on a tantric text associated with Tārā and Valentina Punzi's examination of amulet practices) focus on texts and practices in which spells are an important component. It should thus be acknowledged that there is something *prototypically* "magical" about the case of spells and spell books, as we might want to formulate this (cf. below). My point is simply that the formulation quoted above will not do as a general "definition of Buddhist magic."

Van Schaik's definition also shows a bias that textualist scholarship is not always able to fully avoid: textual materials inform us about their authors or compilers, but one should beware of filtering out the nonliterate or nonspecialist strata of society. It does not make good (at least anthropological but also historical) sense to define the general category of "magic" as consisting solely of textual rituals carried out by "specialists" (point 1 above). What about so-called "popular" forms of magic (or, for that matter, "magical" elements in what Tucci 1980 or Samuel 1993 call "folk religion")? However we may wish to call these elements, they cannot be seen as belonging to a domain hermetically sealed off from the production of textual magic by literate elites (see, for instance,

Berounský 2015: 101). In the Buddhist context more generally, Erick White notes that the magical arts were "often a folk art in terms of their social conditions of production, transmission, and consumption" (2016: 603).

In his proposed definition, van Schaik chooses also to leave aside "magical powers that arise as a side effect of meditation, as these are usually to manifest only after a long period of practice" (point 2). If the aim is to provide a general definition for the category, then "magical powers" arguably should belong to the domain of "magic." The argument provided to justify their exclusion is a *non sequitur*: the length of the training for the *acquisition* of these powers is irrelevant to the definition; what counts is the generally swift character of the results produced by the subsequent *application* of these powers.

For the purposes of the present discussion, one may register a last objection to van Schaik's formulation. The choice to use the term "magic" "to point to rituals entirely performed for 'this-worldly' ends" (point 1) may seem consonant with long-established (although not unquestioned) trends in academic writing on magic. However, it ignores the point that Beyer made half a century ago for tantric Buddhism and that others, as we shall see, have made in various ways: the important place of magical powers and activities on the path toward Enlightenment. Thus, Bailey (in this volume) claims that magic is "vitally necessary" for an understanding of the soteriological dimension of Buddhism (see the section "Magically Storming the Gates of Buddhahood"—a striking formulation by Beyer 1973: 92—in C. Bailey 2020: 545–52).[1] More generally, it is difficult not to see a "magical" character in a number of Buddhist practices (or, for instance, actions ascribed to the Buddha) that are soteriological in their orientation. The Buddha's famous "miracle" at Śrāvastī was an impressive display of magical power that enabled him to defeat the holders of heretical doctrines and convert masses to the Buddhist *dharma* (Strong 1992: 26–7). For Beyer, as summarized by Bailey, "the theory of generation-stage practice is in fact a theory of magic" (2020: 550). We should also keep in mind that tantric exorcisms supposedly liberate demonic beings—the semantics of the verb *dröl* [sgrol], "to liberate," in the context of such rituals has received substantial attention (Cantwell 1997). Faithful adherents of Buddhism are supposedly able to gain liberation through the senses (e.g., liberation through seeing, *tongdröl* [mthong grol]) when they come into contact with certain powerful objects (Gayley 2007). Japanese postmortem consecration rituals and Tibetan practices of ejection of the consciousness principle (*powa* ['pho ba]) are said to enable the deceased to realize Buddhahood or achieve rebirth in a pure land, at least theoretically. Thus, van Schaik's position is arguably reductive. Granted, focusing on a limited subdomain with strong family resemblances to practices and texts that have been documented in a number of other cultural/historical contexts (the Indic Atharvaveda, Greco-Egyptian papyri, medieval Jewish manuscripts, etc.) provides a solid basis for arguing for a transcultural analytical category of "magic"—or, at least, this sets up the basis for a solid discussion in which the "magical" character of the elements under consideration is highly unlikely to be challenged. It is striking, however, that a book subtitled *Magic and Ritual in Tibet* remains outside the scope of *Buddhist Magic*—indeed, the latter does not even mention Beyer's name.

Most of the contributions in this volume take objects that are not spells or spell-centered rites. Nike-Ann Schröder examines "severance" practices (*chö* [gcod]), which may have a more or less "magical" character according to their modalities. C. Bailey presents three rituals, two of which do not have a strongly "magical" character—but the real focus is here on the tantric practitioner's *relations* with deities in matters of magical rites. Rolf Scheuermann presents practices that may seem at first not particularly "magical": "resolute aspiration" prayers (*mönlam* [smon lam]), but these less prototypical manifestations of magical action are rewarding objects of reflection. Eric Mortensen probes into ideas of poison-casting in Gyalthang and their obscure social and conceptual webs. Finally, Samuel Thévoz provides a historical contextualization of the use of "magic" as a key term in Alexandra David-Néel's practices of cultural translation. This multidimensional exploration of both the prototypical core and interesting peripheries of Tibetan "magic" gives this volume, if not a completeness, at least a nicely rounded character.

Beyond "magic"? Reconsidering the usefulness of a category

Of course, as several contributors to this volume have noted, whether "magic" remains a serviceable analytical category is very much debated. Solid scholarly studies of this domain of inquiry have expressed serious doubts in this respect (e.g., M. Brown 1997: 122). The term has a problematic history of derogatory and exclusionary uses and of dubious negative definitions, such as "abortive science devoid of rationality, or private religion devoid of theology" as P. Jorion and G. Delbos sum it up (1980: 91). Although anthropologists and other social scientists have increasingly striven to use this concept without implicit value judgments, academic discourse on "magic" still remains occasionally marked by echoes of now outdated contrasts. Reformulating an observation by White

(2016: 592), one notes that taking academic and other discourses on "magic" as a partly reflexive object of analysis has itself become the focus of substantial scholarship (e.g., Tambiah 1990; Greenwood 2009; Otto and Stausberg 2013; Dubuisson 2016; Jones 2017).

A recent intervention in the debate on the scholarly value of the notion of "magic," particularly relevant for our purposes, is Erick White's essay "Contemporary Buddhism and Magic" (2016), which develops a critical, anthropological take on scholarly as well as Asian modernist uses of this category. White's point of departure is a "minimalist" definition of magic that, contrary to van Schaik's, is quite standard in its breadth of coverage: "ritualized actions and techniques intended to produce discernible yet extraordinary effects in the material and phenomenological world" (ibid.: 593). However, considering the problematic baggage of the term "magic," White suggests using "ritual arts of efficacy" instead (ibid.), a proposal that has met with some measure of interest in recent work on contemporary Buddhism (Joffe 2019: 52; Brac de la Perrière and Jackson 2022: 7; Patton 2022).

"Efficacy" is obviously a key term. Unfortunately, beyond the issue of its rather unwieldy length, White's formulation is arguably too broad. One needs to distinguish between different modes or logics of ritual efficacy, the "magical" being just one of them. Another could be termed a "cultic" mode, for less coercive or mechanistic ritual modalities, centering on the worship and supplication of (human or nonhuman) powers (as in Tibetan *söldep* [gsol 'debs] prayers of supplication). Arguments such as Richard Kieckhefer's ([1989] 2014: 14–16) on the difficulty of distinguishing, sometimes, between coercion and supplication are fair game, but my point is about polar ideal types, not separate domains. Yet another mode of ritual efficacy could be labeled "social conventional," for characterizing what John Austin (1975) has called the "felicitous" character of procedures (typically including speech acts) sanctioned by social conventions (as in oath-taking). These different modalities are probably not an exhaustive list and are not mutually exclusive: one given ritual may mobilize different logics at different moments in the ritual sequence. If one considers this diversity of possible ritual modalities, it appears clearly that "ritual arts of efficacy" cannot function as a replacement for "magic." We will return below to White's text, concerning the issue of the problematic duality of "magic" and "religion."

Rolf Scheuermann's chapter in this volume suggests that we consider another analytical and terminological option, as outlined by Otto and Stausberg (2013: 10–12), who declare that they "have stopped believing" in the category of "magic" (ibid.: 11), even if one attempts to construct it through family-resemblance and prototype approaches (ibid.: 8–10). Scheuermann summarizes their arguments for the use of an alternative approach, based on "patterns of magicity"—aspects of, or patterns displayed by, actions commonly labeled as "magical," such as the particular use of words or the miraculous capabilities that may be attributed to individuals. Otto and Stausberg claim that one may want to consider these patterns in themselves as more promising analytical avenues of empirically based research than the larger and unstable category of "magic." Scheuermann's chapter embraces this strategy and, in the course of his examination of aspiration (*mönlam*) practices, suggests a rather convincing addition to Otto and Stausberg's initial list of patterns. I would argue, however, that this list is heterogeneous and unsystematized. The formulation "patterns of magicity" lumps together quite different planes of analysis: sources of power/efficacy, aims of the act, social evaluation, and so on. In that sense, it strikes one as analytically less useful than more precise formulations, such as for instance the locus of power enabling the action, the modes (or logics) of efficacy, the aims of the action, or the location in the religious field (in Bourdieu's sense). Otto and Stausberg's methodological suggestion (presented in less than two pages) is perhaps still in a preliminary stage and remains in need of a fuller treatment and critical examination.

If "magic" is a problematic category, and if White's or Otto and Stausberg's reformulations are not fully convincing, where to go from here? Daniel Dubuisson proposes the use of "magism(s)" (Catholic and others) as a way of moving beyond the "debased, worn-out word 'magic'" (2016: 5). Is this the way forward, or a scholarly illusionist's trick? My own argument will be that a noun is not what suits best the facts at hand, but obviously there will always be differences in scholarly sensibilities. One thing is clear: despite decades of critiques, today "magic" and its cognates still belong to the vocabulary of social scientists. As a number of authors have noted (e.g., Sørensen 2013: 241), we may have more to lose than to gain from abandoning the term altogether. There are striking cross-cultural family resemblances (such as those that constitute the subject matter of van Schaik's study—see also C. Bailey 2021) and, to this day, apparently no better term to designate this modality of human thought and action.

There have been arguments for the importance of emic understandings of the term. Modern analytical distinctions of what is "magic" and what is not, in terms of the sources of power for instance, may not map well at all onto medieval Western European conceptual distinctions: what, analytically, may appear as "magical" in sacraments or exorcisms was not conceived as "magic" (in either of its two main modalities of demonic or natural magic) at that time

(Kieckhefer 2014: x–xi). But the dual aims of understanding local worlds of conceptions and practices at a given place and time and elaborating serviceable cross-cultural analytical categories are both important. The historically relatively unstable character of conceptions of "magic" in the West (M. Bailey 2006: 2; White 2016: 592–3) is a challenge for the elaboration of a satisfactory analytical category; however, in contrast to this diverse historical trajectory, we should also acknowledge the relative convergence and stabilization of contemporary analytical uses. (In this respect, van Schaik's definition appears as somewhat an outlier in its narrow focus on one particular type of phenomenon.)

Beyond dichotomies: "Magical" *and* "religious"

Remaining with vernacular categories, what sense of the lay of the land may we derive from Tibetan emic notions? A number of Tibetan terms have been identified that can be glossed in relation to "magic" or a "magical" character. Some point more to the domain of magical illusion or display of magic, like *sgyu ma*, *'phrul*, and compounds like *sgyu 'phrul*, *rdzu 'phrul*, or *cho 'phrul* (see Scheuermann in this volume, and van Schaik 2020: 176 n.1).

Some designate "spells": *sngags* (Skt. *mantra*), *rig pa* (Skt. *vidyā*), *gzungs* (Skt. *dhāraṇī*); one finds also numerous compounds of these terms. Books of spells such as those studied by Cuevas (2010), van Schaik (2020), and Brown (in this volume) are often called *be'u bum*, literally "calf's nipple": an old term used for "compilations of useful material" perhaps and, in the context of these compilations of magical spells and rites, more specifically, "handbooks" of "practical magic," or "grimoires" (Cuevas 2010: 166–7). (Bailey and Wenta in this volume also mention the term *las tshogs*, "collection of [ritual] actions," for such compilations.)

The key term *sngags* (which on its own, as opposed to *mdo*, Skt. *sūtra*, may also function as a shorthand designation of the tantras) is found in yet other compound formulations that point toward the domain of sorcery or "black magic." Scheuermann (in this volume) mentions *ngan sngags*, literally "evil mantras," as well as the term *mthu*, which "literally means 'power' but is used to denote aggressive forms of magical ritual" (van Schaik 2020: 176 n.1), or aggressive application of magical power more broadly (Sihlé 2013: 217–18). The combination *mthu (dang) sngags* is another common designation for religious/tantric power, often (but not necessarily: see Sihlé 2009: 160) denoting its aggressive uses.

Another important term in this semantic field is *dngos grub* (Skt. *siddhi*), which refers to the "attainments" of tantric practice—a notion that Bailey and Wenta (in this volume) gloss evocatively as "super powers." These powers or results of tantric practice are often classified and hierarchized, the higher ones being soteriological in nature, the lower ones being more paradigmatically "magical" and including aggressive magic (Skt. *abhicāra*) (Wenta in this volume).

Building upon the basic term *las* (Skt. karma, "act, ritual action"), the compound *las-sbyor* (literally "application of the activities") is an interesting term as well, which has been glossed in diverse ways. It refers generally to the ritual actions, typically classified in four categories (pacifying, augmenting, controlling, and destroying), but it may also refer specifically to the last of these categories (Karmay 1998: 8, 69). Cuevas (2010: 170) has suggested an etymological reading of the term that could imply affinities with Western notions of sympathetic magic, a suggestion that has been followed by Bailey and Wenta in the introduction to the present volume, but regarding which van Schaik (2020: 176 n.1) expresses some reservations.

Magical illusion, spells, aggressive magic, supernormal powers, and results of tantric practice are some of the key themes that are highlighted by this cursory exploration of the rich Tibetan vocabulary showing semantic affinities with our notion of "magic." Scheuermann (in this volume) has noted perceptively that three of the terms examined in his own discussion, namely *mthu*, *rdzu 'phrul*, and *cho 'phrul*, all occur as designating the Buddha's magical powers, and more generally "as qualities acquired along the Buddhist path." In view of the discussion above, one can only subscribe to his (somewhat cautiously worded) conclusion: "a clear delineation between religion and magic is not easy." This brings us back to one of the guiding threads of this discussion: the particularly strong overlap between what, using Western categories, we may want to call "religious" and "magical" elements in the Tibetan (and tantric Buddhist) context.

There are well-known historical developments that illuminate this state of affairs; as summarized by van Schaik (2020: 11–12):

> The literature of spells predated the Vajrayana, and the creators of Vajrayana rituals took aspects of these magical practices—the mantras, mandalas, and ritual implements—and integrated them into a system of salvation. In the tantras, the deity, their mandala, the recitation of their mantra, and the use of hand gestures and special implements are all part of a path toward awakening. It is the power in these methods … [among others] that makes the Vajrayana the swift path to enlightenment.

> Yet the Buddhist tantras also contain rituals for protection, wealth, and love, not to mention destruction. This mixed nature of the tantras … is [partly] the result of how the tantras developed historically, drawing on the powerful magical practices of earlier Buddhist sutras and dharanis. Mantras, for example, began as spells taught by the Buddha for protection from snakebite and other threats to monks and nuns. Later, mantras became linked to specific deities, representing the power of each deity in sound. Later still, the use of mantras was taught as a method for enlightenment itself, rather than just for magical effect.

Faced with these profound Buddhist historical and contemporary links between the "religious" and the "magical," is it analytically tenable at all to argue for the enduring relevance of the old anthropological duality of "religion" and "magic" as, in some important sense, opposed domains? Some formulations by the contributors to this volume show some degree of hesitation here—and one could say that they are in good company: we have here a lingering framework, in much nonspecialist writing of course, but even also in some recent scholarly works.

Erick White's essay, mentioned above, is intriguing in this regard. Its arguments regarding the problematic character of the term "magic" are generally well taken. It is striking, however, that a number of them revolve around one idea: the irreducibly flawed duality of "religion" and "magic" in scholarly and modern thinking. For White, we have in "the observations of scholars and practitioners alike … an analytic frame that is constantly, even obsessively, returning to the modern question of how within Buddhist social worlds 'magical' beliefs, behaviors, and consciousness differ from 'religious' and 'scientific' sensibilities" (2016: 593–4). This assessment appears excessive and one-sided: there is substantial scholarship concerning Buddhist lives and worlds that leaves the relatively unwieldy macro-category of "magic" aside—not to mention the said dualities—in favor of fine-grained and more solid and enlightening analyses. But White's text returns itself repeatedly to this condemnation of a (supposedly dominant) dichotomous mindset and biased use of the category of "magic"; actual examples are not discussed within the strict limits of the space allowed, leaving nonspecialist readers with the impression that the phenomenon might be quite general.

Other voices are more nuanced with regard to the assessment of the current state of the debate. Matteo Benussi (2019) maintains to some extent the notion that the magic vs. religion distinction (understood in a non-dichotomous way) may keep some operational value, but in a cautious way:

> A consensus has emerged amongst anthropologists and religious studies specialists that deciding where religion (e.g. belief in spiritual beings), folk knowledge (e.g. non-biomedical healing systems), or "natural philosophy" (e.g. astronomy) end and magic begins, has more to do with cultural boundary-making and social normativities than with any "objective" reality.

Western processes of categorial boundary-making between "magic" and "religion" have a complex history of their own, in which Protestantism played a not negligible part (Tambiah 1990: 18, 31; Hanegraaff 2016). (Similarly, we know the important influence Protestantism has exerted on Western studies and definitions of "Buddhism": see Gombrich and Obeyesekere 1988; Schopen 1991.)

Yet other scholars have clearly abandoned the idea of two separate domains—as the opening quote of this afterword illustrates. Gustavo Benavides has written an essay (2006) on the overlap and partial inseparability of what is commonly designated as "religion" and "magic," with substantial reference to Buddhist along with Christian (mainly Catholic) traditions. The title of the first section announces clearly the general frame: "Magic within Religion." Some contributors to the present volume voice arguments for abandoning the dichotomy or acknowledging the overlap of the two categories. In their introduction, Bailey and Wenta note: "An esotericist model of magic, which is much more in line with the actual emic viewpoints of the writers and practitioners of the texts and methods we are studying, recognizes magic not as opposed to religion but as a specialized form of it." If we leave aside the literate elites referred to here and consider the broader picture of Tibetan magical practices in general, the same premises regarding an esotericist perspective probably do not hold, but the conclusion arguably remains to quite some extent. Most practitioners of Tibetan magical rituals as well as their clients see these activities as part of Buddhist religion in a very basic, unproblematic way—if at times as a worldly and therefore somewhat inferior orientation within the Buddhist religious fold. But "magical" assistance—warding off misfortune, calling prosperity, fertility, longevity and success, and so on—by the Buddhist religious specialists remains a doctrinally and ethically profoundly legitimate and valued domain of activity, exemplifying (at least ideally) competence, power, and compassion.

Schröder's chapter presents the position of "cultural anthropology" with regard to the duality of "religion" and "magic" somewhat surprisingly in terms of the (obviously outdated) evolutionism of the early thinkers within the discipline, but the chapter's main line of argument is quite compelling. The tantric practice of "severance" presents a whole field of modalities. Some of those—the " 'magic' end" of the continuum—are more typically "magical": practice with objects, and in places and times, suffused with power or powerful symbolism: thigh-bone trumpets, cremation grounds, nightly practice, and so on, with lore going back to transgressive Indic Śaiva practitioners. Other modalities—the "religio-philosophical end"—are less typically "magical": more visualized forms in more neutral places and times, such as a monastic ritual assembly, with associations to standard Mahayana Buddhist philosophical tenets. The analysis suggests there is more, here, than just a polarization of a field: "those contents are not opposites but rather form a field, inform each other, and enhance each other's power of transformation when applied together during the *gcod* practice." We have here a stimulating, clearly more subtle approach to the duality, working not with simple binary oppositions but with a field of polarities that can be seen to interact with each other. There are quite some affinities, here, with the suggestion, presented above, that we should distinguish, within the category of ritual, different poles corresponding to "cultic," "magical," and "social conventional" ritual logics.

The Tibetan practices of "resolute aspirations" analyzed in Scheuermann's chapter are also illuminating in this respect. A preliminary observation is that they need not take always a strong "ritual" character: a *mönlam* may consist of earnest words of aspiration of one's own, voiced spontaneously according to one's inspiration in a given situation; they do not always consist in the recitation of a predefined, known aspiration text such as the Zangchö Mönlam (Samantabhadra's "Aspiration to Good Actions," also known as "The King of Aspiration Prayers"). Generally speaking, "prayers" addressed to invisible beings, beseeching them to grant favors, assistance, or other benefits, belong more to the "cultic" ritual modality—but this is more what Tibetan *söldep*, or prayers of supplication, are about. The logic of *mönlam* is that of an efficacious mechanism, sometimes independent of outside powerful beings, and often building on favorable, auspicious (even powerful, one might perhaps say?) circumstances: a sacred temple, a day with religious significance, or the presence of a venerated master, or of large numbers of participants in the ritual event for instance. As highlighted by Scheuermann, the inherently efficacious utterance of "words of truth" may be one of the logics involved. The inherent efficacy of words places the *mönlam* practices closer to the "magical" than to the "cultic" pole. The results are often perceived as coming in future lives, which makes aspiration prayers less prototypically "magical," but they are valued as ritual techniques for producing these results—powerful techniques that, beyond one's own religious qualities, depend on outside factors like place, setting, and so on. An interesting twist here is to be found in the *dhāraṇī* for accomplishing resolute aspirations (*smon lam 'grub pa'i gzungs*) mentioned at the end of Scheuermann's chapter. This element is more prototypically "magical" due to its spell-like character, and it is sometimes inserted into the text of aspiration prayers. As in Schröder's chapter, we see that a certain "magical" character is generally present, but more or less so, depending on the particular modalities or examples considered.

A well-rounded exposition of Tibetan forms and principles of "magical" activity (which is beyond the scope of the present discussion) would need to go into the main forms it takes and the main analytical subcategories that could be elaborated. A productive point of departure could be found in Bailey's chapter (and previous writings on this topic) and the distinction between "natural" magic and "demonic" magic. The first might be seen as "essentially a branch of medieval science" (Kieckhefer [1989] 2014: 1, quoted by Bailey), or "an extension of natural philosophy," whereas the second "rests upon … religious beliefs and practices" (ibid.)—categories that are not mutually exclusive, however, if we consider the complex composition of certain practices. An echo of this distinction between "natural" and "demonic" magic appears in A. David-Néel's classification of Tibetan magicians: a majority "seek the power of coercing certain gods and demons" while a more "enlightened" minority with knowledge of the "true" nature of reality understand the practitioner to be the source of the production of "magical" phenomena. As Thévoz points out in his chapter, this duality echoes the book's original title, *Mystiques et Magiciens du Tibet*.

A prototype approach to the "magical"

In light of the elements discussed above, what could a definition of "magic" look like? As a first step, I would like to argue for a slight reformulation of the question, and privilege the use of *the adjective "magical."* Analytically, "magic" is less an identifiable domain with its own boundaries than a qualifier for certain types of actions (along with associated material objects, representations, and texts—or sections of texts). Actions with a certain "magical" character are to be found within what, analytically, we would call the domain of "religion," or at its margins, but in other domains too. As Marcel Mauss and Henri Hubert put it ([1902] 2001: 24):

> There is probably not a single activity which artists and craftsmen perform which is not also believed to be within the capacity of the magician. … Magic, in general, aids and abets techniques such as fishing, hunting and farming. Other

> arts are, in a manner of speaking, entirely swamped by magic. Medicine and alchemy are examples.

We could add to the list yet other economic pursuits intertwined with magic: Kula magic, or *yang* practices in Tibet (briefly mentioned above), or even (if we take an example mentioned by Scheuermann in this volume, quoting Malkiel) the "technical analysis" predictive technique used with stock market charts, a technique (according to Malkiel) with a scientific validity comparable to that of alchemy. One could possibly further add a number of social practices or avoidances concerned with luck, fortune, and auspiciousness, such as the avoidance of the left-hand side, the choice or avoidance of certain colors, or certain shared gestures in games or sports. One may refer here to G. da Col and C. Humphrey, who speak more broadly of "technologies of anticipation" (2012: 1).

It might be therefore analytically more solid to speak of a "magical" character of certain activities, without referring to a presumed *domain* that we could call "magic," the contours of which would be exceedingly difficult to outline. There is also arguably more flexibility and possibility of nuance in the approach consisting in talking about a certain (if need be, strongly or weakly) "magical" character in an action (or a section of that action) than in asking, more bluntly, whether something is or belongs to "magic." After this brief excursus, we will remain for the remainder of this discussion in the core of the category of "magical" activity: certain ritual practices, or the application of "magical" powers.

As a second step, adopting a *prototype approach* would seem the methodologically soundest strategy, considering the diversity of elements contained in contemporary definitional attempts (or even just those contained in this volume, which range from the esotericist-inspired, by Bailey, to a creative polyphonic proposal, by Schröder), as well as the great variety of empirical phenomena under consideration. The key arguments for this strategy are, to quite some extent, mutatis mutandis, the ones that Benson Saler has developed with substantial elaboration in favor of a prototype approach to the definition of "religion" (1993, 2000, 2008). (One may also refer here to similar work on definitional approaches to "ritual" by Snoek 2006.) Monothetic definitions, although simpler, and not devoid of heuristic value, essentialize certain features; they operate a selection of definitional criteria that, for complex categories such as "religion" or "magic," may not fit well certain phenomena that should be included (e.g., "supernatural" may not be a category that corresponds accurately to emic understandings; and not all magical spells are based on "sympathetic" logics, as pointed out by van Schaik 2020: 7). They also set up rigid boundaries between the inside and the outside of the category, leading to irresolvable arguments about "borderline" cases (Saler 1993: 156–7). "Family-resemblance" approaches, which derive their inspiration from natural language philosophy (in particular Wittgenstein [1953] 2009), and polythetic grouping (which has roots in the work of biologists) are two similar, and more flexible, strategies. A category is defined by an extended list of features; phenomena are considered to be included to the extent that they exhibit a sufficient degree of matching with these features. (Defining tantric traditions has been approached in a similar way by a number of scholars; a "master list" of features is collated in Wallis 2013.) Prototype theory improves on these approaches by including specifications of "prototypes": the clearest cases of membership in the category. The emphasis here is on defining the core of the category, not its boundaries.

In attempting to define what constitutes "magic," or a "magical" character, a prototype approach could include features such as the following (some of which are mentioned in this volume's introduction or subsequent chapters; see also Otto and Stausberg 2013: 9–10):

- *nature*: ritual actions mobilizing/channeling power (coercion of powerful entities, empowerment of objects, etc.) or direct application of power according to one's will
- *aim*: affecting/changing (or protecting from unwanted change) the state of beings, objects, places or other conditions; manipulating/coercing beings; effects are most commonly of a worldly nature but can include otherworldly aims or extraordinary displays of power (e.g., the Buddha's feats at Śrāvastī); effects are most often perceptible, sometimes less (e.g., protection from misfortune, liberation from *saṃsāra*)
- *time frame*: often swift or immediate efficacy, sometimes lasting effects (protective magic)
- *principles of efficacy*: powerful utterances/writing, powerful substances or empowered devices, action/substances/devices involved according to laws of sympathy (similarity, contagion) or antipathy, recourse—often in a coercive mode—to powerful entities (demonic magic), sometimes unmediated application of power at a distance; may include illusionist techniques (e.g., display of substances supposedly extracted from an ailing body)
- *nature of utterances/writing, if involved*: non-ordinary modalities of speech (Malinowski's "coefficient of weirdness,"[2] foreign words, etc.), spells or other

powerful forms (invocation of sources of power, e.g., truth in Buddhist contexts), symbolical correspondences; procedures or enunciations may also rely on written manuals
- *locus of application of action*: the intended target (being, object, etc.) itself, via contact/ingestion, or material devices such as amulets, effigies, simulacra, objects with symbolical associations to target
- *actors*: very wide range; often noninstitutionalized specialists, but also (as a part of their activity) institutional (e.g., religious) specialists, acting at the solicitation of clients (or in the context of regular activities: e.g., Eucharist, blessings); also nonspecialist actors for simpler forms
- *social setting*: often private, sometimes even secret and/or morally transgressive; but also public, official for certain forms

Prototypical examples include spells, amulets, talismans; healing rituals, exorcisms, war magic, aggressive magic, weather magic, rituals of wealth—or particular sections of all these rituals, involving spells, manipulation of material devices like effigies representing targets that are to be acted upon, and so on.

The last elements of the definition, such as the very wide range of possible actors, are clearly less specific than others (critiques of polythetic definitions sometimes claim that the long lists end up "dissolving" the categories), but altogether these criteria build up a certain profile, the core of which is sharpened by the prototypical examples.

Power and efficacy are obviously key. Some of the chapters in this volume help us move toward finer understandings of Tibetan conceptions of "magical" efficacy. Punzi's chapter provides us with a rare ethnographic attempt to move toward an empirically informed better understanding of emic ideas in this respect. Her arguments regarding the importance of eliciting explicit emic perspectives remind one of Gilbert Lewis's critiques of external observers who, failing in this respect, base themselves on a simple (and inescapably ethnocentric) "look of magic" (1986). An ethnographic attention to detail and commitment to eliciting local specialists' own comments on the ritual process, or its modifications, enable us to sense the importance of pragmatic flexibility on the part of the officiants. From a text-based perspective, Landesman's chapter ("Obstacles to Attainment" section) gives us some sense of how literate religious elites within the Buddhist tantric tradition conceptualized failures in ritual efficacy, here in the sense of not achieving "attainments," or "magical" accomplishments (*siddhi*). Lacking Buddhist ethical qualities on the part of the performer is one of the possible sources of ritual failure.

An empirical dimension is often present in "magical" activity (M. Brown 1997: 128–9). One of the texts presented in Amanda Brown's chapter contains indications that "the practitioner is warned that this recitation will cause boils to rise on his own body, mouth, and tongue; however, he is not to be concerned about that outcome": this might be a reflection of speculations based on empirical observation. Writing from the position of a substantial, prolonged personal engagement with modern instantiations of Tibetan tantric and healing traditions, Ben Joffe notes: "Ignoring the empiricist, experimental, and rational pretensions of magical experts risks flattening the complexities" of the Tibetan Buddhist ritual and theological tradition (2019: 457).

A last note, simply to acknowledge that the complicated ethics of "magical" activity need to be addressed. It is striking that several contributions (most prominently Brown and Wenta in this volume) focus on violent, aggressive "magical" activities. Both authors echo emic normative principles in this respect: the need of highly qualified tantric practitioners and ultimately compassionate action. These principles also inform, to some extent, the actual system of religious training: "Tibetan culture has erected a system wherein the very exercises that allow the acquisition of magical powers [*in short, an extensive regimen of preliminary purifications of the mind*] guarantee their proper use"—in other words, a "ritualization of moral attitudes" (Beyer 1973: 29). But the Buddhist tradition has to be acknowledged as a complex whole in which contradictory elements are found. The ambiguities and internal cultural tensions around the practice of violent ritual activity (powerful exorcisms primarily) constitute a guiding thread in a book-length ethnography of tantric practitioners in a Tibetan-speaking area of northern Nepal (Sihlé 2013).

Conclusion: Toward comparison and larger disciplinary discussions

In the preceding pages, taking my point of departure from the chapters brought together in the present volume and their focus on a category that has been arguably both central in anthropological thinking (Greenwood 2009: 1; Viveiros de Castro 2009: 246) and very challenging to come to terms with, I have made a few simple arguments:

- We need a broader definition of "magic" than the rather narrow textualist paradigm offered by Sam van Schaik's recent book.

- Two recent attempts to replace the category of "magic" with more serviceable analytical tools, White's "ritual arts of efficacy" and Otto and Stausberg's "patterns of magicity," ultimately remain unsatisfactory.
- At the risk of repeating a now well-established understanding: the domains of the "magical" and the "religious" cannot be conceptualized as separate; their overlap is particularly striking in the Tibetan Buddhist context.
- Whereas the noun "magic" suggests a presumed *domain*, the contours of which would be exceedingly difficult to outline, the adjective "magical" may enable more flexibility and nuance. A prototype approach to the definitional question is outlined.

What would be the next step? A. Wenta concludes her chapter in this volume with the observation that comparison "remains a desideratum for the future generation of tantric scholars." In this volume, some doors to comparative exploration have indeed been opened. This is the case with Western esotericism as well as with the so-called "cunning folk" and their "familiar spirits" in medieval and early modern popular religion in the British Isles, in Bailey's chapter (following some of his other recent work). Wenta's chapter in itself has a strong comparative thrust at its core: it examines magical recipes containing very similar prescriptions in the Śaiva and Buddhist tantras, and further explores the links presented by certain literary motives with Brahmanical elements; this enables her to draw conclusions about circulations, as well as to point to probably shared understandings. This kind of work undoubtedly needs to be pursued.

For instance, the centrality of Tibetan tantric Buddhist traditions in the contributions brought together in this volume (including in the present afterword) begs the question of a careful comparison with the place of "magical" features in non-tantric Buddhist traditions. From an anthropological perspective, this could be approached, in part, through a comparative examination of the main specialists associated with practices of a "magical" character in, say, the Tibetan and Burmese religious fields. A particular focus of this discussion could be the figures of the Tibetan tantrists, *ngakpa* [sngags pa], non-monastic practitioners who specialize strongly in tantric rituals, and the Burmese practitioners of the *weikza* Buddhist esoteric path, many of whom focus on exorcism. This will have to wait for another occasion.[3] Ultimately, though, I would like to suggest that, whereas the category of "magic" enables one to outline broad comparative contrasts and arguments at the macro level, for a fine-grained analysis of Tibetan (or Buddhist) rituals and their specialists it remains a broad macro-category and a rather blunt analytical tool. But broad contrasts may be stimulating, important points of departure. Thus, if we go back to general anthropological discussions of "magic" like Brown (1997) or Benussi (2019), which in a sense updates the former in the attention given to the presence of "magic" in modernity or postmodernity, what is striking from a Tibetan studies perspective is that *the strong presence of "magical" elements at the very heart of a "religious" tradition like tantric Buddhism* is a theme that goes unaddressed, in all these works. Moving this notion into mainstream anthropological (or religious studies) discussions of "magic" and "religion"—and perhaps discussions of religious power or authority, or of ritual ethics—should be our next goal.

Notes

1 We should note here A. David-Néel's "choice ... of magic as a defining feature of Tibetan Buddhism as a whole" (in the words of Thévoz, in this volume), "magic" being understood as present in soteriological practices too.

2 Malinowski (1935: vol. 2, 218).

3 One of the first comparative mentions of Tibetan and Burmese specialists of "magical power" is Samuel (2012: 156); similarities between the Burmese *weikza* path and Buddhist tantric traditions have been mentioned already far earlier. There has been ongoing comparative work between specialists of Buddhism, in particular in its Burmese and Tibetan forms, at the CNRS in Paris, France, since 2012. See, for instance, https://himalayas.hypotheses.org/2246.

References

Austin, J. L. (1975), *How to Do Things with Words*, 2nd ed., Oxford: Clarendon.

Bailey, C. (2020), "The Magic of Secret Gnosis: A Theoretical Analysis of a Tibetan Buddhist 'Grimoire,'" *Journal of the Korean Association for Buddhist Studies* 93: 535–70.

Bailey, C. (2021), "Review of Van Schaik, Sam, *Buddhist Magic: Divination, Healing, and Enchantment through the Ages*," H-Buddhism, H-Review. https://www.h-net.org/reviews/showrev.php?id=56639 (accessed July 29, 2021).

Bailey, M. D. (2006), "The Meanings of Magic," *Magic, Ritual, and Witchcraft* 1 (1): 1–23.

Benavides, G. (2006), "Magic," in R. A. Segal (ed.), *The Blackwell Companion to the Study of Religion*, 295–308, Malden, MA: Blackwell.

Benussi, M. (2019), "Magic," in F. Stein (ed.), *Open Encyclopedia of Anthropology [Online]*, Facsimile of the 1st ed. in *The Cambridge Encyclopedia of Anthropology*,

Open Knowledge Press. Available online: https://www.anthroencyclopedia.com/entry/magic (accessed March 5, 2023).

Berounský, D. (2015), "Tibetan 'Magical Rituals' (*las sna tshogs*) from the Power of Tsongkhapa," *Revue d'études tibétaines* 31: 95–111.

Beyer, S. V. (1973), *The Cult of Tārā: Magic and Ritual in Tibet*, Berkeley: University of California Press.

B. Brac de la Perrière, B., and P. A. Jackson (2022), "Introduction. Worlds Ever More Enchanted: Reformulations of Spirit Mediumship and Divination in Mainland Southeast Asia," in B. B. de la Perrière and P. A. Jackson (eds.), *Spirit Possession in Buddhist Southeast Asia: Worlds Ever More Enchanted*, 1–41, Honolulu: University of Hawai'i Press.

Brown, M. F. (1997), "Thinking about Magic," in S. D. Glazier (ed.), *Anthropology of Religion: A Handbook*, 121–36, Westport, CT: Greenwood Press.

Cantwell, C. M. (1997), "To Meditate upon Consciousness as Vajra: Ritual 'Killing and Liberation' in the rNying-ma-pa Tradition," in H. Krasser, M. T. Much, E. Steinkellner, and H. Tauscher (eds.), *Tibetan Studies: Proceedings of the 7th Seminar of the IATS, Graz 1995*, 1: 107–18, Vienna: Verlag der Österreichischen Akademie der Wissenschaften.

Cuevas, B. J. (2010), "The 'Calf's Nipple' (*Be'u bum*) of Ju Mipam ('Ju Mi pham): A Handbook of Tibetan Ritual Magic," in J. I. Cabezón (ed.), *Tibetan Ritual*, 165–86, New York: Oxford University Press.

da Col, G., and C. Humphrey (2012), "Introduction: Subjects of Luck—Contingency, Morality, and the Anticipation of Everyday Life," *Social Analysis* 56 (2): 1–18.

Denwood, P. (1975), "Review of *The Cult of Tārā: Magic and Ritual in Tibet*, by Stephan Beyer," *Bulletin of the School of Oriental and African Studies* 38 (3): 656–57.

Dubuisson, D. (2016), *Religion and Magic in Western Culture*, trans. M. Cunningham, Boston, MA: Brill.

Gayley, H. (2007), "Soteriology of the Senses in Tibetan Buddhism," *Numen* 54 (4): 459–99.

Gellner, D. N. (1990), "Introduction: What Is the Anthropology of Buddhism About?," *Journal of the Anthropological Society of Oxford* 21 (2): 95–112.

Gombrich, R. F. (1971), *Precept and Practice: Traditional Buddhism in the Rural Highlands of Ceylon*, Oxford: Clarendon Press.

Gombrich, R. F., and G. Obeyesekere (1988), *Buddhism Transformed: Religious Change in Sri Lanka*, Princeton, NJ: Princeton University Press.

Greenwood, S. (2009), *The Anthropology of Magic*, Oxford: Berg.

Hanegraaff, W. J. (2016), "Reconstructing 'Religion' from the Bottom Up," *Numen* 63 (5–6): 576–605.

Joffe, B. (2019), "White Robes, Matted Hair: Tibetan Tantric Householders, Moral Sexuality, and the Ambiguities of Esoteric Buddhist Expertise in Exile," Ph.D. diss., University of Colorado.

Jones, G. M. (2017), *Magic's Reason: An Anthropology of Analogy*, Chicago: University of Chicago Press.

Jorion, P., and G. Delbos (1980), "La notion spontanée de magie dans le discours anthropologique," *L'Homme* 20 (1): 91–103.

Kalff, M. (1976), "Review of *The Cult of Tārā: Magic and Ritual in Tibet*, by S. Beyer," *Artibus Asiae* 38 (1): 85–6.

Karmay, S. G. (1998), *Secret Visions of the Fifth Dalai Lama: The Gold Manuscript in the Fournier Collection Musée Guimet, Paris*, London: Serindia.

Kieckhefer, R. ([1989] 2014), *Magic in the Middle Ages*, 2nd ed., Cambridge: Cambridge University Press.

Lewis, G. (1986), "The Look of Magic," *Man, N.S.* 21 (3): 414–37.

Malinowski, B. ([1935] 1966), *Coral Gardens and Their Magic: A Study of the Methods of Tilling the Soil and of Agricultural Rites in the Trobriand Islands. Vol. II: The Language of Magic and Gardening*, 2nd ed., London: George Allen and Unwin.

Mauss, M. ([1902] 2001), *A General Theory of Magic*, trans. R. Brain, London: Routledge.

Otto, B.Ch., and M. Stausberg (2013), "General Introduction," in B.-C. Otto and M. Stausberg (eds.), *Defining Magic: A Reader*, 1–13, Sheffield: Equinox.

Patton, T. (2022), "Special Issue "Buddhist Wizards and Magic." Available online: https://www.mdpi.com/journal/religions/special_issues/buddhist_wizards_magic (accessed March 13, 2023).

Saler, B. (1993), *Conceptualizing Religion: Immanent Anthropologists, Transcendent Natives, and Unbounded Categories*, Leiden: Brill.

Saler, B. (2000), "Conceptualizing Religion: Responses," *Method & Theory in the Study of Religion* 12 (1–4): 323–38.

Saler, B. (2008), "Conceptualizing Religion: Some Recent Reflections," *Religion* 38 (3): 219–25.

Samuel, G. (1993), *Civilized Shamans: Buddhism in Tibetan Societies*, Washington DC: Smithsonian Institution Press.

Samuel, G. (2012), *Introducing Tibetan Buddhism*, New York: Routledge.

Schopen, G. (1991), "Archaeology and Protestant presuppositions in the study of Indian Buddhism," *History of Religions* 31 (1): 1–23.

Sihlé, N. (2009), "The *ala* and *ngakpa* Priestly Traditions of Nyemo (Central Tibet): Hybridity and Hierarchy," in S. Jacoby and A. Terrone (eds.), *Buddhism Beyond the Monastery: Tantric Practices and their Performers in Tibet and the Himalayas*, 145–62, Leiden: Brill.

Sihlé, N. (2013), *Rituels bouddhiques de pouvoir et de violence: La figure du tantriste tibétain*, Turnhout: Brepols.

Snoek, J. A. M. (2006), "Defining 'Rituals,'" in J. Kreinath, J. Snoek, and M. Stausberg (eds.), *Theorizing Rituals. Vol. 1: Issues, Topics, Approaches, Concepts*, 3–14, Leiden: Brill.

Sørensen, J. (2013), "Magic Reconsidered: Towards a Scientifically Valid Concept of Magic," in B.-C. Otto and M. Stausberg (eds.), *Defining Magic: A Reader*, 229–42, Sheffield: Equinox.

Strong, J. (1992), *The Legend and Cult of Upagupta: Sanskrit Buddhism in north India and Southeast Asia*, Princeton, NJ: Princeton University Press.

Tambiah, S. J. (1990), *Magic, Science, Religion, and the Scope of Rationality*, Cambridge: Cambridge University Press.

Tucci, G. (1980), *The Religions of Tibet*, Berkeley: University of California Press.

van Schaik, S. (2020), *Buddhist Magic: Divination, Healing, and Enchantment through the Ages*, Boulder, CO: Shambhala.

Viveiros de Castro, E. (2009), "The Gift and the Given: Three Nano-Essays on Kinship and Magic," in S. C. Bamford and J. Leach (eds.), *Kinship and Beyond: The Genealogical Model Reconsidered*, 237–68, New York: Berghahn Books.

Wallis, Ch. D. (2013), *Tantra Illuminated: The Philosophy, History, and Practice of a Timeless Tradition*, 2nd ed., Petaluma, CA: Mattamayūra Press.

White, E. (2016), "Contemporary Buddhism and Magic," in M. Jerryson (ed.), *The Oxford Handbook of Contemporary Buddhism*, 591–605, Oxford: Oxford University Press.

Wittgenstein, L. ([1953] 2009), *Philosophische Untersuchungen: Philosophical investigations*, trans. G. E. M. Anscombe, P. M. S. Hacker, and J. Schulte, revised 4th ed., Chichester, West Sussex: Wiley-Blackwell.

Contributors

Cameron Bailey is an independent researcher based in the United States. He holds a MA in Religious Studies from Florida State University and a Ph.D. in Tibetan Studies from the University of Oxford and was recently an assistant professor in Indian philosophy at Dongguk University, Seoul. His research specializes in the mythological and ritual aspects of Tibetan protector deity cults.

Amanda N. Brown is a doctoral student and instructor in the Department of Religion at Florida State University. Her research interests focus on magic, narratives of secrecy, and the grotesque. Her current research examines Tibetan revelatory texts that invoke the deity Yamāntaka, particularly texts found in the ritual program of the 'Bri gung bKa' brgyud master Chos kyi grags pa (1595–1659).

Susan Landesman is an independent scholar and educator residing and working in New York City. Her research interests include Indo-Tibetan Buddhism, early Buddhist tantra, Tibetan art, and women in Buddhism, having completed her doctorate in Indian and Tibetan languages and cultures at Columbia University. Her most recent book is *The Tārā Tantra: Tārā's Fundamental Ritual Text (Tārā-mūla-kalpa), Part 1: The Root Tantra* (2020). *The Tārā Tantra, Part 2: The Uttaratantra*, is forthcoming.

Eric D. Mortensen is the John A. Von Weissenfluh Professor of Religious Studies and the Chair of the Department of Religious Studies & Ethics at Guilford College in Greensboro, North Carolina. His research focuses on Tibetan and Himalayan folklore, the religions of the peoples of Northwest Yunnan in Southwest China, divination, magic, the language of Ravens, storytelling, and the roles of animals in religious traditions. His most recent publication is "Of Monsters and Invisible Villages: *Nags myi rgod* Tales of the Tibetans of Gyalthang," in N. Mikles and J. Laycock, eds. *Religion, Culture, and the Monstrous* (2021).

Valentina Punzi is a Ph.D. candidate at the Centre de recherche sur les civilisations de l'Asie orientale, École Pratique des Hautes Études and at the Department of Estonian and Comparative Folkloristics, University of Tartu. Her current research explores contemporary ritual practices among communities in the Sino-Tibetan borderlands. She received a double Ph.D. from the University of Naples L'Orientale (Asian Studies) and Minzu University of China (Tibetan Studies) in 2014. From 2016 to 2020, she was a postdoctoral fellow at the University of Naples L'Orientale. She has conducted extensive fieldwork in Qinghai and Sichuan (PRC) on oral history, ethnic identity, and folk religion.

Rolf Scheuermann is a Tibetologist who works as a research area coordinator at the Käte Hamburger Centre for Apocalyptic and Post-Apocalyptic Studies at the University of Heidelberg. His research interests focus on Buddhist philosophy, Tibetan meditation traditions, Tibetan strategies for coping with the future, and Buddhist eschatology. He has published on the early bKa' brgyud tradition, Tibetan divination, Buddhist end-time narratives, and eco-Buddhist movements. Recently, he coedited the volume *Glimpses of Tibetan Divination* (2019) with Donatella Rossi and Petra Maurer.

Nike-Ann Schröder holds a magister degree in Tibetology and a Ph.D. in cultural anthropology. After completing her Ph.D., she served as a faculty member and teacher in Tibetology at Humboldt University, Berlin. Currently she prepares her postdoc research project on female agency in tantric rituals. Her research interests focus on ritual healing, pilgrimages, female practitioners in Tibetan Buddhism, individual and collective traumatic experiences and cultural strategies of coping/transformation, and decolonized research and theory approaches. Her most recent book chapter is The Cremation Ground, the Battlefield, and the Path of Compassion: What Makes the Fabric of an Individual's Tantric Encounter (2023).

Nicolas Sihlé is a research fellow in anthropology at the Centre national de la recherche scientifique (CNRS, France); he also teaches at INALCO and EHESS in Paris. His research interests focus on ritual, religious specialists, Tibetan religion, and the comparative anthropology of Buddhism. His book *Rituels bouddhiques de pouvoir et de violence* (2013), on Tibetan tantrists, non-monastic specialists of powerful, sometimes violent tantric rituals, like exorcisms, addresses questions of ritual violence and religious specialization. He has coedited a special issue on the Buddhist gift (*Religion Compass* 2015) and a special section on the anthropology of Buddhism (*Religion & Society* 2017).

Samuel Thévoz is an independent scholar associated with the THALIM-research unit at la Sorbonne nouvelle and a visiting fellow in the Department of Religious Studies at the University of Vienna. His research interests focus on travel literature to Tibet and on the reception of Buddhism and yoga in literary, theatrical, artistic, scholarly, and esoteric milieus from a global perspective, with special attention to fin de siècle France up to the 1960s. He is the author of *Un* *horizon infini: explorateurs et voyageurs français au Tibet* (2010). He has also edited forgotten travel narratives to Asia and the formerly unpublished first novel written by Alexandra David-Neel (1868–1969).

Aleksandra Wenta is Lecturer in Indology and Tibetology at the University of Florence, Italy. She holds an M.Phil. and a Ph.D. from the University of Oxford, and a Vidyāvāridhi (Ph.D.) degree from Benares Hindu University. She was assistant professor and a founding faculty at Nalanda University (2016–20). She researches the history, ritual, and literature of tantric Buddhism and Śaivism and Indo-Tibetan Buddhism. She coedited with Purushottama Bilimoria the volume *Emotions in Indian Thought-Systems* (2015, reprint 2018, 2020). She is the author of *The Vajrabhairavatantra: A Study and Annotated Translation* (forthcoming).

Index

Page number followed by n reference note

Abhicāra, 16, 28, 37, 53n23, 61, 63, 64, 67, 71, 79n4, 230
Abhidharma 174
affinity group 141–2
aggressive magic 16, 28, 61, 63, 67, 68, 71, 120n10, 229, 230, 237, 238
Agrippa, Heinrich Cornelius 4, 105
alchemy 48, 86, 205, 235
altered states 112, 174, 175, 176
amulets 97, 117, 127–36, 130, 2, 133, 134, 136, 142, 147n6, 224, 237
  efficacy of 118, 130, 131, 132, 133, 143, 145
  textual- 127–9, 140, 144
  types of 128
Amye Drakar mountain 130
ancestors 68, 79n10, 156
animated corpse (*vetāla*) 48, 58n145
apotropaic 16, 64, 91–2, 105, 106, 107, 133
arapacana 92
Archenemies 19
  the logic of 73
Āryākṣayamatiparipṛcchānāma-Mahāyānasūtra 90
Asaṅga 108
ashes 39, 45, 46, 48, 54n76, 68, 69, 70, 74, 136
astrology 19, 26, 95
Āṭānāṭiya Sutta 106
Atharvaveda 63, 64, 65, 104, 226
attraction 25, 26, 61, 67, 75
attainments see *siddhi*
auspicious
  circumstances 223
  days 27
  substances 67, 117, 121n18
  symbols 147n5
  words 136, 140
authority 3, 111, 113, 129, 141, 143, 145, 197, 213n8, 240

Bai 149, 157, 158, 164
Baima 129, 133, 134, 136, 140, 143
Banshul monastery 129
Bcud len 114, 115
Bden tshig see words of truth
Bdud 'joms gling pa 109, 110
Bembo 133, 140
Beyer, Stephen 29n5, 221–2, 225, 226, 238
Bhūtaḍāmara Tantra 106, 107
Bka' brgyud 94
Black Beryl 26
Black magic 26, 87, 152, 158, 162, 164, 206, 207, 229
Black Moon's Mystery Tantra 14, 23, 26, 28
blessing 95, 115, 116, 131, 132, 237
blood 19, 22, 23, 25, 27, 43, 46, 69, 70, 106, 108, 110, 155
Blue Beryl 153, 154
Bodhgayā 91, 94, 95
Bodhicaryāvatāra 91, 92, 93
Bodhicitta 37, 50
Bon/Bön 129, 147n6, 153, 164n4, 169, 172, 176, 185
Buddhism 14, 15, 28, 88, 93, 97, 103, 106–9, 114, 119, 151, 172, 179, 187, 197–8, 202, 206–8, 211–12, 216n21, 221, 223, 225, 227, 232, 240
  Mahāyāna 50, 63, 90, 91, 96, 108, 109, 216n21, 233
  Vajrayāna 108, 109, 151, 188, 230
burnt offering 39, 40, 41, 42, 43, 44, 45, 46, 47, 48, 49, 53n23, 56n112, 56n121
Bu ston 35

Cakrasaṃvara 210
camel-magic 76–8
cancer 150, 155, 156, 160, 161, 162, 163, 164
colonialism 3, 14, 170, 171, 172
communism 151, 152, 154

creating dissent (*vidveṣaṇa*) 61, 63, 73–4, 80n18
cremation/charnel ground 38, 46, 47, 48, 49, 68, 69, 73, 77, 169, 170, 179, 180, 181, 182, 183, 184, 185, 186, 233
crow-magic 67–71
cultural revolution 129
curse charts 17, 18
cursing 21, 22, 88, 150
  collection of 26

Dalai Lama: Fifth 26, 177, 189n10
  Fourteenth 94, 113
  Seventh 111
dance (*'cham*) 173–9, 183, 184, 185, 186, 189n10
David-Neél, Alexandra 170, 183, 193–212
Ḍākinīs 93, 108–10, 130, 131, 169, 173–4, 177–8, 186, 200
Dbang du 'gyur see subjugation
decolonization 171, 173
demons 3, 16, 17, 23, 28, 29n11, 47, 54n75, 93, 105–20, 130, 154–5, 159, 164, 174, 197, 198, 207, 208, 213n8, 225
design grammar 140–2
destructive magic, see *abhicāra*
Dge lugs 61, 110, 112, 113, 114, 129, 133, 151
Dhāraṇī 30n23, 96, 229, 233
divination 88, 91–3, 98n29, 153, 210
Dīgha Nikāya 106
Dmag zor rgyal mo 114
driving away 61, 68, 69, 70, 71, 76, 77, 80n18
drums 134, 140, 172, 175, 176, 177, 179, 182, 188, 208
Dug, see also cancer, or poison 149–64, 174
Durkheim, Émile 2, 106, 162, 199, 221
Durkheim's concept of magic 3, 86, 88

efficacy 21, 25, 65, 67, 73, 80n18, 94, 128, 129, 132, 141, 142, 143, 144, 145, 188, 211, 221, 227, 228, 236, 237, 239
efficacies of words 89, 92, 96, 233
  of places 89, 96
  of objects 89, 94, 96
  of special time 89, 96
effigy 18, 19, 20, 21, 22, 24, 25, 28, 29n13, 42, 43, 44, 45, 46, 47, 54n75, 55n94, 57n121, 66, 106, 224, 237
emic 2, 4, 5, 15, 103, 125–6, 127, 145, 146, 197, 228, 229, 232, 235, 237
empowerment 37, 88, 104, 115, 118, 131, 132, 134, 143, 177, 178, 181, 188, 189n10, 236
enactment 170, 173, 176, 177, 179, 180, 182, 183, 185, 186, 188
esotericism 2, 3, 4, 103, 112, 170, 196, 198, 199, 206, 207, 208, 210, 211, 213n10, 214n13, 223, 232, 235, 239
etic 4, 16, 62, 63, 125, 126, 146
Evans-Wentz, Walter 183, 196, 197, 210–11
exorcism 54n75, 224, 225, 228, 237, 238, 239

familiar spirit 104, 107–10, 112, 114, 119, 120
Fashi 140
Ficino, Marsilio 105
flight 51
folk 61, 67, 68, 71, 78, 140, 224, 225, 232
folklore 19, 107, 152, 160, 161, 164n2, 198
folkloric 150, 162, 164n2
footprint 42, 44, 54n74
France, *see also* French 195, 196, 197, 198, 200, 202, 203, 204, 207, 208, 209, 211
Frazer, James 2–3, 62, 86, 171, 183, 199, 213n8
Frazerian 5
frogs 18, 19, 21, 22, 23, 25, 153

Gaṇḍavyūha-Sūtra 91, 92, 108
Garuḍa 18–21, 26
Gcod 169–88, 195, 198, 204–5, 210
Gesar 119, 121n25
Gnubs chen Sangs rgyas ye shes 14, 23, 27, 28n1
  Gnubs's reincarnation 30n27
Greek Magical Papyri 5, 226
grimoire 4, 5, 13, 16, 106, 110, 193, 197, 202, 206, 212, 212n2, 214n12, 121n21, 229
Gsang ba ye shes 110, 112, 115, 116, 118, 121n21
Gshin rje be'u bum see Yama's handbook
Guhyasamājatantra 67, 75

Guhyasūtra of the *Niśvāsatattvasaṃhitā* 61
Gulikā see pills
Gyalthang 149, 150, 151, 152, 153, 154, 156, 157, 158, 159, 160, 163, 164, 164n2, 165n25

hailstorm 13, 16, 23, 24
healing 46, 47, 88, 92, 93, 115, 127, 133, 143, 169, 185, 238
Hevajratantra 77

Iamblichus 105, 206
impurity 68, 71, 80n17, 162
insect 149, 159
interdependent origination 4, 40, 103
inversion 13, 19, 20, 25, 26, 27
invisibility 47, 48, 49, 51, 88

'Jam dpal bshes gnyen 28n1
'Jigs med gling pa 99n38, 173

Kālī 184
karma 62, 63, 64, 65, 79n4, 95, 104, 161, 182, 230
Kaṭutaila 56n107, 67, 68, 79n15
'Khor lo *see* wheels
Khyung see *Garuḍa*
King of Resolute Aspirations of Samantabhadra 91, 92
Kings 35, 36, 42–7, 44, 46, 56n97
  nāga-king 19, 30n17, 115
Klong chen rab 'byams dri med 'od zer 210
Klu/nāga 13, 16, 17, 18, 19, 20, 23, 27, 28, 30n19, 31n34, 115, 147n5, 150, 153, 154, 163, 165n25
  bla klu 161

Las bzhi 16
legitimacy 31n30, 141, 142
leprosy 16, 17, 22, 23, 24, 27, 31n34, 154, 161, 165n25
Liṅga see effigy
Lisu 149. 152, 153, 157, 158
literature 68, 71, 74, 79n8, 107, 108, 109, 119, 170, 176, 193, 195, 196, 211, 213n10, 230
logocentric 88, 224
logocentrism 142

magic
  cross-culturality of 1, 2, 3, 13, 16, 28, 78, 89, 97, 125, 126, 127, 146, 224, 229
  definitions of 1–5, 15–16, 25–6, 36, 37, 62, 63, 86–9, 92, 97, 103, 127, 146, 170–3, 179, 182, 186, 188, 194, 197, 209, 222–40
  demonic 104–7, 228
  as law of sympathy 2, 5, 16, 18, 20, 21, 24, 26, 62, 67, 69, 73, 74, 76, 78, 156, 160–1, 199, 213n9, 230, 236
  natural 104, 199, 228
  and religion 1–5, 15, 23, 62, 63, 85, 86–9, 96, 97, 105, 126–7, 146n2, 170–3, 183–5, 187, 221, 222, 226, 227, 230–2, 234, 235, 240
  as ritual 2, 3, 4, 5, 13, 14–28, 35–51, 61–72, 74, 75, 76, 78, 87–8, 95, 103, 105, 107, 109, 110, 112, 116, 119, 126. 127, 128. 134, 141, 142, 170, 183, 187, 188, 201, 207, 223, 224, 225, 226, 227, 229, 230, 233, 236, 237, 239, 240
  and science 1, 3, 4, 15, 86, 87, 89, 97, 104, 170, 171, 187, 202–5, 210, 211, 213n9, 226, 234
  as semiotic domain 140–2
  tantric 62–5
magical recipes 22, 43, 61, 62, 64, 65, 66, 67, 68, 69, 70, 71, 72, 73, 74, 75, 76, 77, 78, 79n15, 80n19, 80n26, 159, 222, 224, 239
Mahākāla 107, 110
Maitreya 108
manipulation 3, 5, 6, 13, 16, 17, 24, 36, 65, 66, 70, 74–6, 78, 103, 142, 236, 237
Mañjuśrī 92, 108
  Mañjuśrī-Yamāntaka, 15
  wrathful form of 13, 28
Mañjuśrīmitra 14
Mañjuśriyamūlakalpa/Mañjuśrīmūlakalpa 48, 58n146, 61
mantra 4, 16, 18, 19, 20, 21, 22, 23, 24, 25, 28, 31n30, 36, 37, 38, 39, 40, 41, 49, 51, 52n16, 62, 63, 65, 67, 68, 69, 73, 74, 75, 76, 77, 78, 87, 92, 104, 106, 107, 109, 117, 118, 119, 121n22, 130, 131, 132, 143, 229, 230, 231
merit 88, 91, 92, 94, 95, 96, 223

Milarepa 108–9, 196–7, 213n7, 214–15n16, 215n17
miraculous 171
capabilities 90, 94, 96, 228
powers 16, 29n10, 51
monks 37, 50, 106, 113, 161, 177, 231
Mosuo 149, 153, 155, 156, 158
Mthu 87, 229, 230
mustard seed 22, 40, 43, 44, 45, 46, 48, 53n23, 53n36, 54n74, 55n94, 73, 121n28
oil 56n107, 67, 68, 69, 70, 71, 79n7, 80n18
mystics and mysticism 37, 48, 165n17, 194, 195, 198, 200, 204, 205, 206, 210, 213n10, 214n12, 215n19

Nāga, see *klu*
Naxi 149, 151, 152, 153, 157, 158, 164n4, 165n25
Netratantra 71
Nimba/Neem Tree 43, 46, 56n97, 68, 70, 71, 74, 79, 80
novice 37, 50
Nyi ma gzhon nu 110–20

obstacles 48, 50–1, 57n134, 72, 116, 178
occult 2, 3, 4, 57n145, 104, 194–7, 199, 200, 204–9
omens 48
oracles 112, 113, 152
orientalism 3, 172, 201, 207, 215n17
ostracization 150. 156, 157
Otto & Stausberg 2, 3, 85, 87, 88, 89, 92, 95, 96, 97, 127, 146n1, 223, 227, 228, 236, 239

pacification 16, 37, 39, 40, 47, 53n28, 57n135, 230
Padmasambhava, *see also* Guru Rinpoche 21, 108, 114, 115, 116, 118, 130, 133, 169, 177, 179, 186, 189n10, 208, 214–15n16
painted cloth 37, 38, 39, 40, 41, 47, 48, 49
*Pāramitā*s 90
patterns of magicity 2, 85, 89–98, 91, 92, 96, 97, 127, 228, 239
'Pho ba 180, 182, 195, 213n7, 225
Picatrix 4–5
pills 39, 49, 53n37, 71, 131
Platonism 3, 5, 105, 106
poison 19, 23, 25, 43, 45, 46, 54n74, 56n97, 69, 70, 73, 106, 149, 151, 153, 154, 156, 157, 155, 158, 159, 160, 161, 162, 163, 164, 165n15, 165n19, 222, 226
pollution 25, 160, 161–2, 165n27
power(s) 2, 16, 21, 24, 28, 39, 46, 49, 93, 94, 106, 109, 117, 118, 143, 150, 175, 186, 188, 228, 229, 230, 232, 233, 236, 237
accumulation of 158, 182
activation of 20, 22, 25–7
of the Buddha 87
of coercing 197, 234
of entities 16, 105
evil 157
extraordinary 95
of *gcod* 171
of God 29n11
magical 36, 37, 47, 51, 87, 88, 93, 223 225, 229, 230, 235, 238, 240n3
materials 24
mechanism of 26
miraculous 16, 119
mystical 37
of objects 207, 215n19
occult 58n145, 104, 196
over spell 71
place 116
protective 93
religious 240
of ritual 26
special 128, 194
superior 37, 48
supernatural 1, 47, 87, 180, 208
super 4, 230
supernormal 1, 4, 200, 230
supplication of 227
tantric 229
transference of 216
of transformation 91, 170, 180, 182, 187
of *vidyādhara* 48
wander-working 29n10
of words 104
of words of truth 93, 94
of worldly deities 110
of worshipped deities 13, 180, 231
Prajñāpāramitā 170, 184
Praṇidhāna see *smon lam*
prayer 1, 85, 90, 91, 95, 106, 111, 233

prayer-flag 27, 154
of supplication 227
wishing 90
prosperity 37, 40, 41, 47, 53n23, 72, 80n21, 224, 232
protection 19, 20, 22, 57n135, 94, 106, 107, 128, 132, 133–40, 145, 236
amulets 130
of animals 147n6, 129–33
genre 106
mantras for 131
rituals for 143, 231
protector deities, *see also* Dharma protectors 27, 28, 48, 108–20, 121n25, 154, 177, 178, 179
Pure Land 31n29, 48, 90, 91, 180, 225
Puṣṭi/Pauṣṭika 63, 71, 72 *see also* prosperity
psychism 198, 202–4, 205, 207, 208, 209, 210, 211, 214n13, 215n19
psychology 66, 202, 203, 204, 205, 211
purity 25, 160

Qinghai Province 129, 130

Rāhula 23, 28, 30n16, 31n35
Ratnakuṭa Collection 91
Ravens 107, 151
Rdo rje legs pa 110
Rdo rje shugs ldan 154, 161
Resolute aspirations 85, 90, 91, 92, 93, 94, 95, 96, 97, 226, 228, 233, 234
Rdzogs chen 188, 200, 201, 206
Rdzu 'phrul 87, 229, 230
Rgya Zhang khrom 14, 29n4, 30n27
Rgyas pa see prosperity
Ril bu see pills
Rnying ma 14, 23, 28, 80n22, 108, 109, 110, 113, 114, 118, 133, 169
Rnying ma rgyud 'bum 14, 23, 30n19
Roerich, George 195
Rwa lo tsā ba 61

Sādhana, see also *sgrub thabs* 36, 37, 47, 63, 80n28, 169, 173–80, 182, 186, 209
salt 43, 44, 45, 46, 47, 53n28, 75
semiotic 31n33, 67, 140, 141, 142, 144
Śākta/Śaiva tantras 61, 63, 65, 66, 67, 68, 69, 71, 74, 76, 79n2, 79n3, 80n28, 180, 184, 210, 222, 233, 239
Sangs rgyas gling pa 118
Sangs rgyas rgya mtsho 26, 153
Śāntika/śānti 63, 71, *see also* pacification
Sa skya 61
Serpent, see *Klu*
Sichuan Province 129, 133, 156, 164
Siddhi 4, 35, 36, 37, 40, 41, 47, 48, 49, 50, 51, 54n55, 57n134, 63, 64, 79n3, 230, 237
Śiva 70, 75, 109, 110, 111, 120n8, 184
as Bhairava 184
as Mahādeva 48, 109
as Rudra 177
Skrod pa see driving away
Shamanism 119–20, 146n3, 172, 189n5
Sle lung Bzhad pa'i rdo rje 4, 110–20
Smon lam see resolute aspirations
snakes 27, 28, 73, 153, 155, 156, 160, 161, 231
sorcery 16, 20, 26, 28, 29n11, 64, 158, 159, 164, 197, 199, 206, 207, 229
soteriology 4, 13, 62, 63, 88, 90, 103, 184, 225, 230, 240n1
spirits (*bhūtas*) 19, 31n31, 48, 49, 56, 181, 186, 199
Śrī Devī 107, 110
Stūpa 20, 27, 38, 39, 40, 41, 42, 50, 94, 95
subjugation 16, 36, 37, 42, 43, 44, 45, 46, 47, 49, 54n74, 55n97, 63, 75, 76, 107, 174, 175, 177, 178, 179
substances: 21, 23, 24, 43, 44, 63, 65, 66, 73, 78, 87, 104, 131, 114, 115, 117, 118, 129, 130, 132, 144, 142, 143, 145, 147n8, 236
contaminated 13, 17, 25, 26, 31n31, 31n32
curative 72
eight auspicious 121n19
foul-smelling 68
fragrant 40
harmful 19
natural 128
peaceful 71
precious 106, 118
red 46
sixteen auspicious 117
three pungent 45, 56n107, 67
word- 144
substitution 70, 71, 125, 132, 143, 144, 179, 215n17
Sukhāvatī 48, 49, 51, 92

supernatural 1, 47, 87, 107, 158–9, 180, 203, 208, 215n17, 235
supernormal 1, 4, 38, 47, 57n134, 103, 104, 106, 200, 208, 215n19, 230
superstition 61, 86, 89, 96, 151, 203
Sūtras 91, 108, 160, 170

Talismans 160, 237
tantra 2, 14, 23, 26, 31n33, 35, 36, 43, 61–84, 106–7, 113, 169, 172, 173, 179–91, 199–200, 208, 210, 221–6, 229–31, 236, 238, 240
Tārā 35, 36, 37, 52n8, 108, 224
Tārā-mūla-kalpa 35, 38, 58n146
The Moon's Mystery Handbook 13, 16–24, 25, 27, 28
The Ritual Text of Ūrdhvajaṭā 35, 36, 52n4, 52n8, 52n17
theosophy 206, 207, 209
theurgy 206–7
Third Law 86
three metals 49
three sweets 19, 22, 30n18, 71–2, 80n21
three whites *see* three sweets
toads 107, 155
transgression 25, 26, 29n7, 71, 181, 184, 185, 187, 233, 237
transubstantiation 144–5
travel 127, 172, 195, 196, 200, 206, 213n12
treasure 14, 27, 30n27, 40, 110, 113, 117, 118
  finding 88, 107
  immobilization of 72
Trungpa, Chögyam 171, 188
Tsong kha pa 47, 91, 108
Tylor, Edward B. 86, 171, 183, 199

Uccāṭana see driving away
Udumbara 40, 41, 45, 53n35, 71, 72
Umā 106

Vaiśravaṇa 106
Vajrabhairava 29n2, 30n16, 61, 210
Vajrabhairavatantra 61
Vajrakīla 177
Vajrayoginī 77, 78, 110
van Schaik, Sam 1, 10n1, 29n5, 30n23, 87, 88, 92, 95, 97n1, 98n16, 98n18, 127, 147n4, 222, 223, 224, 225, 227, 228, 229, 230, 236, 238
Vaśīkaraṇa see subjugation
Vasubandhu 174
victim 17, 18, 20, 21, 22, 24, 67, 75, 76, 153, 157, 158, 159, 163, 164
Vidyā 35, 36, 37, 38, 51, 52n16, 71, 229
Vidyādhara 37, 42, 47, 48, 49, 51, 53n21
Vimalakīrti Sūtra 108
Vīṇāśikhā Tantra 61, 68
violation 31n34, 50
violence, *see also* war 74, 106, 116, 224, 237, 238
visualization 15, 36, 63, 76, 77, 78, 114, 115, 117, 118, 176, 179, 180, 181, 183, 184, 185, 186, 233
Visuddhimaga 57n134
vows 40, 41, 42, 46, 50, 90
  vow-breaker 17, 18, 20, 22, 26, 27, 50, 174

wealth 6, 40, 47, 72, 88, 107, 116–19, 131, 158, 159, 231, 237
wheels 17, 19, 65, 76, 77, 130, 131, 132, 143, 147n7
  action- 17
White Beryl 26
witchcraft 29n11, 75, 107, 109, 112, 119, 120, 157, 158, 159, 162, 163, 165n15, 165n19
Wittgensteinian "family resemblances" 1, 88, 127, 226, 228, 236
worldly ends 57n128, 87, 88, 92, 97, 223, 224, 225, 236
words of truth 93–4

Yama 28, 68, 76
Yama's Handbook 13
Yamāntaka 13, 24, 26, 29n2, 30n16, 31n35
  of Rnying ma tradition 14
Yamāri 23, 24
Yantra see wheels
Ye shes 'od 172, 187
Yi 149, 156, 157, 158
Yoga 48, 72, 117, 203, 206, 207, 208
  sexual 20, 113, 115
Yogi(nī) 64, 106–10, 117–18, 175, 177–8, 184, 196, 197, 200, 202, 212
Yunnan 149, 156, 158, 163, 164

Zhi ba see pacification
Zla gsang be'u 'bum see *The Moon's Mystery Handbook*
Zla gsang nag po'i rgyud see *Black Moon's Mystery Tantra*